Anna Uhl Chamot

Joan Baker de Gonzalez

Isobel Rainey de Diaz

Richard Yorkey

 Heinle & Heinle Publishers
A Division of Wadsworth, Inc.
Boston, Massachusetts 02116

TEACHER'S EDITION

Publisher: Stanley J. Galek
Editorial Director: Christopher Foley
Project Editor: Anita L. Raducanu
Content Editor: Kathleen Sands Boehmer
Assistant Editors: Erik Gundersen
Nancy A. Mann

Production Supervisor: Patricia Jalbert
Production Manager: Erek Smith
Designed and Produced by: Publishers' Graphics Inc.
Prepress Color and Integration:
FinalCopy Electronic Publishing Services
Cover: The Graphics Studio/Gerry Rosentswieg

Acknowledgments

The authors and publisher would like to acknowledge the contributions of the following individuals who reviewed the *Intercom 2000* program at various stages of development and who offered many helpful insights and suggestions:

• Mary J. Erickson and Galen Shaney, *English Language Institute, University of Texas, Pan American*
• Toni Sachs Hadi, *New York City Board of Education*
• Katy Cox and Alexandre Oliveira, *Casa Thomas Jefferson, Brasília, Brazil*
• Ronald A. Reese, *Long Beach (CA) Unified School District*
• Ruthann Hilferty, *Paterson (NJ) Board of Education*

• Lúcia de Aragão, Sonia Godoy, and Rosa Erlichman, *União Cultural, São Paulo, Brazil*
• Peggy Kazkaz, *William Rainey Harper College*
• Roland G. Axelson, Diane Hazel, and Mary Wayne Pierce, *Hartford (CT) Public Schools*
• Keith A. Buchanan, *Fairfax County (VA) Public Schools*
• Robert Saitz, *Boston University*

Contents

COMMUNICATION GRAMMAR SKILLS

COMMUNICATION	GRAMMAR	SKILLS

COMMUNICATION	GRAMMAR	SKILLS

PHOTO CREDITS

TEXT CREDITS

INTRODUCTION

INTERCOM 2000 is a four-level basic course for secondary and adult students of English. Situations in the lives of a multicultural group of characters provide natural contexts in which a carefully selected and graded structural syllabus is integrated with common communicative functions. INTERCOM 2000 features a spiraled approach to language learning with presentation, reinforcement, expansion, and regular review of communication forms and structures. This approach promotes the gradual but secure development of listening, speaking, reading, and writing skills. The four levels of INTERCOM 2000 develop language skills generally included in elementary through low intermediate programs.

Each level of INTERCOM 2000 features:

- Student Text
- Workbook
- Teacher's Edition
- Tape Program
- Testing Program

NEW FEATURES OF *INTERCOM 2000*

The most popular features of the NEW INTERCOM series have been retained and in many cases expanded in INTERCOM 2000. A number of totally new features have been integrated into the new edition. Some of the new features are:

- Colorful student texts with enhanced graphics.
- An entirely new illustration program for all levels.
- Expanded exercises in the student text for abundant practice in all four skill areas.
- Clearly listed objectives at the beginning of each unit, providing a useful reference and organizational tool.
- Real-life readings and activities focusing on building reading strategies.
- Authentic and simulated authentic reading and listening activities, focusing on building reading and listening strategies.

- Final Activities, at the end of each unit, that help students synthesize what they have learned and encourage cooperative learning.
- Expanded Workbooks with extra practice in grammar, vocabulary building, writing, and cooperative learning.

THE RATIONALE

Communicative competence is the primary goal of INTERCOM 2000. Because of this, grammatical meaning and grammatical form are given equal weight. Following a carefully sequenced syllabus, grammatical structures and common communication functions are presented in natural contexts. Students learn new forms and functions in clear presentation segments and practice activities (Unit Opener, Presentation, Practice, Listening) and then build to less controlled language activities that are more student-initiated (Interactions, Reading, Writing, Final Activities). In this way, each unit moves from a receptive focus to a productive one, in which students use English to actively communicate in meaningful ways.

INTERCOM 2000's spiraled approach enables students to develop higher level language abilities through a wide variety of meaningful experiences and communication tasks. Activities include dialogs, role plays, interviews, group discussions, and real-life reading situations (maps, advertisements, schedules, menus, etc.). Each unit has a unifying context that provides the topics and situations for the new forms to be learned.

ORGANIZATION OF THE TEXT

In Book 4, each of the 12 units of INTERCOM 2000 begins with a colorful Unit Opener. The Unit Opener, which is often a dialog, motivates learning through the natural use of practical language in diverse settings. Openers are intended for comprehensible input and exposure to natural language, rather than for memorization. In the Openers, the emphasis is on the main idea of the dialog or reading, and as in a natural language learning situation, students learn to deduce meaning from context.

In the Presentation, Vocabulary in Context, Pronunciation, and Practice sections that follow the Unit Opener, language is controlled so that students can focus on and practice the new functional and structural forms. This controlled practice gradually leads to activities that encourage students to use their newly acquired language skills more independently in varied situations.

In the more challenging language tasks in Listening, Reading, Writing, Interaction, and Final Activity sections, the emphasis is on meaningful communication and student interaction. Interactions provide semi-structured activities and are a natural bridge from the more controlled activities at the beginning of the unit to the open-ended Final Activity at the end. Reentry sections recycle previously learned material in new contexts. The General Guidelines at the end of this introduction give more details about each section and general procedures to follow for each one.

FEATURES OF EACH COMPONENT

STUDENT TEXT

- Colorful, high-interest content
- Graphics to enhance real-life reading and writing situations
- Content relating to a wide variety of subjects
- Easy-to-use format
- Abundant practice of functions and structures in a variety of situations
- Vocabulary List of productive and receptive words

TEACHER'S EDITION

- General Guidelines for each section as well as suggested procedures for every page
- Detailed comments and notes for each student page
- Language Notes and Cultural Notes for useful background information
- Answers for Practice, Reentry, Reading, and Writing exercises
- Additional Expansion Activities within each unit and at the end of the Teacher's Edition
- Listening Scripts for the Tape Program
- Cross-referencing of student text and workbook activities
- Workbook Answer Key

STUDENT WORKBOOK
- Wide variety of exercises relating to each Presentation in the student text
- Recycling and reinforcement of vocabulary and structures
- Cross-referencing with student text
- Additional writing practice, emphasis on writing from personal information and experience
- Final Activity in each unit that can be used as a cooperative learning activity
- Exercises suitable for homework or in-class work

TAPE PROGRAM
- Listening practice with native speakers at natural speed
- Opportunities for listening and repetition
- Includes the following sections: Unit Opener, Comprehension Questions (and answers), Presentation, Vocabulary in Context, Pronunciation, and Listening
- Suitable for the language lab, in-class use, or independent work

TESTING PROGRAM
- Two volumes: one containing the testing program for Books 1 and 2 and the other for Books 3 and 4
- Each volume contains: two placement tests, oral interviews, and 3 achievement tests for each level of the series.

USEFUL CLASSROOM TECHNIQUES

PAIR WORK AND GROUP WORK

Pair work and group work are an integral part of INTERCOM 2000, and teaching students to work together successfully will contribute to their success in learning to communicate in English. Here are some suggestions for handling pair and group work.

- It will take time for students to get accustomed to working in pairs and groups if they have never done so before. Work it into the program little by little.
- Show students how to set up for pair and group work. Students should work with a variety of partners, not always the same person.

- Always go over the instructions for pair or group work carefully. Taking time to demonstrate exactly what is to be done will make the experience productive and pleasant for everyone. Before starting pair work, it is recommended to have pairs of students do the first few items to make sure students understand the activity.
- All tasks should be within the English level of the students if they have done the preceding practice. Help students keep their interactions entirely in English.
- Be helpful, not critical. Give students time to get started in the task. Then move from group to group, listening and helping only as needed.
- Finish with a teacher-class feedback period. Have several pairs of students do items from the practice.

CHAIN DRILLS

Chain drills provide a good format for practicing new patterns, especially question and answer patterns. Going in a "chain" around the class, each student asks the next person a question or adds on to a list. Chain drills can be used to practice something new, review a structure, or simply to warm up at the beginning of class.

> A: Where's Paris?
> B: It's in France. Where's Milan?
> C: It's in Italy. Where's Miami?
> D: It's in Florida, in the United States. Where's Toronto?

> A: I'm wearing a blue and white blouse.
> B: *A* is wearing a blue and white blouse and I am wearing a green shirt.
> C: *A* is wearing a blue and white blouse, *B* is wearing a green shirt, and I am wearing black pants.

DICTATION

Dictations can be excellent learning activities and can be used in a variety of ways. Dictations help students focus on listening, remembering, and writing. In the beginning, you may want to concentrate

on students' listening, and not require accurate spelling. Easier dictations can include words, numbers, spelling out words letter by letter, and short sentences. Gradually build to longer dictations with longer sentences and short paragraphs. With longer dictations, first just read the sentence or passage and have students listen. Then read two more times for students to write. Give students time to check their spelling and punctuation.

Dictations can be handed in for correction or corrected in class. For in class correction, students can: work in small groups to check their work and reach agreement, and then check with the class; write the dictation on the board and have other students help correct errors; dictate the sentences or words to the teacher at the board and check for errors.

CLOZE EXERCISES

In a cloze exercise, every fifth, sixth, or seventh word of a paragraph or dialog is deleted and replaced with a blank. This format encourages students to read for comprehension using contextual clues and shows students that they don't need to understand every word of a passage to understand it. Reading or Listening texts from the book may be converted to the cloze format, or you can make up your own exercises. If using material from the book, students can do the cloze exercise before doing the Reading or Listening in the book, or do it afterwards as a reinforcement. When possible, to check their work, have students share and discuss their answers. Often more than one word can be an acceptable answer.

PRONUNCIATION

SOUND-LETTER CORRESPONDENCE

The English spelling system presents difficulties for all users of the language, especially learners, because letters or combinations of letters do not consistently represent the same sound. The teacher's notes give the pronunciation of some of the more difficult and unfamiliar words with phonetic symbols so you can be sure of the pronunciation in Standard American speech. These symbols are for your reference.

Vowel Sounds

Common spellings		Uncommon spellings
/ə/	but, up	d<u>oe</u>s, l<u>o</u>ve
/iy/	meet, eat, see, me	p<u>ie</u>ce, happ<u>y</u>
/i/	it, in	
/e/	egg, get	h<u>ea</u>d
/ey/	date, say, rain	gr<u>ea</u>t, n<u>ei</u>ghbor
/a/	not, hot	f<u>a</u>ther
/æ/	man, ask	
/uw/	pool, new	d<u>o</u>, wh<u>o</u>, bl<u>ue</u>
/u/	good, put	w<u>ou</u>ld
/ow/	road, home, old	gr<u>ow</u>, kn<u>ow</u>
/ɔ/	call, dog	b<u>ough</u>t
/ɔy/	boy, voice	
/ay/	smile, die, try	h<u>igh</u>, b<u>uy</u>
/aw/	pound, house	

Consonant Sounds

Common Spellings		Uncommon spellings
/p/	pan, map, please, supper	
/b/	but, job, blouse	
/t/	time, hot, try, butter	
/d/	dime, bad, dry	
/k/	car, back	
/g/	go, big, great	
/f/	fine, if, fry	<u>ph</u>oto, lau<u>gh</u>
/v/	very, love	
/θ/	think, with	
/ð/	that, father	
/s/	see, miss	
/z/	zoo, jazz	doe<u>s</u>, i<u>s</u>
/š/	shirt, dish	<u>s</u>ure, <u>s</u>ugar
/ž/	televi<u>s</u>ion, A<u>s</u>ia, gara<u>g</u>e	
/č/	church	
/ǰ/	June, George	
/m/	man, am	
/n/	now, run	
/ŋ/	sing	
/l/	like, all, milk	
/r/	rice, car	
/h/	hello	
/y/	yes	
/w/	went	
/hw/	what, where, when	

GENERAL GUIDELINES

UNIT OPENER

The purpose of the Unit Opener is to introduce students to the language to be presented in the unit. Comprehension Questions (given in the Teacher's Edition and in the Tape Program) help students focus their listening. The Unit Opener, in conjunction with the Presentation and Vocabulary in Context sections that follow it, constitutes the "receptive" stage that leads to active oral production in the Practice and Interaction activities. Students are not expected to master, memorize, or perform the Opener initially. However, it is a good idea to come back to the Opener later in the unit for review and reinforcement.

The Unit Opener and Comprehension Questions are recorded in the Tape Program.

Here are some suggested guidelines for using the Opener.

1. Have students read the title and look at the picture(s) that accompany the Unit Opener. Have them identify the characters and talk about what they notice about the picture. Use the picture for vocabulary review, if appropriate.
2. Read or play the tape for the introductory lines. Encourage students to make intelligent guesses about the topic(s) of the conversation that follows.
3. Have students listen as you read or play the tape for the Opener. Student books can be opened or closed, as you prefer.
4. Ask one or two Comprehension Questions (given in the teacher's notes of each unit). Tell students to listen for the answers as they listen again to the Opener.
5. Read or play the tape for the Opener again.
6. Now read the Comprehension Questions given in the teacher's notes and check the answers. If you prefer, play the tape which gives the questions and answers.
7. Give students a chance to ask questions about vocabulary.
8. As a class, have students answer the Discussion Questions given in the teacher's notes. Encourage students to give their own opinions.
9. *Optional.* Model each line of the Opener, and

have students repeat as a class, in groups, and individually. You can use the tape as a model for repetition.

PRESENTATION

Presentations teach new functions and structures. They contain the models for Practice and Interaction sections that follow. It is important that students understand the new functions and structures and have time to practice the language models before moving on to the more challenging Practice sections.

All Presentations are recorded in the Tape Program.

1. Follow any suggestions given in the teacher's notes for introducing the target structure before going to the book.
2. Point to the picture and target structure or dialog in the book. Read or play the tape for this new material and have students repeat. Students can repeat chorally, in groups, and individually.
3. When possible, have students add examples of their own. Specific suggestions for this are given in the teacher's notes. Students can use their own experience and personal information.
4. If the Presentation contains a short dialog, have students practice reading the dialog in pairs or small groups for additional oral practice before going on to the Practice section.

VOCABULARY IN CONTEXT

In Book 4 there are two types of Vocabulary in Contexts—those that present vocabulary from the Unit Openers and those that present new word sets. Both are recorded in the Tape Program.

Vocabulary from the Unit Openers: A variety of exercise types are used to check students' comprehension of words or expressions in the Opener. In addition to completing definitions or a paragraph, students frequently practice inferring or guessing the meaning of a word or expression from context. Follow these guidelines:

1. Teach students to use linguistic, situational, and discourse clues when they infer meaning from context. Linguistic clues include: the part of speech; singular, plural, or mass noun; definitions in appositives, etc. Situational clues include those

that come from our general knowledge of the world and from the immediate situation (occupation of speaker, where the speakers are, etc.). Discourse clues include what we know about how specific language is used for a specific type of communication (for example, *Once upon a time* is used with fictional narratives, usually of the class fairy tale) and what was said previously in the present situation. Teaching students to infer the meaning of words and expressions from context makes them more independent language learners.

2. Do these exercises with the whole class to begin with. As soon as possible, have students do them with a partner or do them individually and check them with a partner.

Vocabulary sets: A vocabulary set, such as table items, is presented.

1. When possible, introduce new vocabulary using realia or materials as suggested in the teacher's notes.
2. Hold up your book and point to each word or phrase as you read or play the tape. Have students repeat several times.
3. Point to pictures and ask *What's this? / What's A? / What's B?*
4. When appropriate, model and have students repeat short dialogs.
5. See the teacher's notes for other suggestions specific to the vocabulary.

PRONUNCIATION

Pronunciation sections help students focus on sounds, intonations, and rhythms of the language. Spend about five to ten minutes on Pronunciation. Several short, well-spaced practices are better than one long session. A guide to the phonetic alphabet is found on page 177 of Student Book 1.

PRACTICE

Practice exercises follow all Presentations. Many provide activities for pairs or for small group work.

1. Read the instructions. Model the boxed example or the first item in the exercise. Model it again with a student taking one of the roles. Then have a pair of students model the first item.

Students take turns or change roles as appropriate.
2. Go over several more items, having pairs of students do items in the exercise for the class. This helps students understand how to do the activity before starting pair practice. Make corrections as needed. When suggested, go over the whole exercise as a class before pair practice.
3. When students seem comfortable with the exercise, have them work in pairs and do the Practice. Circulate in the classroom. Listen carefully to students as they practice and make important corrections when necessary. Make sure students are taking turns or changing roles.
4. Regroup for a teacher-class feedback. Ask pairs of students to perform selected items.

INTERACTION

Interactions generally offer freer conversation practice. Interaction and Final Activities often feature information gap activities. In these activities, each student has some information that the other student does not have but needs. Therefore, there is a gap of information between students. It is important that students rely totally on their oral English communication skills to find out the needed information. Remind students not to show written information or speak in their native language. In the beginning, to help students understand an activity you may wish to model some of it with another student before students start.

When the Interaction or Final Activity has a role play follow these general guidelines:

1. Read the instructions with the class and talk about the general task.
2. Have students discuss and answer planning questions in their groups.
3. Have them write out the conversation and practice it. Require memorization if you like, otherwise students can write cues for their lines on 3 x 5" cards to use during the dramatization as necessary.
4. Role play as many conversations as time permits.

Option: If and when students are able, teach them to make a plan for the role play rather than write out the exact words. A plan consists of a functional statement for each line, for example:

SALESPERSON: Greet the customer.

CUSTOMER: Say you want to return a shirt that you don't like

REENTRY

Reentry activities review and reinforce material introduced and practiced earlier in the unit or in a previous unit. They can be done in many ways: orally as a class, individually, in small groups, on the board, or as written homework.

1. Read the instructions. Briefly review the target structure or function on the board. Ask students for example sentences. See suggestions in the teacher's notes.
2. Students can do the exercise individually or in pairs.
3. Check answers with students. You can review answers orally, have students write answers on the board, or have students work in groups to review answers before you check their work.

LISTENING

Listening activities in Book 4 focus on global comprehension. The tape scripts are provided in the teacher's notes in the Teacher's Edition. All listening activities are recorded in the Tape Program.

1. Most listening activities have First and Second Listenings. First have students prepare their papers for answering, copying the format or numbering their papers according to instructions.
2. Tell students briefly what they will be listening to. Encourage them to tell you things they might hear on the tape given the general situation.
3. Play the tape or read the script for the example when provided. Check the answers.
4. Play the tape or read the script for the First and Second Listenings, following instructions in the teacher's notes. In some cases, the First Listening should be corrected before doing the Second Listening. In others, both can be corrected at the end.
5. Play the tape or read the script for either the First or Second Listening more than once if your students need repetitions in order to do the task.
6. Use the conversations in the Listening activities with a more limited focus of your choice. For example, make a cloze listening dictation from a conversation by removing every sixth or seventh word or words of your choice.

READING

The Reading selections relate to the topic of the unit, and where possible incorporate functions and structures from the units. Students are presented with a wide variety of types of reading, including various newspaper articles and columns, a poem, personal essay, and an interview. There are also a variety of reading tasks suggested in the *First Reading* and *Second Reading* activities.

1. Readings start with *Before You Read* questions that activate students' background knowledge about the topic. Encourage class discussion and contributions from as many students as possible. Write notes and vocabulary from the discussion on the board. Add any other background knowledge your students might need. If appropriate, these pre-reading questions can be discussed in small groups and checked with the whole class.
2. Have students read the instructions and questions in the *First Reading* silently. Then have them tell you in their own words what they are going to look for as they read the first time.
3. Give students time to read the selection. Remind them to read straight through the selection and try to guess from context the meaning of words and expressions they don't know.
4. Discuss the answers to the questions in the *First Reading* with the whole class. Encourage students to show you where they got answers in the text when the answers are not obvious.
5. Give students time to read the selection again. (This can be assigned for homework.)
6. Have students read and follow the instructions for the *Second Reading* activity. Check answers.
7. Answer students' questions about the selection. Encourage them to ask about things, linguistic or cultural, that do not make sense to them.
8. Give students an opportunity to react to the selection in their own way. Possibilities include: (a) a class discussion using one or more of the questions suggested in Reacting to the Reading in the teacher's notes, (b) copying one or two quotes from the selection and writing a personal reaction to them, or (c) drawing a picture about the reading.

Note: In some readings, there will be vocabulary unfamiliar to students. Students do not need to know all of the vocabulary in the reading in order to do the Reading exercises. Encourage students to read for the main idea and derive meaning from context. If you want, you can go over additional vocabulary after students have completed the Reading exercises.

WRITING

Writing activities give students a chance to communicate in writing, using new structures and vocabulary. Follow the detailed instructions in the student text, which always suggest three parts for writing activities: (a) preparing for writing, (b) drafting, and (c) talking about what we have written. When possible, allow time for rewriting, editing, and sharing of final drafts.

FINAL ACTIVITY

The Final Activity is designed to help students synthesize new material and work cooperatively; it also provides closure to the unit. It often requires students to use many different communication forms. See the notes about information gap activities under Interaction, page x.

1. Read the instructions with the class. If necessary, give examples by doing part of the Final Activity together. You may want to ask several volunteers to demonstrate part of the Final Activity. Make sure students understand what they are to do.
2. Follow any specific instructions given in the teacher's notes.
3. As students do the activity, move around the room and help them as needed. Make note of any important errors, but do not correct at this time.
4. Go over the results of the Final Activity as suggested in the unit.
5. Encourage students in their work and talk about areas for improvement. You may want to give additional practice for language points that caused students trouble.

CORRELATING *INTERCOM 2000* WITH *BUILDING BRIDGES*

BUILDING BRIDGES: CONTENT AND LEARNING STRATEGIES FOR ESL is a three-level content-based series that parallels and complements INTERCOM 2000. BUILDING BRIDGES teaches students the essential concepts and skills they will need for success in mainstream science, mathematics, literature, and social studies classes.

BUILDING BRIDGES is based on the Cognitive Language Learning Approach (CALLA) in which high priority content, academic language development, and direct instruction in learning strategies are integrated into lessons that encourage student analysis and critical thinking.

The following chart summarizes the content presented in BUILDING BRIDGES and correlates this series with INTERCOM 2000:

BUILDING BRIDGES Levels		Content	INTERCOM 2000 Levels
Book 1	High Beginning	• school survival • community life • academic language • learning strategies	Book 2
Book 2	Low Intermediate	• major concepts and academic language associated with math, science, social studies, and literature • learning strategies	Book 3
Book 3	Intermediate		Book 4

Intercom 2000

The People

Tom Logan

MARITAL STATUS: married; 3 children

OCCUPATION: travel agent (Wells Travel Agency)

PASTIMES: working in the yard, listening to music

Adela Logan

MARITAL STATUS: married; 3 children

OCCUPATION: student and homemaker

SCHOOL: Winfield Technical Institute

MAJOR: computer programming

PASTIMES: listening to music, going to the movies, sewing

Sam Logan

AGE: 20 years old

MARITAL STATUS: single

OCCUPATION: mechanic (Winfield Garage) and student

SCHOOL: Winfield Community College

MAJOR: engineering

SPORTS: running, swimming, soccer

Bob Logan

AGE: 17 years old

SCHOOL: Winfield High School

SPORTS: basketball, soccer, tennis

PASTIME: playing chess

BEST FRIEND: Mike Young

Lisa Logan

AGE: 12 years old

SCHOOL: Winfield Elementary School

ABILITIES: sings well

SPORTS: ice skating

PASTIME: sewing, playing chess

BEST FRIEND: Joyce Young

Elinor Young

MARITAL STATUS:
married; 4 children

OCCUPATION: doctor
(Winfield Hospital)

PASTIMES: playing
tennis, going for
long walks, going to
museums

Howard Young

MARITAL STATUS:
married; 4 children

OCCUPATION:
engineer

PASTIMES: playing
tennis, swimming

Liz Young

AGE: 21 years old

MARITAL STATUS:
single

OCCUPATION:
international
telephone operator

LANGUAGES: German,
French, Spanish

Mike Young

AGE: 17 years old

SCHOOL: Winfield
High School

SPORTS: soccer,
basketball, tennis

PASTIMES: dancing

BEST FRIEND: Bob
Logan

Ted Young

AGE: 15 years old

SCHOOL: Winfield
High School

SPORTS: soccer,
swimming

PASTIME: playing
chess

Joyce Young

AGE: 12 years old

SCHOOL: Winfield
Elementary School

ABILITIES: draws well

SPORTS: soccer,
basketball, tennis

PASTIME: dancing

BEST FRIEND: Lisa
Logan

Pablo Nava

MARITAL STATUS: married; 2 children

OCCUPATION: architect

ADDRESS: Calle Paloma, 5 Mexico, D.F., Mexico

Melanie Nava

MARITAL STATUS: married; 2 children

PLACE OF BIRTH: Los Angeles, California

OCCUPATION: English teacher

PASTIMES: travel, photography

Carlos Nava

AGE: 18 years old

PLACE OF BIRTH: Mexico, D.F., Mexico

OCCUPATION: student (last year of high school)

LANGUAGES: Spanish and English

Ana Nava

AGE: 14 years old

PLACE OF BIRTH: Mexico, D.F., Mexico

OCCUPATION: student

LANGUAGES: Spanish and English

Maria Gomez de Nava

MARITAL STATUS: widowed; 1 child (Pablo Nava)

ADDRESS: Calle Paloma, 5 Mexico, D.F., Mexico

Gino Leone

PLACE OF BIRTH:
Naples, Italy

MARITAL STATUS:
Married

OCCUPATION: cook
(Roma Restaurant)
and cooking teacher
(Winfield
Community College)

SPORTS: swimming

PASTIMES: reading,
painting

Cristina Silva Leone

PLACE OF BIRTH:
Bogota, Colombia

MARITAL STATUS:
Married

OCCUPATION: cashier
(Roma Restaurant)
and student

SCHOOL: Winfield
Community College

MAJOR: art history

PASTIMES: dancing,
playing chess

Gloria Rivera

AGE: 16 years old

SCHOOL: Winfield
High School

PLACE OF BIRTH: New
York City

SPORTS: volleyball,
tennis

ABILITIES: plays the
guitar well, sings

LANGUAGE: Spanish

Toshio Ito

PLACE OF BIRTH:
Kyoto, Japan

OCCUPATION: flight
attendant (World
Airlines)

LIKES: travel,
working with people

SPORTS: swimming,
running

Nhu Trinh

PLACE OF BIRTH:
Saigon (currently
Ho Chi Minh City),
Vietnam

OCCUPATION: flight
attendant (World
Airlines)

PASTIME: going to
the movies

Sekila Manzikala

PLACE OF BIRTH:
Kinshasa, Zaire

OCCUPATION: student

SCHOOL: Winfield
Community College

ABILITIES: sings well

LANGUAGES: French,
Lingala, English

Useful materials: newspaper ads for business openings; pictures that suggest possibilities (see p. 10); pictures for comparisons (e.g., three or more of the same object)

The Grand Opening

PROCEDURE

1. Refer to General Guidelines for Opener, page ix.
2. Read or play the tape for the introductory lines. Ask students to speculate on what Adela and Tom will talk about.
3. Read or play the tape for the conversation. Follow the guidelines.
4. Before listening to the ad, ask students what information they expect to find in it. List their suggestions on the board (*Where is it?*, etc.)
5. Read or play the tape for the ad and have students check to see if their questions were answered.
6. After following the guidelines, read the script or play the tape for the Comprehension Questions and their answers.

COMPREHENSION QUESTIONS

Now answer these questions about Tom and Adela's conversation.

1. What do Tom and Adela want to do this weekend? *Tom wants to work in the yard. Adela wants to go to the Grand Opening of the new mall.*
2. What does Adela think Tom will enjoy at the mall? *The car show.*
3. Why does Adela want to go to the fashion show? *She wants to get some ideas for clothes.*
4. Do the kids want to go to the Grand Opening? *We don't know. Maybe.*
5. What is Tom a little worried about? *He's afraid they will spend too much money.*

Now listen to these sentences about the ad for the Winfield Mall. Say *Yes, that's right, No, that's wrong,* or *I don't know. Maybe.*

6. This is the first shopping mall in Winfield. *Yes, that's right.*
7. There are thirty or more stores in the mall. *Yes, that's right.*
8. There were special activities Monday through Thursday. *I don't know. Maybe.*
9. There are old and modern cars in the car show. *Yes, that's right.*
10. There are fashion shows on Sunday. *No, that's wrong.*

UNIT 1

COMMUNICATION
Talking about plans for the weekend ▪ Talking about possibilities ▪ Talking about preferences ▪ Agreeing reluctantly ▪ Refusing politely

GRAMMAR
Might/may + verb ▪ *Would rather* + verb ▪ The superlative

SKILLS
Listening to ads for businesses ▪ Reading a modern folk tale ▪ Writing a narrative

The Grand Opening

It's Friday evening. Adela and Tom Logan are in the living room of their new home reading the newspaper.

ADELA: Tom, what are we going to do this weekend?

TOM: I was planning to work in the yard. Why?

ADELA: Maybe we should take a look at the new Winfield Mall. The Grand Opening's this week.

TOM: Already? Amazing! That place sure went up fast. Hmm . . . Well, . . . I'd rather finish the yard work, but if you really want to . . . Anything special going on?

ADELA: You might be interested in the car show. The ad says it's the biggest and the best in Winfield history.

TOM: C'mon. You know ads always exaggerate.

ADELA: I know, but there's a fashion show I'd like to see, too. I might get some good ideas.

TOM: OK. Sounds good to me. Let's see if the kids want to go. But let's try not to spend too much money.

DISCUSSION QUESTIONS

1. What is there to interest the following people at the Grand Opening: children, people who want to make their homes or apartments prettier, people who like clothes, people who like cars?
2. What kind of people do Tom and Adela seem to be? Do you think they have a good marriage? Why or why not?

LANGUAGE NOTES

1. *Ad* is the common short form of *advertisement*.
2. *Sure* is used here for emphasis.

CULTURAL NOTE

Displays of automobiles, fashion shows, and other exhibits are common in the walkways of American shopping malls. Weather permitting, a special event like a Grand Opening sometimes includes a few amusement rides, especially for children, out in the parking lot.

1 Vocabulary in Context

PROCEDURE

1. Refer to General Guidelines for Vocabulary in Context, page ix.
2. Have students work in pairs on Part A.
3. Do Part B with the whole class, and teach students what context is and how to use it to infer meaning.

Answers: **A.** 1. improvement 2. convenient
3. latest 4. economical 5. sponsored 6. luxurious
7. creative 8. safest 9. exaggerate **B.** 1. f 2. d
3. i 4. g 5. b 6. h 7. a 8. c 9. e

Workbook: *page 1, exercises A, B*

---

1 Vocabulary in Context

A. **Find words in the conversation and the ad on pages 6-7 to complete these sentences.**

1. When you make something better, you make a/an _____ on it.
2. If parking is close to a business, it is _____ parking.
3. If the car models or fashions are from this year, they are the _____ models or fashions.
4. If a car doesn't cost a lot of money to run, it is _____ .
5. If a business pays the cost of a show or exhibit, the show or exhibit is _____ by that business.
6. If a car has beautiful and expensive equipment, we say it is _____ .
7. If a person has talent to make new and beautiful things, the person is _____ .
8. The _____ cars are the ones in which you are protected. You are not going to get hurt in these cars.
9. When ads say more than is true, they _____ .

B. **Can you guess the meaning of these words or expressions from the way they are used in the conversation or the ad? Match each expression with its meaning.**

1. **Route** 25   **a.** happening
2. **It went up** fast.   **b.** I like that idea.
3. **amusement rides** for kids   **c.** make nice or pretty
4. **Don't miss it!**   **d.** they built it
5. **Sounds good to me.**   **e.** together
6. **Amazing!**   **f.** highway
7. Anything special **going on?**   **g.** Be sure you see it.
8. ways to **decorate** your home   **h.** I can't believe it.
9. sponsored **jointly** by   **i.** carnival entertainment;
   Warner's and Ray's   for example,
                                               a merry-go-round

2 Presentation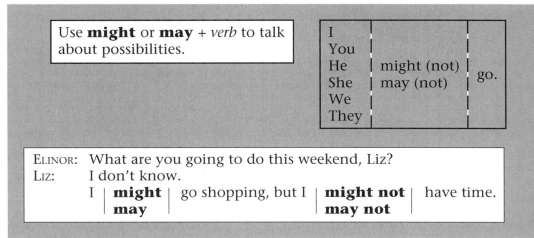

Talking about possibilities

> Use **might** or **may** + *verb* to talk about possibilities.

I You He She We They	might (not) may (not)	go.

ELINOR: What are you going to do this weekend, Liz?
LIZ: I don't know.

I | **might**
may | go shopping, but I | **might not**
may not | have time.

3 Practice

A. Read the situation. Discuss what *might* or *might not* happen. You can also use *may* or *may not*.

> It's very cloudy today.
>
> A: It might rain.
> B: We might not be able to play the baseball game.

1. Dr. Young is working at the hospital tonight. There was a serious car accident in Winfield about fifteen minutes ago.

2. Smoke and Fire, a famous British rock group, is giving a concert in New York tonight. They were late to the airport in London, so their instruments and equipment had to go on another plane.

3. Bob has two tests this morning; math and English. He wasn't feeling well last night so he didn't finish studying for math, and he forgot to read one of the stories for English.

4. Winfield High School's girls' basketball team is playing Westlake this weekend. The game is going to decide the area championship. Two of Winfield's very good players have bad colds. Their parents don't want them to play.

2 Presentation

PROCEDURE
1. Refer to General Guidelines for Presentation, page ix.
2. To reenter modal auxiliary verbs, write *can*, *should*, and *will* on the board and have students ask and answer questions using them in the context of the Grand Opening. For example: *When can you go to the Grand Opening on Friday? Should you bring your little brother?*
3. Read or play the tape for the Presentation. Have students repeat chorally, in groups, and in pairs.
4. Point out that the vertical bars mean students can use either expression.
5. To expand the Presentation, ask students what they are going to do at some rather distant time in the future. They are probably unsure and should respond *I might/may ____, but I might/may not.*

LANGUAGE NOTES
1. *Might* and *may* are interchangeable in statements to express a future possibility. Like *can*, *should*, and *will*, they precede the base form of a verb.
2. For yes/no questions about future possibilities, Americans usually ask *Do you think you/he/she/they might ____? Might you/he/they*, etc. is rare in the U.S. (*May I go?* is a request for permission.)

3 Practice

PROCEDURE
1. Refer to General Guidelines for Practice, page x.
2. Do as a whole class practice or have students work in pairs and check answers with the whole class.
3. In this type of Practice, be prepared to help students with vocabulary that they ask for.

Possible answers: **A. 1.** Dr. Young might be at the hospital all night. She might not get any sleep. **2.** The group might not be able to play. They might borrow some instruments. **3.** Bob might fail both tests. The teacher might not ask about the story he didn't read. **4.** The girls might not play, and the team might lose. They might feel better on Saturday, and they might play. The team might lose anyway.

B: **1.** The bear might climb down and attack the man (hiker). The man might not see the bear, and then the bear will go away. **2.** The man and woman might run out of water. They might see a shark. Someone might come to rescue them. **3.** Either horse might win. One jockey might try to cheat. One of the horses might fall down. **4.** The police might not stop the driver. They might stop the driver and give him/her a ticket. The driver might slow down.

4 Interaction

PROCEDURE

1. Refer to General Guidelines for Interaction, page x.
2. Read the conversation with the class and elicit suggestions for words to fill the blanks.
3. Ask one student to model the conversation with you. Then have one or two pairs of students demonstrate it. Offer help as needed.
4. Give pairs time to practice both parts. Circulate and help students.
5. Regroup as a class. Ask pairs of students to do the conversation for the class.

■ EXPANSION ACTIVITY: What I might do this summer

1. Have students write a short composition about what they might do this summer (or another rather distant vacation). Your students may have indefinite ideas about the summer right now, so *might/might not (may/may not)* would be appropriate auxiliaries to use to discuss them. For more definite plans, students must use *be going to* or *will/will not probably. Want to* and *would like to* can also be used.
2. Before students write, brainstorm possibilities for things to do during vacation: work, study, travel, get into shape, etc.
3. Have some students read their compositions. Others can ask questions to get more specific information.

Workbook: *page 2, exercises C, D*

B. Talk with your classmates about what *might* happen to the people in the pictures. Use your imagination and create a story.

1.
2.

3.
4.

4 Interaction

Try to make plans for a future activity with another student. Talk about various possibilities but make no final decision.

A: What're you doing _____ , _____ ?
B: I'm not really sure. I | might | _____ , but
              | may |
     I | might | not because _____ . What about you?
      | may |

A: I was thinking | I | might _____ .
           | we |
B: ____ , but let's wait and see. I'll let you know _____ .

5 Presentation 🔲

Talking about preferences

Use **would rather** + *base form of a verb* to talk about preferences.

Contraction:

'd rather

A

1. I like to play tennis, but I **would rather** swim.
   I**'d rather** swim than play tennis.
2. Dr. Young sometimes works nights, but she **would rather** work days.
   She**'d rather** work days than nights.
3. Mike and Bob play soccer, but they **would rather** play basketball.
   They**'d rather** play basketball than soccer.

B

LISA:	**Would** you **rather** study architecture or medicine?
JOYCE:	I**'d rather** study architecture.
LISA:	Why **would** you **rather** study architecture?
JOYCE:	Because I like to draw. For me, artistic things are more interesting than science.

6 Pronunciation

Pronounce these sentences.

1. I'd rather drink juice than milk.
   /aɪ dræð ər/
2. She'd rather study in the afternoon than at night.
3. He'd rather work on Sunday than Saturday.
4. A: Would you rather play basketball or volleyball?
   B: We'd rather play volleyball.
5. A: Would the Youngs rather go to Mexico or Canada?
   B: They'd rather go to Mexico. They'd like to see the Navas again.

7 Practice

A. **Talk about what the people in each situation *would rather* do. Use sentences like those in model *A* in *5*.**

1. Dung Nguyen works from 3 PM to 11 PM as a security guard at a factory. She's a sports fan, but she can't go to most sports events because she has to work.
2. Mary is studying Japanese because her company wants to send her to Japan. Her company also has an office in Germany. She already knows a little German, and wants to learn to speak it well.

5 Presentation

PROCEDURE
1. Refer to General Guidelines for Presentation, page ix.
2. Put the choices from sections A and B on the board, for example *play tennis OR swim*.
3. Read or play the tape for A and B. Have students repeat chorally, in groups, and individually.
4. To expand the Presentation, have students suggest choices such as *read in English OR native language*. Ask students to state their preference or ask another student for his or her preference.

LANGUAGE NOTE
The auxiliary expression *would rather*, like *might*, is used before a base verb. Only the word *would* is moved before the subject in forming questions.

6 Pronunciation

Focus: Intonation on sentences with *would rather*; pronunciation of *would* in contractions

PROCEDURE
1. Refer to General Guidelines for Pronunciation, page x.
2. Model the sentences or play the tape and have students repeat.
3. Emphasize the choices with a hand gesture.

7 Practice

PROCEDURE
1. Refer to General Guidelines for Practice, page x.
2. Have students read the situations in part A aloud. Ask simple questions to check comprehension.
3. Have students write statements using *would rather* with a partner. Then have them share their statements with the class.
4. For part B, have students practice with a partner. Then check some of the completions with the whole class.

Possible answers: A. 1. Dung Nguyen /den nuyEn/ would rather work from 7 AM to 3 PM (than from 3 PM to 11 PM). She'd rather go to sports events than work. 2. Mary would rather go to Germany than to Japan. She'd rather learn more German than start to study Japanese.

3. The children would rather do something else than work on Saturday. Ana would rather swim than work. Helena would rather play her flute (than work). Pedro would rather read (than work).
B. 1. I like to cook, but I'd rather go to a restaurant. **2.** I know how to play basketball, but I'd rather play volleyball. **3.** My father is a salesperson, but he'd rather be a teacher.

8 Practice

PROCEDURE
1. Refer to General Guidelines for Practice, page x.
2. Review model B in Presentation 5, page 11.
3. Have two students demonstrate #1 or ask a student to demonstrate it with you.
4. Have students practice in pairs. Circulate and offer help as needed.
5. Regroup as a class. Have some students demonstrate their conversations.

Workbook: *page 3, exercises E, F*

9 Presentation

PROCEDURE
1. Refer to General Guidelines for Presentation, page ix.
2. Read or play the tape for model A and have students repeat.
3. Ask if Tom is very happy to do what Adela wants. (Not very happy. He would rather finish the yard work. He also says *I guess we can go,* which shows he is not too eager.)
4. Read or play the tape for model B and have students repeat.
5. Ask if Sekila feels like going to the mall. (No, she doesn't. She hates crowds.)

LANGUAGE NOTE
The negative of *would rather* is *would rather not.* It is heard most commonly in polite refusals.

CULTURAL NOTE
The polite refusal *I'd rather not* is usually accompanied by further explanation, such as *I hate crowds.* It is usually used among friends and when the invitation is informal or on the spur of the moment. If Sam were inviting Sekila on a date, she would say, *I'm sorry I can't. I would like to, but I have to ____.*

3. Ana, Helena, and Pedro Alvarez have to help their parents with the house and yard work on Saturday mornings because both their parents have full-time jobs. Ana is a great swimmer, Helena plays the flute, and Pedro loves to read.

B. Complete these sentences about yourself and people you know.

1. I like to _____ , but I'd rather _____ .
2. I know how to _____ , but I'd rather _____ .
3. My _____ is a _____ , but he'd/she'd rather _____ .

8 Practice

Work with a partner. Find out his or her preference for each pair of activities below. Continue your conversation and find out his or her reasons, too. Follow model *B* in *5*.

1. live in a house / apartment
2. work days / nights
3. have Saturday / Sunday free
4. eat meat / vegetables
5. drink milk / lemonade
6. be married / single
7. go to China / Japan
8. study during the day / late at night
9. be a flight attendant / engineer
10. run / walk for exercise

9 Presentation

Agreeing reluctantly; refusing politely

A
| ADELA: | Let's go to the Grand Opening tomorrow. |
| TOM: | I'd rather finish the yard work, but if you really want to go, I guess we can go. |

B
| SAM: | I might take a look at the Grand Opening, Sekila. Do you want to come along? |
| SEKILA: | Thanks, but I'd rather not. I hate crowds. |

10 Interaction

Work with a partner. Write a conversation in which you discuss plans for the weekend. Choose one of the following situations.

A. One person mentions some possibilities. The other person always has something he or she would rather do. They never come to an agreement.

B. One person mentions some possibilities. The other person isn't excited about the suggestions, but finally agrees to one of them.

11 Reentry

Compare the two women, their clothes, and their dogs. Use adjectives such as: *elegant, casual, tall, short, thin, heavy, pretty, beautiful, large, small,* **and** *long.*

Anna   **Beth**

12 Presentation

Using the superlative

> When talking about a group of people or things, use the superlative to describe the one having more of a quality than all the others.

A

the tallest building

B

the best actor

C

the most expensive car

D

the worst singer in the world

---

10 Interaction

PROCEDURE
1. Refer to General Guidelines for Interaction, page x.
2. Encourage students to answer these questions before beginning to write: a. *Who are the speakers?* (their personalities, interests); b. *Where are they at the moment?*
3. Have students work in pairs. Circulate and offer help as needed.
4. Have as many pairs as possible role play their conversations for the class.

Workbook: *pages 4–5, exercise G*

11 Reentry

PROCEDURE
1. Refer to General Guidelines for Reentry, page x.
2. Ask students to compare things in the pictures using *small*, *pretty*, and *beautiful*. Write their sentences on the board. Ask students for the rules for using *-er* and *more*.
3. Have students work with a partner or in a small group and write 5-10 sentences.
4. Have students share their sentences with the class.

Possible answers: Beth is more elegant than Anna. Anna is wearing more casual clothes than Beth. Beth is taller/heavier than Anna. Anna is shorter/thinner than Beth. Anna's skirt is shorter than Beth's. Anna's dog is larger/heavier/more beautiful than Beth's. Beth's dog is smaller/prettier than Anna's.

LANGUAGE NOTE
In addition to the rules given in the chart on page 14, there are a few two-syllable words that follow either system, among them: *narrow, noble, common, handsome, stupid.*

12 Presentation

PROCEDURE
1. Refer to General Guidelines for Presentation, page ix.
2. Point to the pictures as you read the descriptions or play the tape. Call students' attention to the fact that in each case, the person/thing is #1 in its group. Have students repeat the descriptions.

3. Read or play the tape for sentences #1-4. Have students repeat. Comment that the new mall is #1 *in the area.* Another common phrase used with the superlative is *in the world.*
4. Go over the rules in the grammar box. Then give students an adjective and ask them to say the comparative and superlative forms. Do some with books open; some with books closed.
5. Have students make sentences with some of the superlative forms in the grammar box.

LANGUAGE NOTE

The superlative form marks the #1 position in a ranking of usually three or more things. However, people sometimes rank two things. For example, two brothers might be arguing, and one might say *Mom and Dad love me best.*

13 Practice

PROCEDURE

1. Refer to General Guidelines for Practice, page x.
2. Ask students some questions that focus on the different sections of the map or chart, for example: *How far is ____ from Winfield? How many stores does ____ have? When did ____ open?, How are the prices at ____?*
3. Ask students to study the map and make comparisons, such as *Middlesex is farther from Winfield than Riverview.*
4. Read the instructions on page 15 and have two students read the example. Do as a whole class practice.

	Base	Comparative	Superlative
One-syllable adjectives	old nice big	older than nicer than bigger than	the oldest the nicest the biggest
Two-syllable adjectives ending in **-y**	pretty ugly	prettier than uglier than	the prettiest the ugliest
Irregular adjectives	good bad far	better than worse than farther than	the best the worst the farthest
Adjectives of two or more syllables that don't end in **-y**	boring elegant	more boring than more elegant than	the most boring the most elegant

1. Winfield Mall is **the newest** mall in the area.
2. The new mall is going to be **the best** place to shop in Winfield.
3. Winfield Mall is **the most modern** in the area.
4. The parking at Winfield Mall is **the most convenient** in the area.

13 Practice

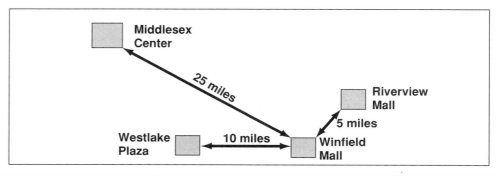

Area Shopping Centers	Size	Year Opened	Location	Prices
Winfield Mall	31 stores	1991	in Winfield	$$
Middlesex Center	21 stores	1975	25 miles from Winfield	$$$
Westlake Plaza	15 stores	1980	10 miles from Winfield	$$
Riverview Mall	10 stores	1984	5 miles from Winfield	$

Study the information in the chart. Then ask and answer questions about the malls, following the example.

> large
> A: Which shopping center is the largest?
> B: Winfield Mall is the largest. It's larger than all the others.

1. old
2. close to the Logans' house
3. big
4. small
5. new
6. far from the Logans' house
7. large
8. close to Middlesex Center
9. good prices
10. high / bad prices

14 Practice

A. Complete the recommendations and warnings with the superlative form of one of these adjectives. There is always more than one correct answer.

boring	exciting	outgoing
comfortable	expensive	(un)reasonable
(in)considerate	hardworking	(un)reliable
(in)convenient	(un)interesting	(un)romantic
(un)crowded	luxurious	(un)selfish
elegant	modern	
energetic	old-fashioned	

1. You really should try the Winfield Mall. It's _____ mall in the area.
2. I don't recommend Midtown Mall. It's _____ .
3. Don't buy a Spirit DL. It's _____ car on the market.
4. Buy the Demgo instead. It's _____ car you can get.
5. You should buy your clothes at Wilson's. They have _____ clothes in town.
6. I don't recommend Harold's. They have _____ clothes in town.
7. You should see that movie. It's _____ of the year.
8. Don't waste your time on that movie. It's _____ of the year.
9. You should meet Howard Young. He's one of _____ people I know.
10. I really don't care much for Mrs. White. She's one of _____ people I know.

B. Compare your answers with a classmate's. How many are the same? How many are different? Do all of your partner's answers make sense?

Answers: Questions and second sentences follow the example. Here is the first sentence for each answer. 1. Middlesex Center is the oldest shopping center. 2. Winfield Mall is the closest to the Logans' house. 3. Winfield Mall is the biggest. 4. Riverview Mall is the smallest. 5. Winfield Mall is the newest. 6. Middlesex Center is the farthest from the Logans' house. 7. Winfield Mall is the largest. 8. Westlake Plaza is the closest to Middlesex Center. 9. Riverview Mall has the best prices. 10. Middlesex Center has the highest/worst prices.

Optional: Give additional practice of *the farthest* using the map on page 14 or a map of your country. Have students ask and answer questions like *Which city is the farthest from Riverview?*

14 Practice

PROCEDURE
1. Refer to General Guidelines for Practice, page x.
2. Have students work alone and complete the sentences. Have them write only the missing words for the whole sentence.
3. As suggested in part B, have students check each other's work. Then check the exercise with the whole class.

Possible answers: 1. the most convenient/modern 2. the most expensive/crowded in town. 3. the most expensive/unreliable 4. the most comfortable/reasonable/reliable 5. the most comfortable/elegant 6. the most old-fashioned/expensive 7. the most exciting/interesting/romatic 8. the most boring/uninteresting/romantic 9. the most energetic/hardworking/interesting/outgoing 10. the most selfish/boring

■ EXPANSION ACTIVITY 1A: They take the prize! They're #1!
(page 189)

Workbook: *page 6, exercise H*

15 Reentry

Note: This Reentry reviews the vocabulary necessary for Interaction 16. It can also be used to review and develop vocabulary related to stores.

PROCEDURE

1. Refer to General Guidelines for Reentry, page x.
2. Write the following questions on the board. *What services can you get in a ____? What can you buy in a ____?*
3. Answer these questions with the whole class for businesses you choose (as examples or if vocabulary is not well-known). Then have students answer the questions for other businesses in pairs or small groups.

Optional: Select a store(s) and have groups compete to see which can make the longest list of items or services.

CULTURAL NOTE

A unisex hair salon styles both men's and women's hair. They have not replaced barbers, who cut men's hair and give shaves, and beauty salons or parlors that are only for women.

16 Interaction

PROCEDURE

Note: Statements describing the location of the different stores in the Winfield Mall appear on page 171 of the text. Have students make copies of the floor plan (1 for every 4 students) if they cannot write in their books. If you do not have copying facilities, write the statements on page 171 on the board in advance of the activity and have one quarter of the students copy A, one quarter B, etc.

1. Refer to General Guidelines for Interaction, page x.
2. Assign students to groups of four. Assign each a letter (A, B, C, and D) and give them appropriate copies of the statements on page 171.
3. Have each group choose a leader and a secretary. The leader directs the cooperative effort. The secretary writes the names/descriptions of businesses on the floor plan when agreed upon.
4. Have students read their own statements silently. When students believe they have information that will help the group, they read a statement aloud. *Students should not show each other their written statements.* This is an oral activity.

15 Reentry

The new Winfield Mall is opening with one or more of the following businesses. With your class or in a small group, talk about what you can buy in each store or the service(s) you can get.

1. bank
2. bookstore
3. camera shop
4. clothing store
5. department store
6. electronics store
7. fast food restaurant
8. gift shop
9. hardware store
10. ice cream parlor
11. jewelry store
12. kitchen shop
13. lamp store
14. music store
15. office supply store
16. pharmacy
17. shoe store
18. sporting goods store
19. supermarket
20. toy store
21. unfinished furniture store
22. unisex hair salon

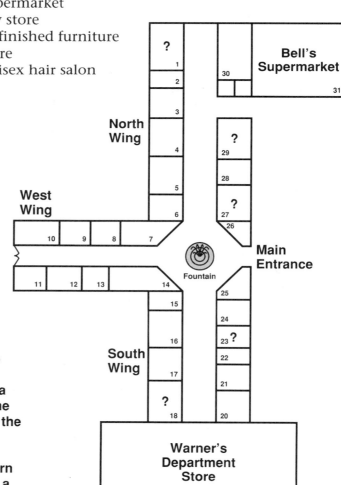

16 Interaction

Work in a group of four students. Make a copy of the floor plan of the mall. Your teacher will give each of you a set of six statements about the location of different stores in the new Winfield Mall. Share the information and identify each store in the mall. You will learn about the stores marked with a ? in the next activity.

17 Listening 🎞️

Write the following numbers of the unidentified stores in the new mall on your paper: 1, 18, 23, 27, and 29. Leave four blank lines between numbers.

First Listening

Listen to the ads and identify each of the five businesses. Write the name next to the appropriate number.

Second Listening

Listen again and find answers to these questions:

1. Does the business make a superlative claim? If so, what?
2. Does the ad include an obvious exaggeration? If so, what?
3. Does the business have a special offer for the Grand Opening? If so, what is it?

#27 — Carmen's Boutique

1. Superlative claim: _____the best quality for the price_____

2. Obvious exaggeration: _no_

3. Special offer: _15% discount on the latest spring fashions_

Answers: **2.** Ellen's Unisex Salon **3.** Small World **4.** toy store **5.** Rosemary's Boutique **6.** office supply store **7.** bookstore **8.** Burger Place **9.** Taco Place **10.** hardware store **11.** Value Slacks **12.** Music Lovers, Inc. **13.** Smart Shoes **14.** Sports Shop **15.** Jenson's Jewelry **16.** Mary Jo's Women's Store **17.** Allen's Men's Store **20.** Hal's Electronics Store **21.** Lamps and Lighting **22.** Kitchen Shop **24.** Fast Photo **25.** ice cream parlor **26.** bank **28.** Harlan's Shoes **30.** Nelson's Pharmacy

17 Listening

PROCEDURE
1. Refer to General Guidelines for Listening, page x.
2. Play the tape or read the script for the Listening. The tape includes the directions and example on page 17.
3. For script and answers see, page 197.
4. If you are reading the script: For the First Listening, give students 10 seconds after each ad to identify the business. For the Second Listening, read the instructions and examples again, giving the answers to the example questions. Then read the ads and give students 30 seconds after each ad to answer the questions.

■ EXPANSION ACTIVITY 1B: Recommendations and warnings
(page 189)

PROCEDURE

1. Refer to General Guidelines for Reading, page x.
2. Talk with students about the questions in "Before You Read." Then have students read the first paragraph on p. 19.
3. Have students read the instructions and questions in the "First Reading" silently. Then have them tell you in their own words what they are going to look for as they read the first time. Teach the useful vocabulary at this time.
4. Ask students what they can already tell about the story from questions 2 and 3.
5. Be sure students understand the difference between paying cash and buying on credit.
6. Give students time to read the story. Remind them to try to guess the meaning of words/expressions they don't know.
7. Discuss the answers to the questions in the "First Reading" with the whole class.
8. Give students time to read the story again (can also be assigned for homework).
9. Have students work with a partner and find the words defined in the "Second Reading" exercise.
10. Answer students' questions about the language in the story or about its meaning.
11. Give students an opportunity to react to the reading in a personal way. Consider using some of the discussion questions in "Reacting to the Reading" on page 20.

18 Reading

Before You Read

1. What is folklore? What is a folk tale or a folk song? Can you name an old folk tale? Can you name a modern folk singer?

2. Discuss or share a folk tale from your country with a partner.

First Reading

Read the following questions and try to find answers to them as you read this modern folk tale. Try to understand the main ideas in the story and guess the meaning of new words and expressions, if necessary. Then discuss the answers to the questions with your classmates.

> **Useful vocabulary:**
>
> 1. **setting:** where the story takes place (including details of weather, size of city, etc.)
> 2. **characters:** the people in the story
> 3. **plot:** the action; what happens in the story

1. What details about the setting are important?

2. Who are the characters in the story? How are they similar? How are they different from each other?

3. The plot of the story:
   a. Where do the Petits and Legrands shop before the mall is built?
   b. Where do they shop after?
   c. What happens to change their lives?
   d. How does the change affect what they can and can't do?

4. Which of these sayings do you think best expresses the main idea of this story? What are your reasons?
   a. You never know from where the wind will blow.
   b. The biggest isn't always the best.
   c. Good friends are with you in bad weather.

1   When most people think of folklore, they think of old stories, songs, sayings, proverbs, and practices of the common, and usually more rural, people of a country. But folklore doesn't have to be old or rural. People today write and sing songs about the problems, thoughts, and values of modern people, both urban and rural. What do you think a modern folk tale might be like?

A Tale of Big and Small

2   There was once a family named Petit who lived in a small city, in a nice, old neighborhood with a small business area on a street nearby. On that street, they shopped in a nice grocery store owned by one of their neighbors, bought medicine at the local drugstore owned by another of their neighbors, and filled up their gas tank with gasoline at a neighborhood garage.

3   Living next door to the Petits were the Legrands. The Legrands, of course, could shop at those same neighborhood businesses, and they did until the big chains and the big shopping malls came along. As soon as they had the opportunity to shop at the largest supermarket in town at the ultra-modern mall, they did. As soon as they could save a little on their medicine at the big chain pharmacy at the mall, they did. As soon as they could save a penny a gallon on their gas at the station in the mall, they did.

4   In spite of this difference in consumer habits, the Petits and the Legrands were good friends and neighbors. When they got together, the conversation often turned to how to get the most for your money, and the Legrands were right in there pushing the big chains.

5   "You really should try the mall, Petit," said Legrand. "It's the easiest place to shop. They've got the latest in everything and the largest variety —all under one roof. You're making a big mistake if you don't shop out there." "And," said Mrs. Legrand, "mall merchants buy and sell in such large quantities that the prices just have to be better."

6   "There's no doubt they have more variety than the stores here in the neighborhood, but as for the prices, I'm not so sure I agree with you," said Mr. Petit. "It seems to me that some of those business people out at the mall jack up the prices so they can lower them later and make you think things are on sale." "Maybe we're old-fashioned," said Mrs. Petit, "but we can get almost everything we need right here in the neighborhood, and we'd rather deal with people we know. Business people here in the neighborhood count on our business and if worse comes to worst, I know we can count on them."

7   Then one day something quite unexpected happened. The local clothing factory where the Petits and the Legrands worked was closed. Businesses half way around the world could make better and cheaper clothing, so 300 people were out of work. Times were hard. Savings were used up quickly. There were hopes for a new factory, but negotiations were slow.

Possible answers: First Reading **1.** The characters live in a small town in an old residential area. Their neighbors run the businesses in a small business area nearby. There is a large, new shopping mall in town. **2.** Characters: the Petits and the Legrands. Similarity: they live in same neighborhood. Difference: They like to shop in different places. **3. a.** in their neighborhood **b.** Legrands - the mall; Petits - the neighborhood **c.** The local clothing factory closes. **d.** The Legrands can't get to the mall. They have to shop near home. Neither family can find work easily. **4.** There is no one correct answer. All are true in part and relate to the events of the story. However, the choice of words in the story; the frequency of comments about bigness, perhaps make **b** the best choice. The main idea of the story is more related to bigness than to adversity or friendship.

Possible answers: Second Reading   **1.** a chain, chain store
2. pushing; to push one type of business or product
3. to jack up prices   **4.** old-fashioned   **5.** deal with
6. count on   **7.** negotiations   **8.** tough   **9.** afford
10. purchases

Reacting to the Reading: Discussion Questions
1. In what other areas of life is it true that the biggest isn't necessarily the best?
2. Are there times when the biggest has an advantage?
3. One way businesses sometimes try to trick customers is to jack up prices and then reduce them so people think there is a sale when there really is none. What are some other ways some businesses try to trick customers?
4. How can we prepare for adversity, for unexpected things in our lives?

19 Writing

Note: This Writing reinforces the three elements of a story presented in the reading: setting, character, and plot. We cannot expect that all students will be good story tellers, but we can point the way by showing them that they need to make the setting, characters, and plot clear to a reader or listener through details.

PROCEDURE
1. Refer to the General Guidelines for Writing on page xi.
2. Help students think about what to write by having them do part A.
3. Encourage students to think about the details they will include. Have them write notes to answer the questions on page 21 *before* they write a first draft of the story.
4. Have students exchange papers and read another student's story. Have them share their reactions to their partner's story and make suggestions.
5. If time permits, have students incorporate any suggestions and make a final copy.

8   Not long after the closing, the Petits and the Legrands met at their neighborhood grocery. While they were waiting to check out, they talked. "Things are really tough," said Mr. Petit. "Yeah," said Legrand. "I can't even afford the gas to get to the mall anymore."

9   Then it was the Petits' turn. "Twenty dollars and forty-five cents," said the grocer, Mr. Font, as Mrs. Font bagged their few purchases. "Things are really bad, Pedro," said Mrs. Petit. "Ten is all we have. Can we pay you the rest next week? We've got a job this weekend." "No problem," said Mrs. Font. "Thanks a lot," said the Petits. After saying good-bye to the Legrands, they picked up their bag and went out.

10   Mr. Font turned to the next customers, the Legrands. "That'll be thirty-one dollars and eighty-five cents, sir," said Font. "Things are very bad," said Mrs. Legrand. "Fifteen is all we have. Can we pay you the rest next week? We have work this weekend."

"Sorry," said Mr. Font coldly. "We don't give credit."

Second Reading

Read the story again. Then talk with a partner and try to find a word or expression that means the same thing as the following:

1. stores with the same name and owned by the same company (3)
2. speaking in support of *(a slang expression)* (4)
3. to raise; make prices higher *(a slang expression)* (6)
4. out-of-date, not modern (6)
5. do business with (6)
6. depend on (6)
7. business talks (7)
8. difficult (8)
9. have enough money to pay for (8)
10. things you buy (9)

19 Writing

A. Tell a partner about something funny or interesting that happened to you or someone you know.

B. Write a short story about that event. Your story can be a recommendation or a warning. Before you write the story, answer the following questions in note form to be sure you included the best ideas and details possible.

1. Where does the story take place? What are the important details about the setting?
2. Who are the characters in your story? What are the important details about them?
3. What happens to the characters? What is the plot?

C. Now share your story with a small group or the class. Ask them for suggestions to improve it. Did they understand the whole story? Were certain parts confusing?

20 Final Activity

Work with a small group of students. Choose one of the businesses in the new Winfield Mall and plan a one-minute television advertisement to announce its Grand Opening. Be sure all members of your group participate in the advertisement as announcer, business owner(s), customers, etc. Remember to tell what the business is, where it is located, when it will open, and why people should patronize your business and come to the Grand Opening. Use comparatives or superlatives in your ad. For other suggestions listen to the ads in *Listening 17* again.

■ EXPANSION ACTIVITY: Sharing stories
1. Have students attach their stories to a slightly larger piece of paper and tape them to the wall.
2. Keep them there several days so students can read them.
3. If possible, help students edit their stories and make a booklet of them.

20 Final Activity

PROCEDURE
1. Refer to General Guidelines for Final Activity, page xi.
2. With the class, brainstorm a list of selling points heard in most ads. For example: service, quality of merchandise, large selection, easy to get to, convenient parking and hours, low prices, special prices.
3. Form groups and have students discuss and answer the planning questions first.
4. Have the group write out what each person is going to say and practice it. Students can memorize their ads or make 3 x 5 cards with their comments on them.
5. Have students role play as many ads as time allows.

Workbook: *page 7, exercises I, J*

Useful materials: pictures of motor vehicles, interiors and exteriors; posterboard, marking pens

At the Car Show

PROCEDURE

Refer to General Guidelines for Opener, page ix.

COMPREHENSION QUESTIONS

Now answer these questions.

1. Are there many people at the Grand Opening? *Yes, there are. About half the population of Winfield.*
2. What does Bob like about the car? *It's beautiful. It's economical. It's got everything.*
3. What is Tom's first reaction to the car? *It's expensive.*
4. Does Tom think that $14,900 is a bad price for the car? *No, he doesn't.*
5. Does Sam have enough money to buy the car? *No, he doesn't.*

Now listen to these sentences. Say *Yes, that's right, No, that's wrong,* or *I don't know. Maybe.*

6. Tom thinks it's a good idea to buy a new car. *No, that's wrong.*
7. Bob has his driver's license. *No, that's wrong.*
8. Bob is not a careful driver. *I don't know. Maybe.*
9. Bob had a problem when he was learning to park. *Yes, that's right.*
10. Bob is sure that he won't fail the road test. *Yes, that's right.*

DISCUSSION QUESTIONS

1. What lesson do you think Bob learned?
2. What are some reasons to buy a brand new car? To buy a used car?
3. Should parents teach their children to drive or should the children learn from another person?
4. Should teenagers have their own cars? Why or why not?

UNIT 2

COMMUNICATION
Talking about wishes and imaginary situations ▪ Checking facts and observations ▪ Talking about the parts of a car ▪ Talking about desirable and undesirable qualities

GRAMMAR
Imaginary condition: *if* + past, *would/could* ▪ Tag questions with present tense of *be* ▪ Adjective + *enough* ▪ *Too* + adjective

SKILLS
Writing a paragraph about an imaginary situation ▪ Reading about an organization ▪ Listening to traffic-related reports

At the Car Show

Half the population of Winfield seems to be at the Grand Opening of the new Winfield Mall. There's a terrific car show sponsored by Winfield's only local dealer, Wilson Motors. Tom, Sam, and Bob Logan are looking at the new Spirit DL.

BOB: It's a beauty, isn't it, Dad? And economical, too. Look at that — 40 miles to the gallon.

TOM: Yeah, but look at the price!

BOB: But it's got everything, Dad — power steering, power brakes, cloth upholstery, air-conditioning . . . the works. $14,900 really isn't bad, is it?

TOM: No, I guess not for a good medium-sized car. But nobody pays cash for a car these days, so you have to add a few thousand dollars in interest, too. What do you think, Sam?

SAM: I'd have to work ten years to pay for this one. Would you buy this Spirit if you could, Dad?

TOM: No, I don't think I would.

BOB: Why not?

TOM: Because, in my opinion, it's not wise to buy a new car at all. A new car depreciates very fast. It loses a couple thousand dollars in value the minute you drive it off the lot. It's better to buy a good used car, especially if you know the previous owner.

BOB: I don't care what I drive. I just wish I had my license. When do you think I can take the road test, Dad?

TOM: I don't know. I'm not sure you're ready to drive alone, Bob. You're just not careful enough.

BOB: Not careful enough? Dad, you're not still upset about the dent I made in the car when I was learning to park, are you?

TOM: Well, I'm sure glad you weren't driving a new car.

BOB: C'mon, Dad. Give me a break . . . Other guys my age have their licenses. I learned my lesson. I drive carefully now. You can bet I won't fail the road test.

TOM: Well, we'll see.

1 Vocabulary in Context 🔲

A. **Complete the definitions with words from the conversation and the introduction (pages 22–23).**

1. When something loses value it _____ .
2. Money that you pay to borrow money is called _____ .
3. A business person who sells cars is called a car _____ .
4. The place where the dealer keeps cars is called the _____ .
5. A permit to drive a car is called a _____ .
6. When you stop your car and leave it for a while, you _____ it.

B. **The following underlined words and expressions appear in the conversation. What do they mean?**

1. Nobody pays <u>cash</u> for a car these days.
2. <u>You can bet</u> I won't fail that test.
3. When can I take the <u>road test</u>?
4. I don't think it's <u>wise</u> to buy a new car.
5. The <u>previous</u> owner of this car was a couple with eight kids.
6. I'd like a <u>medium-sized</u> car.

LANGUAGE NOTES
1. A **dent** is a hollow place especially in metal made by an impact of something else hard. Draw or demonstrate the meaning with a gesture.
2. **The works** is a slang expression meaning *everything*. In the Opener it means all possible accessories and luxuries.
3. *C'mon, Dad. Give me a break.* means *Stop giving me problems about the dent.* or *Not that old story again.*

CULTURAL NOTE
In the U.S. most new cars are financed by a bank or the car manufacturer's finance company. Typical financing from a bank on a $15,000 car might be 25% down ($3750) and $308 per month for four years.

1 Vocabulary in Context

PROCEDURE
1. Refer to General Guidelines for Vocabulary in Context, page ix.
2. Have students work with a partner or in a small group. Check answers with the whole class.

Answers: **A. 1.** depreciates **2.** interest **3.** dealer **4.** lot **5.** license **6.** park. **B. 1.** money in the form of coins and bills **2.** You can be sure **3.** the test on the road, when you have to drive the car **4.** intelligent, a good idea **5.** last **6.** not big and not small

Workbook: *page 8, exercise A*

2 Reentry

Note: Students first practiced wishes in *Book 2* (*Liz wishes she could find a better job.*) This Reentry prepares students for imaginary conditional sentences in Presentation 3 by reminding them that the past tense in a wish shows that it is imaginary or unreal.

PROCEDURE
1. Refer to General Guidelines for Reentry, page x.
2. Write the real situations on the board with the beginning of each wish, e.g., *I don't have a job. I wish _____.* Ask students to provide the completions. Call attention to the change in verb forms.
3. Do Part A as a whole class. Encourage many different completions.
4. Have students do B in small groups. Demonstrate a good completion of each item before they practice alone. Circulate and help as needed.
5. Regroup the class. Ask for examples of each item.

Possible answers: **A.** **1.** Bob wishes he had his driver's license. Bob wishes he could take the road test today. Bob wishes he didn't have to drive with his dad. Ted wishes he knew how to drive. Ted wishes he were 16. Ted wishes he didn't have to wait a year to learn to drive. **2.** Lisa wishes she didn't have a cold/could swim in the meet/were well. She wishes Dr. Young could help her/had a perfect medicine/knew how to make her well fast. **3.** They wish they had more money/could find a cheaper place/their present apartment were better. **4.** He wishes he could do everything/the party were next weekend/didn't have so much homework.

Possible answers: **B.** **1.** I can't speak English perfectly. I wish I could (speak it perfectly). **2.** I have a headache. I wish I didn't have a headache. **3.** I don't know how to draw. I wish I knew how to draw. **4.** I am not tall. I wish I were tall.

LANGUAGE NOTE
Formal writing requires *were* in all persons, singular and plural, to express imaginary or unreal wishes with the verb *to be.* Even educated people, however, are heard to say *was* in the first and third person singular in speech. For example, *I wish I was taller* or *Ted's not happy. He wishes he was 16.*

2 Reentry

Expressing wishes

	Use past tense forms to express wishes.

Reality	**A wish**
1. I can't have the car this weekend.	I wish I **could** have the car this weekend.
2. I'm not 21.	I wish I **were** 21.
3. I'm too tall.	I wish I **weren't** tall.
4. Lisa doesn't know how to drive.	She wishes she **knew** how to drive.
5. The Riveras don't have a car.	They wish they **had** a car.
6. I have a cold.	I wish I **didn't have** a cold.

A.   Read each situation and tell what people wish were true.

1. Bob Logan is 17 and has a learner's permit, but he can't drive the family car alone. His friend Ted is 15. He can't drive at all.
   Bob wishes he (had) (could) (didn't have to) _____ .
   Ted wishes he (knew how to) (were) (didn't have to) _____ .
2. Lisa Logan has a cold so she can't participate in today's swimming meet.
   Lisa wishes she (didn't have) (could) (were) _____ .
   She wishes Dr. Young (could) (had) (knew how to) _____ .
3. Gino and Cristina aren't happy with their apartment, but they can't find a better one. They can't afford more than $500 a month rent and most of the apartments they looked at were more expensive than that. They wish _____ .
4. Mike has a lot of homework this weekend, and he also has a soccer game and an invitation to a party. He can't possibly do everything. He wishes _____ .

B.   Share your wishes with a small group of classmates. Use sentences like these. Talk about school or work, your family responsibilities, or other things.

1. I can't _____ . I wish I _____ .
2. I | have / don't have | _____ . I wish I _____ .
3. I don't know how to _____ . I wish I _____ .
4. I | am / am not | _____ . I wish I _____ .

3 Presentation 📼

Talking about imaginary situations

> Use the *past tense* in the *if*-clause; use **would** or **could** + *verb* in the result clause.

Note:
If I **were** . . .
If he/she **were** . . .

A The Logans **aren't** rich.
If the Logans **were** rich, they **could get** a better car.
(They would be able to do it, but they might not do it.)
If the Logans **were** rich, they **would get** a better car.
(They would do it.)
If the Logans **were** rich, they **wouldn't have** any money problems.

B My family **doesn't have** a car.
If my family **had** a car, I **could learn** to drive.
If my family **had** a car, I **would learn** to drive.
If my family **had** a car, I **wouldn't have to** walk so much.

C My family **has** a car.
If my family **didn't have** a car, I **would have to walk** a lot more.
If my family **didn't have** a car, I **could learn** to drive somebody else's car.

4 Practice

A. Complete the sentences with the past tense of the verb in parentheses to show the idea is not true.

1. If I _____ (know) how to speak Russian, I could go to Russia and learn a lot about the people and culture.
2. If Sam _____ (win) a big prize in the lottery, he could buy a car.
3. If somebody _____ (give) me $100, I would buy a radio.
4. If Bob _____ (have) his driver's license, he would be able to drive alone.
5. If Lisa and Joyce _____ (be) 16, they could learn to drive.
6. If Gloria _____ (have) a brother or sister, she would be happy.
7. If Sekila _____ (win) the lottery, she would fly to Africa to see her family.
8. If I _____ (lose) my wallet, I would report it to the police.
9. If I _____ (be) a car dealer, I would sell small cars.
10. If I _____ (buy) a new car, I would have to pay interest.

3 Presentation

PROCEDURE
1. Refer to General Guidelines for Presentation, page ix.
2. Write the words *Real* and *Imaginary* at the top of two columns on the board. Have students read the sentences in the Presentation and tell you in which column to write them.

LANGUAGE NOTES
1. The past tense in the if-clause shows the condition is not real.
2. Using *would* in the result clause means something would be sure to happen or to be if the condition were true. *Could* means it is a possibility.

4 Practice

PROCEDURE
1. Refer to General Guidelines for Practice, page x.
2. Do as a whole class practice.

Answers: **A.** 1. knew 2. won 3. gave 4. had 5. were 6. had 7. won 8. lost 9. were 10. bought

Answers: **B.** 1. would/could go (*would,* for sure; *could,* a possibility) 2. could watch 3. wouldn't take 4. would buy 5. would move 6. couldn't swim/participate 7. wouldn't go 8. would be

5 Practice

PROCEDURE
1. Refer to General Guidelines for Practice, page x.
2. After students read the imaginary sentences about Gino, ask them for other ways to complete the sentence.
3. Have students work with a partner and write at least two different ways to complete each imaginary situation 1-5.

Possible answers: 1. If Liz were married, she wouldn't be living at home/couldn't depend on Mom and Dad so much/could start a family.   2. If Lisa and Joyce were in high school, they would be in the same school as Bob and Mike/could take algebra/could go to high school dances.   3. If Bob had his driver's license, he could drive the family car alone/would feel great/would be very careful.   4. If the Logans had more money, they could buy a new car/Tom wouldn't work overtime/Adela could take more courses/Sam would go to college full-time/Bob could take a trip to Mexico/Lisa would buy a new bike/maybe, they wouldn't do anything differently   5. If the Youngs lived in New York City, they would ride the subway a lot/Howard and Elinor would go to the theater often/Liz could get a new job/Mike would go to a new high school/Ted wouldn't have to take the bus to school/Joyce could go to the top of the World Trade Center every weekend

Workbook: *page 9, exercises B, C*

B. Complete the sentences using *could, would, couldn't,* or *wouldn't,* and an appropriate verb. Sometimes there are two correct answers that have different meanings.

1. If I had some free time, I _____ to New York.

2. If our class had a television, we _____ the news every day, but we might not.

3. If Adela knew how to fix her computer, she _____ it to somebody else.

4. If Sam Logan won $5000 in the lottery, he _____ a car because he wants one very badly.

5. If Gino and Cristina found a better apartment, they _____ for sure.

6. If Lisa had a cold today, she _____ in the swimming meet.

7. If Dr. Young had to work tonight, she and Howard _____ to the movies.

8. If Lisa lost her wallet, she _____ very sad.

5 Practice

Work with a partner. Complete the *if*-clause, showing that the situation is not true. Then talk about ways to complete the result clause.

Gino isn't a mechanic.	
If Gino were a mechanic,	he could fix his own car.
	he would get dirtier at work than he does now.
	he wouldn't have to work late at night.
	he couldn't work at the Roma.

1. Liz isn't married. If Liz _____ married, she _____ .

2. Lisa and Joyce aren't in high school. If they _____ in high school, they _____ .

3. Bob doesn't have his driver's license. If he _____ it, he _____ .

4. The Logans don't have a lot of money. If they _____ more money, they / Tom / Adela / Sam / Bob / Lisa _____ .

5. The Youngs don't live in New York City. If they _____ in New York City, they / Howard / Elinor / Liz / Mike / Ted / Joyce _____ .

6 Presentation

Asking about imaginary situations

> A: If you had the money, would you buy a new car?
> B: Yes, I would, and I would take very good care of it.
>   No, I wouldn't. I would buy a good used car instead.

7 Practice

Complete both clauses of the questions. Use the verbs in parentheses, as appropriate. Then ask and answer the questions in a small group.

1. If someone _____ you the opportunity, _____ you _____ to the moon? (go / give)

2. If you _____ a trip to any country in the world, where _____ you _____ to go? (win / want)

3. If you _____ a space creature on the street, _____ you _____ to him/her/it? What would you talk about? (see / talk)

4. If you _____ an invitation to meet the president of your country, _____ you _____ ? What would you say to him/her? (accept / get)

5. If you _____ your wallet, what _____ you _____ ? (do / lose)

6. If someone _____ you a really terrific job in Alaska, _____ you _____ it? (accept / offer)

7. If you _____ be really famous, what _____ you _____ to be? (can / want)

8. If you _____ the mayor of your city, what _____ you _____ to improve it? (do / be)

9. If you _____ a gift of $5000, what _____ you _____ with it? (receive / do)

10. If you _____ a magic lamp, what two things _____ you _____ for? (wish / have)

6 Presentation

PROCEDURE
1. Refer to General Guidelines for Presentation, page ix.
2. Expand the Presentation with other questions related to students' experiences, for example: *If we had a test tomorrow, would you study tonight?*

7 Practice

PROCEDURE
1. Refer to General Guidelines for Practice, page x.
2. Have students work on the completion of the questions alone or with a partner. Check answers with the class before forming small groups.
3. Have students discuss one question at a time in a small group. Each student should have a chance to answer each question if he or she wants.

Answers: **1.** gave / would / go **2.** won / where would / want **3.** saw / would / talk **4.** got / would / accept **5.** lost / would / do **6.** offered / would / accept **7.** could / would / want **8.** were/ would / do **9.** received / would / do **10.** had / would / wish

■ EXPANSION ACTIVITY: Survey the class
1. Have students work in pairs and write three or four questions using the imaginary conditional. From these questions, they select one and survey the class.
2. Teach students to make a simple multiple choice answer form for the most likely answers so it is easier to count and report results. The last choice can be *Other*.
3. Each partner surveys half the class and they combine results and report to the class.

Optional: Have students survey people in the community.

Workbook: *page 10, exercise D*

8 Writing

1. Refer to General Guidelines for Writing, page xi.
2. Have students read the three topic choices silently. Ask students for examples of what they would write about the pictures.
3. Have students tell a classmate about the person, place, or thing they are going to write about. Encourage classmates to help each other with ideas.
4. Have students make notes to answer the guide questions before writing their paragraphs.
5. Have students read their paragraphs to the class, using the word ZING. The class tries to guess the person, place or thing.

Optional: Have students work in teams of three to play ZING. The teacher reads the paragraphs aloud. Team members confer and write their guesses. The team with the most correct answers wins. Paragraphs could also be put on the wall and read by students.

9 Presentation

Note: Tag questions are presented in *Book 4* gradually. There is no need to work for mastery at this time.

PROCEDURE
1. Refer to General Guidelines for Presentation, page ix.
2. Write *It's a beauty.* and *The Demgo isn't Japanese.* on the board. Underline the verb and put a + or - above it. Add the tags and demonstrate (using + and -) how the tag uses the opposite verb form and uses a pronoun that refers to the subject of the original statement.
3. Reread the functional explanation in the top box. Have students practice the expected responses for A and B. Then ask each question in the paradigm and have students give the expected response.
4. Have students practice the unexpected responses for A and B. Then ask each question in the paradigm and have students give the unexpected response.

8 Writing

A. Choose one of the situations. Take notes to answer the questions. Then discuss your topic with a classmate.

1. Imagine you are a famous person. If you were that famous person, where would you live? What would your daily life be like? What could you do that you can't do now?

2. Choose a city or a country. If you lived in that place, how would your daily life be different from what it is right now? What could you do that you can't do now?

3. Think about something that you don't have. If you had that thing, what would you do with it? How would your life be different if you had it?

B. Use your notes to write a paragraph that includes answers to the questions.

C. Play a game, called ZING, and share your paragraph with your classmates. Read your paragraph, but substitute the word ZING for the name of the person, place, or thing you wrote about. Your classmates will try to guess the person, place, or thing.

9 Presentation

Checking facts and observations using tag questions

> Use tag questions to check facts or observations when you believe you are correct and expect the other person will agree.

I'm not late, **am I?**	We're late, **aren't we?** We're not late, **are we?**

You're Mexican, **aren't you?**
You're not studying Spanish, **are you?**

He's a doctor, **isn't he?** Mary's not here, **is she?** This car's not Japanese, **is it?**	They're students, **aren't they?** Bob and Mike aren't freshmen, **are they?**

EXCEPTION: I'm late, **aren't I?**

A

BOB:	It's a beauty, **isn't it,** Dad?	
TOM:	Yes, it is, but look at that price!	(expected response)
	No, it isn't. It's ugly.	(unexpected response)

B

LIZ:	The Demgo isn't Japanese, **is it?**	
TOM:	No, it isn't. It's American.	(expected response)
	Yes, it is, but it's made in the U.S.	(unexpected response)

10 Pronunciation

> Use *falling* intonation on the tag question when you are quite sure you are right.
> Use *rising* intonation if you are less sure.

The Winfield Mall is brand new, isn't it? (Quite sure)

The Winfield Mall is brand new, isn't it? (Not sure)

LANGUAGE NOTES
1. Tag questions use a verb that is opposite (affirmative or negative) from the main verb in the statement. The tag is set off by a comma.
2. *Yes* is the expected answer when the statement is affirmative. *No* is the expected answer when the statement is negative.
3. Checking facts or observations when one is reasonably sure he/she is correct or the other person will agree is probably the most common function for tag questions. When you aren't sure (or don't know) you ask an information question. Tag questions are also used to open conversations (See Unit 9).
4. Adding *Right?* to any statement is a simpler, but informal way to check or verify information or opinions. (*You're studying French. Right? You went to the party. Right?*) Overuse of this form should be discouraged.

10 Pronunciation

PROCEDURE
1. Refer to General Guidelines for Pronunciation, page x.
2. Model or play the tape for the examples. Use a hand gesture to accompany the falling or rising intonation. Have students repeat.
3. Practice the falling and rising intonation patterns separately first. Then cue students with the item number and *quite sure* or *not sure* (Student uses falling/rising intonation.)

11 Practice

PROCEDURE
1. Refer to General Guidelines for Practice, page x.
2. Do Part A with the whole class. Have students read statements silently. Remind them to think about which intonation pattern to use.
3. Check to be sure the intonation used fits what the students know about the characters or their classmates. The more likely intonation is indicated in the answers.

Answers: **A.** 1. isn't she? (falling) 2. aren't they? (falling) 3. aren't you? (either) 4. aren't we? (falling) 5. isn't it? (rising) 6. aren't I? (either) 7. is he? (falling) 8. are they? (falling) 9. are we? (either) 10. is she? (rising) 11. are they? (either) 12. is it? (falling) **B.** #2 is true; #4 is false, Talahassee is the capital of Florida.

> **Workbook:** *pages 10–11, exercise E*

Say each sentence twice, first using falling intonation and a second time using rising intonation.

1. The Logans are at the Grand Opening, aren't they?
2. Bob's looking at cars, isn't he?
3. We aren't late for the fashion show, are we?
4. You're coming to the opening, aren't you?
5. It's about 8:00, isn't it?

11 Practice

A. **Read the sentence. Add the correct tag question and ask for a classmate's confirmation. Use falling intonation if you are quite sure; use rising intonation if in doubt.**

1. Adela is at the mall.
2. Sam, Bob, and Tom are looking at cars.
3. You're a secretary.
4. We're next.
5. The mall is open until 10:00.
6. I'm in your group.
7. Tom isn't interested in a new car.
8. The Logans aren't rich.
9. We aren't late for the fashion show.
10. Liz isn't at the mall.
11. The cars in the mall aren't for sale.
12. The Spirit DL isn't very expensive.

B. **Now work with a partner and write six tag questions to check information or observations with your classmates. Then ask another pair your questions.**

1. Check a fact about a classmate.
   (You're from Peru, aren't you?)
2. Check facts about famous people.
   (Michael J. Fox is Canadian, isn't he?)
3. Check facts about places in your city.
   (The library is on First Street, isn't it?)
4. Check facts about other cities or countries, their people, geography, location, etc.
   (Miami isn't the capital of Florida, is it?)
5. Check the time, the day, or the date.
   (Today's Thursday, isn't it?)
6. Check the day or time of some activity, a test, a concert, a TV show, etc.
   (Our next test is Friday, isn't it?)

Talking about the parts of a car

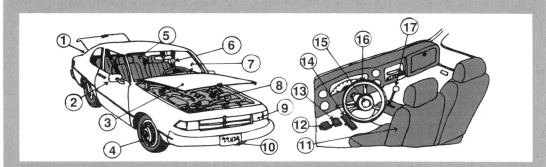

1. trunk	**7.** windshield	**13.** brake
2. mirror	**8.** engine / motor	**14.** gas pedal / accelerator
3. hood	**9.** headlight	**15.** horn
4. tire	**10.** license plate	**16.** steering wheel
5. back seat	**11.** front seat	**17.** (gear)shift
6. seat belt	**12.** clutch	

Complete each sentence with the correct part of a car.

1. You won't be able to see other cars in front of you well if you don't keep your _____ clean.

2. There's a truck behind us. I can see it in the _____ .

3. When you drive at night, you must turn on your _____ .

4. The driver sits in the _____ .

5. When you drive, keep both hands on the _____ .

6. When the Logans take a trip, the children usually sit in the _____ .

7. The _____ has numbers and letters on it. Some plates have only letters on them. **828·TMS** NEW YORK **HOW·R·U** NEW YORK

8. Check your _____ occasionally to be sure you have enough air in them.

9. When you get in the car, be sure to fasten your _____ .

10. You have to open the _____ to put oil in the engine.

11. Don't put your luggage on the seat. Put it in the _____ .

12. If you want to go faster, you press the _____ .

13. If you want to go slower you use the _____ .

14. If you want to change from one gear to another in a standard shift car, you have to step on the _____ and move the _____ .

---

12 Vocabulary in Context

PROCEDURE

1. Refer to General Guidelines for Vocabulary in Context, page ix.
2. Do the sentence completion exercise as a whole class or have students work in pairs and then check the answers as a class.
3. Discuss the value of knowing automobile vocabulary, even if students don't drive. Cars are a general topic of conversation. Furthermore, students may need to use some of these words if they are ever witnesses to an accident or crime involving a car.
4. There are two kinds of mirrors on a car: side-view mirror(s) and a rearview mirror.
5. You might want to illustrate how dialects differ in vocabulary (and spelling) using the following British words for parts of a car. Put these words on the board and have students match them with their American equivalents: *numberplate, tyre, boot (trunk), windscreen, bonnet (hood), wing (fender), gear lever, petrol tank.*

Answers: **1.** windshield **2.** mirror **3.** headlights **4.** front seat **5.** steering wheel **6.** back seat **7.** license plate **8.** tires **9.** seat belt **10.** hood **11.** trunk **12.** gas pedal/accelerator **13.** brake **14.** clutch/(gear)shift

■ EXPANSION ACTIVITY: Parts of a car (Vocabulary building project)

1. Have students find/draw detailed pictures of the exterior and interior of a car. (Check newspaper and magazine ads and car dealers' brochures.)
2. Have students prepare a poster on which they draw lines to the various parts of the car and label them clearly. (To change the poster to a vocabulary testing picture, have students tape pieces of index cards over the words. Vocabulary can be checked by lifting the flaps.)

13 Practice

PROCEDURE

1. Refer to General Guidelines for Practice, page x.
2. Demonstrate the Practice using the picture on page 31 or large pictures of cars from magazines. Be sure to give a plural example too. (*These are the headlights, aren't they?*)
3. Have students practice with a partner or in a small group. Circulate and offer help as needed.

> **Workbook: *page 11, exercise F***

14 Reentry

PROCEDURE

1. Refer to General Guidelines for Reentry, page x.
2. Review the adjectives in the box before students read the model questions and answers. Ask for additional adjectives.
3. Have students practice with their partners and write down their four best questions.
4. Have students ask and answer questions as a whole class. See how many different questions they can ask without repeating.

Answers: Questions and answers follow the models in the box.

> **Workbook: *page 12, exercise G***

---

13 Practice

Practice with a partner. Cover the words naming the parts of a car in *12*. Point to a part of the car in the picture. Name it and ask for your partner's confirmation.

> steering wheel
> A: This is the steering wheel, isn't it?
> B: Yes, it is.

14 Reentry

Making comparisons

Practice with a partner. Ask and answer questions about the vehicles, using *which* and the adjectives in the list on the right.

Useful vocabulary:	
safe	dangerous
economical	expensive to run
cheap	expensive
fast	slow
large (big)	small
good	awful/terrible
strong/powerful	light
heavy	quiet
loud/noisy	ugly
pretty	

1.
motorcycle

2.
pickup truck

3.
compact car

4.
station wagon

5.
van

6.
sports car

> A: Which vehicle is the most economical?
> B: The motorcycle is. It gets about 40 miles per gallon.
> A: Which vehicle is larger, the van or the pickup truck?
> B: I think the van is larger.

15 Presentation ☐━○

Talking about desirable and undesirable qualities

Desirable:
adjective + **enough**

Undesirable:
too + adjective

1. This car is **big enough** for the family.

2. This car is **too small** for the family.

A: Would you buy a motorcycle?

B: No, I wouldn't. It's **too dangerous.**

A: I agree. A motorcycle isn't **safe enough.**

16 Interaction

Talk with your classmates about which vehicle in *14* you would or wouldn't buy and give your reasons. Use *too* or *enough* with some of the adjectives in *14*. You can also use the comparative and superlative forms.

A: Would you buy the _____ ?

B: ____ . | It's _____ .
          | It's too _____ .
          | It's not _____ enough.

A: I | would, too. | It's _____ .
     | wouldn't either. |

---

15 Presentation

PROCEDURE
1. Refer to General Guidelines for Presentation, page ix.
2. Have students look at the pictures as you read the sentences or play the tape. Ask them what kind of car the families want. (A big car is desirable. A small car is undesirable.)
3. Ask if the car on the left will be good for the family in #1. (*Yes, it will. They want a big car and this car is* **big enough.**) Repeat for #2. (*No, it won't. They want a big car and this car is* **too small.**)

LANGUAGE NOTE
Too and *very* cause problems for many students. *Very* is a general intensifier. *Too* has the specific meaning of *for some purpose.* For example, *Lisa is very young. She is too young to drive a car.*

16 Interaction

PROCEDURE
1. Refer to General Guidelines for Interaction, page x.
2. Encourage students to give additional information as well.

Possible completions:
1. A: Would you buy the compact car?
   B: No, I wouldn't. It's too small. (I would buy a bigger vehicle.)
   A: I wouldn't either. It's not big enough. (I need a larger car, too.)
2. A: Would you buy the van?
   B: Yes, I would. It's a nice, big vehicle. (You can carry lots of things in it.)
   A: I wouldn't buy it. It's too big for me. (I would buy a smaller vehicle.)

■ EXPANSION ACTIVITY 2A: He's not tall enough (page 189)
■ EXPANSION ACTIVITY 2B: Who gets what? (page 189)

Workbook: *page 13, exercise H*

17 Reentry

PROCEDURE

Refer to General Guidelines for Reentry, page x.

Answers: **A.** 1. well 2. hard 3. carefully
4. quickly, fast 5. clearly 6. correctly **B.** 1. good,
well 2. rude, politely 3. safely 4. smoothly
5. quick 6. correct 7. careless 8. slowly
9. carefully 10. completely

Workbook: *pages 13–14, exercise I*

17 Reentry

Using adjectives and adverbs

Adjectives (What kind of?)	Adverbs (How?)
1. Bob is a **careful** driver.	He drives **carefully.**
2. He's not a **reckless** driver.	He doesn't drive **recklessly.**
3. He's a **good** driver.	He drives **well.**
4. He's not a **fast** driver.	He doesn't drive **fast.**
5. The written driver's test isn't **hard.**	Bob didn't study **hard** for it.

A. Complete the sentences with the adverb form of the word in parentheses.

If you want to do a good job on the written test, follow these instructions:

1. Read the *Driver's Manual* _____ (good).
2. Study _____ (hard) for the test.
3. Read the questions _____ (careful).
4. Read and think about all the choices. Don't answer too _____ (quick). If you work too _____ (fast), you might make mistakes.
5. Mark your answers _____ (clear).
6. Of course, try to answer _____ (correct).

B. Complete the sentences with either the adjective or adverb in parentheses.

If you want to pass the road test, follow these instructions:

1. Bring a _____ (good/well) car to the test. Drive _____ (good/well).
2. Don't be _____ (rude/rudely). Speak to the test official _____ (polite/politely).
3. Drive _____ (safe/safely).
4. Start and stop your vehicle _____ (smooth/smoothly).
5. Don't come to a _____ (quick/quickly) stop.
6. Check to be sure you are in the _____ (correct/correctly) lane for turns.
7. Don't be _____ (careless/carelessly) when you park.
8. Check the mirror and back up _____ (slow/slowly).
9. Look _____ (careful/carefully) before you pull out of a parking place.
10. When you stop on a hill, put on the emergency brake _____ (complete/completely).

Before You Read

1. What is an acronym? Do you know what the letters UN, WHO, or UNICEF stand for?
2. What organizations do you know that try to help other people or try to help solve serious problems facing your country or the world?

First Reading

Read these questions and try to find answers to them as you read the article. Discuss the answers with your classmates.

1. Who started SADD and why?
2. What is the purpose of the organization?
3. Has SADD been successful?
4. How does SADD encourage better communication between young people and their parents?
5. Why do students join SADD?
6. What kinds of projects do SADD chapters carry out in their schools?

SADD

1   In 1981, Robert Anastas was a high school teacher and athletic coach in Wayland, Massachusetts. That year two of his students were killed in highway accidents. From that tragedy grew an organization called SADD — Students Against Driving Drunk. This organization is dedicated to encouraging students, parents, and community leaders to work together to end underage drinking, to eliminate alcohol and drug abuse, and to eliminate death due to drinking and driving.

2   The key to combating teenage alcohol and drug abuse, says Mr. Anastas, is strong family communication. So, the heart of the SADD program is its "Contract for Life," which parents and young people discuss and sign. When young people sign this contract, they agree to call their parents "for advice and/or transportation at any hour from any place if (they are) ever faced with a situation where a driver has been drinking or using illicit drugs." Parents agree to come and get their children "at any hour, any place, no questions asked and no argument at that time, or (they) will pay for a taxi to bring (their children) home safely."

3   Since 1982, SADD has grown to over 20,000 active chapters in the United States. In these local chapters, sponsored by local businesses and community leaders, young people plan and carry out many different projects to communicate their message. One SADD chapter, for example, operates a booth at the school health fair, and distributes notebooks listing "50 Ways to Say No to Drinking" on

---

18 Reading

PROCEDURE
1. Refer to General Guidelines for Reading, page x.
2. Talk with students about the questions in "Before You Read." **UN** stands for *United Nations,* **WHO** for *World Health Organization*, and **UNICEF** for *United Nations International Children's Emergency Fund.*
3. Have students discuss answers to the "First Reading" questions in small groups or as a whole class.
4. Give students an opportunity to react to the reading in a personal way. Consider using some of the discussion questions in "Reacting to the Reading".

Answers: First Reading: **1.** Robert Anastas, when two of his students were killed in highway accidents; he wanted to do something to stop that kind of tragedy **2.** to encourage students, parents, and community leaders to work together to end underage drinking, to eliminate alcohol and drug abuse, and to eliminate death due to drinking and driving **3.** Yes. Teenage deaths have been cut from about 6,000 to 2,000 a year. **4.** through the "Contract for Life" **5.** Students have different reasons, among them it's the mature thing to do and you can help save lives. **6.** They operate booths at school fairs, print their message on notebooks, put a crashed car in front of the school.

Second Reading: **1.** abuse **2.** underage **3.** tragedy **4.** combat **5.** argument **6.** heart **7.** contract **8.** illicit **9.** key **10.** prom **11.** chapter **12.** join **13.** mature **14.** a great deal of

Reacting to the Reading: Discussion Questions
1. Is alcohol abuse a problem where you live? If not, are there other problems that need attention?
2. Why do people abuse alcohol and drugs?
3. What can an individual person do if he or she knows someone with this kind of problem?
4. Do you know any people who have made something good from a tragedy? Tell their story to the class.
5. What makes good communication between parents and children or brothers and sisters?

■ EXPANSION ACTIVITY: Writing for information
Have students write for SADD's packet of information at the address given in the article. The packet includes information on how to start a chapter and a copy of a newsletter. Students will have the background information to read some of the articles in the newsletter so you might select one for a test.

PROCEDURE

1. Refer to General Guidelines for Listening, page x.
2. Play the tape or read the script for the Listening. The tape includes the directions on page 37.
3. *If you are reading the script*: For the First Listening, give students 10 seconds after each report to write the letter of the report. For the Second Listening, give students 20 seconds after each report to write T, F, or NG for the statements.

Script

Report 1:

ANNOUNCER: Our next item concerns another automobile accident on Winfield streets and roads. Ray Molino is at the scene of the accident out on Route 25 near the new Winfield Shopping Mall.

REPORTER: Thank you, Sally. Ladies and gentlemen, just about twenty minutes ago a 1990 van and a small pickup truck loaded with vegetables crashed near the intersection of Route 25 and Hillside Road. Apparently the driver of the van was trying to pass and didn't see the truck approaching.

Fortunately, no one in either vehicle was hurt. The driver of the van, Ron Martin of Lakewood, and his wife and older child were all wearing seat belts at the time of the crash. Their one-year-old baby was riding in a car seat. Martin and his family are under observation at Winfield Hospital. The driver of the truck refused to be checked.

Report 2:

Good morning everyone! This is Ann Riley with the morning traffic report from the police helicopter high above Springfield. It looks like you early birds won't have any problems today. Traffic is moving well on all the main highways leading into Springfield. There's a lot of traffic downtown at Main and Westlake Boulevard, but if you can stay clear of that one intersection, you should have an easy drive in to work, at least at the moment. I'll be back with our next report in fifteen minutes. That's all for now.

the cover. Among the suggestions they have for saying NO are:

It's never as much fun as it looks in the commercials.
If I wanted the high life, I'd rather go skydiving.
I think therefore I'm not going to drink.
Just plain NO.

Maybe their strongest message is the crashed car they put on the front lawn of the school during prom week.

4   Why do young people join a club with the primary goal of convincing other teens NOT to drink alcohol? As one student says, "It's the mature choice. The other kids know it and respect it." Another student says, "We all have different reasons. If you can save a life by getting someone not to drink, it's a lot better than winning a homecoming game."

5   After a number of years of hard work, all those associated with SADD can be proud of their organization and its work. When Robert Anastas started SADD in 1981, death due to drinking and driving was killing young people age 16-19 at the rate of over six thousand each year. In 1989 the number was just over 2000. But as Mr. Anastas tells SADD members and friends, "We still have a great deal of work to do, but we have the formula; that is the dedication and caring of each SADD student who gives a moment of time to make a lifetime of difference to others."

Students Against Driving Drunk
P.O. Box 800
Marlboro, MA 01752

Second Reading

Work with a partner. For each of the words or expressions below, find a word or expression with a similar meaning in the reading.

1. wrong use of (1)
2. too young (1)
3. a very sad event (1)
4. fight against (2)
5. disagreement, fight in words (2)
6. the most important part of (2)
7. a formal written agreement (2)
8. illegal; against the law (2)
9. answer; solution to a problem (2)
10. a high school dance (3)
11. an individual club in a large organization (3)
12. become a member of an organization (4)
13. adult (4)
14. a lot of (5)

19 Listening 📼

First Listening

You will hear three short radio and TV announcements related to traffic and cars. Listen and write the letters of the reports you hear.

a. a police officer in a car talking to the station

b. a news reporter at the scene of an accident

c. a report about the safety of passengers in automobiles

d. a police officer at the scene of an accident

e. a report of traffic conditions

Second Listening

Now write on your paper *Report 1, Report 2,* and *Report 3* in three columns, and the numbers 1-4 under each. Listen to the reports again and write *T* (True), *F* (False), or *NG* (Not Given) for each statement.

Report 1

1. A van crashed into a bus.

2. One vehicle was trying to pass another.

3. A child was hurt in the accident.

4. The accident happened at night.

Report 2

1. It's early morning.

2. The reporter is also a police officer.

3. The traffic is terrible today.

4. Another report will be made in 15 minutes.

Report 3

1. The report is about the safety of all passengers in a car.

2. In one year, 1,681 children from birth to four years of age died in car crashes.

3. A baby is safe in a person's arms.

4. Children from one to six years of age should ride in a car safety seat.

Report 3:
Good afternoon, ladies and gentlemen. This is Officer Harry Williams of the Winfield police department with the safety commentary of the week. Today I'd like to talk with you about your responsibility to protect children riding in your motor vehicle.

Did you know that traffic accidents are the leading killer of children and young adults? Over 68,000 children under the age of five were injured in car accidents over a span of just four years. In one year alone, 681 children from birth to four years of age died in car crashes.

One of the principal reasons for the deaths of small children is that many people think they are safe in an adult's arms. The fact is, that's the most dangerous place for a child to be. In even a low-speed crash at only 30 miles per hour, the child can hit the windshield with the same force as falling from a three-story building.

Infants and young children under the age of five should always ride in a car safety seat. Not only is it the law in all fifty states of the nation, but it is the best way you can protect the children you love. Older children should wear a properly adjusted seat belt.

Please take your responsibility to children seriously and help me save children's lives.

Answers: First Listening: Report 1: b. a news reporter at the scene of an accident *Report 2:* e. a report of traffic conditions *Report 3:* c. a report about the safety of passengers in automobiles.

Second Listening: Report 1: **1.** F **2.** T **3.** F **4.** NG *Report 2:* **1.** T **2.** NG **3.** F **4.** T *Report 3:* **1.** F **2.** F **3.** F **4.** NG

20 Final Activity

PROCEDURE
Refer to General Guidelines for Final Activity, page xi.

Workbook: *page 14, exercise J*

20 Final Activity

Work in a small group of three to five students. Role play an accident scene. Two students can be police officers, the others can be drivers and/or witnesses to the accident. Plan your role play using the questions below as a guide.

Useful vocabulary:

Could I see your driver's license?
It was your fault.
It wasn't my fault. I was _____ .
Did you see what happened?

1. What kinds of vehicles crashed? Where and at what time of day?

2. What were the weather conditions?

3. Was anybody hurt?

4. Was one driver at fault? Did he or she run a red light, make a wrong turn, drive too fast?

UNIT 3

Making Ends Meet

While Tom and the kids were looking at cars, Adela was at the new Warner's Department Store looking for some clothing bargains. It isn't easy for the Logans to make ends meet, so Adela spends their money very carefully. One way she economizes is by checking the latest fashions in the stores and copying their designs. At Warner's, Adela runs into Liz Young looking at dresses.

LIZ:	I don't believe it. This is ridiculous. $90 for a cotton dress.
ADELA:	Talking to yourself, Liz?
LIZ:	Oh . . . Hi, Adela! Yeah. I just can't believe it. They want $90 for this cotton dress.
ADELA:	It *is* pretty, and that's the best fabric you can get. Why don't you try it on?
LIZ:	Are you kidding? I can't afford $90 for a dress.
ADELA:	*(to salesperson)* Excuse me, miss. My friend would like to try this dress on. Where are the fitting rooms?
LIZ:	Adela, forget it.
ADELA:	Shhh! The fitting rooms, please.
SALESPERSON:	Right over there. Five items maximum.

Useful materials: pictures of people in different places doing different things; pictures of clothing, ordinary and bizarre, credit card brochures and applications

Making Ends Meet

PROCEDURE
1. Refer to General Guidelines for Opener, page ix.
2. Have students infer the meaning of *make ends meet* from the context of the introductory paragraph.

COMPREHENSION QUESTIONS

Now answer these questions.
1. Do the Logans have a lot of money? *No, they don't.*
2. What surprises Liz? *The price of the dress.*
3. How much is the dress? *$90.*
4. What is the dress made of? *Cotton.*
5. Is the dress good quality? *Yes, it is.*
6. Does Liz want to try on the dress? *No, she doesn't.*
7. Why doesn't Liz want to try on the dress? *She can't afford $90 for a dress.*
8. Can Adela make a copy of the dress? *Yes, she can.*
9. Does Liz like the dress? *Yes, she does.*
10. How much will the dress that Adela makes cost? *Under $25.*

DISCUSSION QUESTIONS
1. Why do some people place a lot of importance on clothes? How important is it to be in style?
2. What are some other ways people can economize or save money on clothes?
3. What other things can we economize on? How?

LANGUAGE NOTES
1. Adela's conversation opening is an informal shortening of *Are you talking to yourself, Liz?* She doesn't expect an answer. Adela makes this little joke because they are close friends.
2. *They* in "They want $90 for this cotton dress" is the general *they*, here referring to store owners.

U.S. stores limit the number of items you can take into a fitting room; three and five items are common. Clerks usually give customers a tag that shows the number of items they take into the fitting room. They must return or buy that number of items.

1 Vocabulary in Context

PROCEDURE

1. Refer to General Guidelines for Vocabulary in Context, page ix.
2. Call students' attention to the need to change the form of some verbs, which makes this exercise a subtle form of grammar reentry.
3. Have students read the passage silently and write the completed paragraphs or their choices. Check answers with the whole class.

Answers: **1.** make ends meet **2.** sew **3.** looks at
4. fabric **5.** pattern **6.** bargain **7.** styles **8.** wear
9. fitting room **10.** try … on **11.** fits **12.** put … back

---

Workbook: *pages 15-16, exercises A, B, C*

LIZ: What are you doing? I told you I can't afford it.

ADELA: Liz, try it on. If you like it, I'll help you make it.

LIZ: I didn't know you could sew.

ADELA: I taught myself the basics from a book I got out of the library. Later I took advanced classes at the Technical Institute. . . . So how does it fit? Do you like it?

LIZ: It fits perfectly. I love it. What do you think?

ADELA: It's terrific. C'mon. Put it back and let's get over to the fabric department. You choose the fabric you like, I'll make the pattern, and you'll have your dress for under $25!

1 Vocabulary in Context

Complete the sentences with one of the words or expressions in the list. Change the verb form if necessary. Use a word or expression only once. Not all are used.

fabric	sew	try . . . on	look for
afford	fit	put . . . back	look at
pattern	style(s)	fitting room	run into
bargain	wear	make ends meet	

Most people today don't have enough money to buy all the things they need. In other words, it's difficult to (1) _____ . One way to economize is to (2) _____ some of your own clothes. Adela Logan goes to department stores and (3) _____ the latest styles. When she knows what she wants, she buys the (4) _____ she likes. She doesn't need to buy a/an (5) _____ because she knows how to make one. In the end, her clothes are a real (6) _____ . They cost her much less than if she had bought them in a store.

If you buy your clothes in a store, you can learn to get the most for your money. First, for most of your clothes, choose (7) _____ that you can (8) _____ for a long time. If you aren't sure that you like a piece of clothing, go to a/an (9) _____ and (10) _____ it _____ . Be sure that it (11) _____ well and you like the way it looks. Also buy the best quality you can afford. Good quality clothes will last longer. If you like something, but you won't wear it very much, (12) _____ it _____ on the rack.

2 Reentry

Checking information with tag questions

How much do you know about *Intercom 2000*? Check the information in the statements with a partner by adding a tag question. The information in all the statements is correct, so use expected responses.

1. Winfield is in New York State.
2. Winfield isn't far from New York City.
3. A new mall is opening in Winfield this week.
4. Cristina and Gino aren't at the mall.
5. The Youngs are from Winfield.
6. Liz is the Youngs' oldest child.
7. Liz isn't happy with her job.
8. Ted isn't in college.
9. Ted is younger than Mike.
10. Joyce isn't in high school yet.

3 Presentation

Checking your memory about something

To check your memory about something, use tag questions with the past tense of **be.**

A: Liz wasn't looking for pants, **was she?**
B: No, she wasn't. She was looking for a dress.

A: Tom and his sons were looking at cars, **weren't they?**
B: Yes, they were.

2 Reentry

PROCEDURE
1. Refer to General Guidelines for Reentry, page x.
2. Do the exercise in a chain drill with the whole class. Students can continue to check information about other characters.
3. Remind students that if they are quite sure the statement is true, they use falling intonation on the tag. If not sure, rising intonation.

Answers: **1.** isn't it?/Yes, it is. **2.** is it?/No, it isn't. **3.** isn't it?/Yes, it is. **4.** are they?/No, they aren't. **5.** aren't they?/Yes, they are. **6.** isn't she?/Yes, she is. **7.** is she?/No, she isn't. **8.** is he?/No, he isn't. **9.** isn't he?/Yes, he is. **10.** is she?/No, she isn't.

3 Presentation

PROCEDURE
1. Refer to General Guidelines for Presentation, page ix.
2. To expand the Presentation, put other statements on the board and have students add tag questions. For example: *The weather was nice yesterday.* (wasn't it?), *You weren't absent yesterday.* (were you?), ____ *was sick last week.* (wasn't he/she?), *We were doing the reading at the end of class yesterday.* (weren't we?).

4 Practice

PROCEDURE
1. Refer to General Guidelines for Practice, page x.
2. Write these words in a column on the board: *Liz, Adela, Tom and the kids, the salesperson, the dress, the fabric, the fitting rooms.* Have students suggest an example and put it on the board before they write their questions.

Optional: Students can write tag questions about the pictures on pp. 39–41. For example, *Liz was wearing a purple sweater, wasn't she?*

Workbook: *pages 16–17, exercise D*

5 Presentation

PROCEDURE
1. Refer to General Guidelines for Presentation, page ix.
2. To expand the Presentation, write additional sentences on the board for students to combine. For example: *Pablo is at the principal's office. He is getting some chalk.*

6 Practice

PROCEDURE
1. Refer to General Guidelines for Practice, page x.
2. Have students do Part A with a partner.
3. For Part B, have partners write four questions to ask the class.
4. Put half the pairs on one side of the room, half on the other. Questions from one side are answered by students on the other side.

Answers: **A.** Answers follow this pattern. **1.** A: Where is Bob tonight? B: He's at the Roma celebrating his birthday. **2.** A: Where is Joyce this afternoon? B: She's at the pool practicing for a race. For **3-10** students use any appropriate time phrase in the question.

4 Practice

How much do you remember about the situation and conversation that begins this unit? Without looking back, write five statements with tag questions. Then work with a partner and check each other's memory. Try to make statements that will get expected and unexpected responses. Ask about *Intercom 2000* characters, the salesperson, the dress, the fabric, the fitting rooms, etc.

5 Presentation

Talking about something at a location

> To talk about something at a location, use:
> **be** + location + verb + -*ing* phrase.

A
> A: Where's Adela?
> B: She's at the Grand Opening.
> She's looking for clothing bargains.
> A: Oh, that's right. She's at the Grand Opening looking for clothing bargains.

B
> A: Where are Tom and his sons?
> B: They're at the mall.
> They're enjoying the car show.
> A: Oh, that's right. They're at the mall enjoying the car show.

6 Practice

A. **Work with a partner. Use the cues to ask and answer questions about the *Intercom 2000* characters. Tell where the people are and what they are doing in one sentence.**

> the Youngs this weekend // New York / do some shopping
> A: Where are the Youngs this weekend?
> B: They're in New York doing some shopping.

1. Bob tonight // the Roma / celebrate his birthday
2. Joyce this afternoon // pool / practice for a race
3. Sam // garage / fix his car
4. Liz // drugstore / pick up some medicine

Continue, but now tell what *you* think these people are doing.

5. Ted and Mike // athletic field
6. Howard // kitchen
7. Adela // library
8. Gino and Cristina // airport
9. Sekila // home
10. Tom // office

B. Now use your imagination and ask about famous people you know.

> Tom Cruise
> A: Where do you think Tom Cruise is?
> B: Maybe he's in California making a movie.

7 Interaction

Write the names of two or three family members or friends on a piece of paper, and give it to your partner. Find out where the people are and what they are doing. Continue to ask questions about the people and get as much information as you can.

> my brother Pablo
> A: What's ___your brother Pablo___ doing these days?
> B: ___He's in New York working for an advertising company.___
> A: Oh, what / when / where / why, etc.

■ Expansion Activity: What are they doing?

1. Have students bring pictures of people doing different things in different places. Try to get several pictures of the same place (office, kitchen, countryside, etc.) with small differences. The more action in the pictures, the better. Put the pictures on the wall.
2. Divide the class into two teams. Students on team A choose a picture and give clues. (*A person is in the country riding a horse. A man is at a party dancing with a short woman.*) Students on team B try to guess which picture is being described in the fewest number of guesses. Have students give clues in two sentences like those in Presentation 5. Then permit other clues only after Team B guesses once. The team that needs the fewest guesses on an equal number of pictures wins.

7 Interaction

PROCEDURE
1. Refer to General Guidelines for Interaction, page x.
2. Demonstrate the model using one of your relatives. Have students ask you questions.
3. Have students write and exchange their lists and talk to their partners.
4. To recap the activity, ask who learned about a really interesting person. Put the names of the interesting people on the board. Have the class talk with the students who know these people using the model.

Workbook: *page 17, exercise E*

8 Presentation

PROCEDURE
1. Refer to General Guidelines for Presentation, page ix.
2. Write sentence #1 on the board. Draw an arrow from *himself* back to *Bob* and ask for a paraphrase of the meaning. (*Bob wrote a note to Bob/himself.*)
3. Ask students to show or tell you to whom each reflexive pronoun refers.

LANGUAGE NOTE

Reflexive pronouns show that someone does/did/will do something to or for himself/herself. They are not used for reciprocal action. Teach the phrase *each other* for reciprocal action. Contrast the following sentences: (a.) *John and Sue talk to themselves during exams. / John and Sue talk to each other during exams.* (b.) *In order to love each other, we must love ourselves.*

9 Practice

PROCEDURE
1. Refer to General Guidelines for Practice, page x.
2. Do with the whole class.

Answers: **1.** himself **2.** herself **3.** myself **4.** themselves **5.** yourself **6.** itself **7.** themselves **8.** ourselves **9.** himself **10.** themselves **11.** myself **12.** herself.

8 Presentation

Reflexive pronouns

(I)	**myself**	(we)	**ourselves**
(you)	**yourself**	(you)	**yourselves**
(he) (she) (it)	**himself** **herself** **itself**	(they)	**themselves**

A

B

1. **Bob** wrote **himself** a note so he wouldn't forget to do what his mother asked.
2. **Liz** put the dress on and looked at **herself** in the mirror.
3. A **computer** can now program **itself.**
4. **We** should introduce **ourselves** to our neighbors.
5. Watch out! **You**'ll fall and hurt **yourselves.**
6. **Adela** and **Tom** taught **themselves** to play Ping-Pong.

9 Practice

Complete the sentences with the correct reflexive pronoun.

1. Toshio always introduces _____ to the passengers on his flights.
2. Gloria never had a music teacher. She taught _____ to play the guitar.
3. Maybe I'm crazy, but I like to talk to _____ .
4. They were very rude. They invited _____ to the party.
5. When you pass a mirror, look at _____ to see if your posture is good.
6. That's a very advanced robot. It can repair _____ .
7. People sometimes talk to _____ when they are alone.
8. As we read, we should ask _____ questions about the reading.

9. Mike wasn't careful when he was cooking and he burned _____ .
10. Parents must watch small children carefully so they don't hurt _____ while playing.
11. I never get any letters. Maybe I should write _____ one.
12. Lisa wasn't careful and she cut _____ with a sharp knife.

10 Interaction

Share answers to the following questions with a small group of your classmates. You can talk about yourself or people you know. Ask questions with *when, where,* and *why* to get more information.

a. Do you ever talk to yourself?
b. Do you ever write notes to yourself?
c. Do you ever read out loud to yourself?
d. Do you ever introduce yourself to a stranger?
e. Did you ever teach yourself something?
f. Did you ever hurt yourself seriously?

Do you ever =
Do you at any time

11 Reentry

Phrasal verbs

Intransitive	Transitive	Intransitive or Transitive	
come back	look at	get up	stand up
come in	look for	sit down	wake up
go away	run into		

1. Verbs that are not followed by an object (noun/pronoun) are called *intransitive*. They can be followed by an adverb.
   Paul **is coming back.**
   Paul **came back** early.

2. Verbs that are followed by an object (noun/pronoun) are called *transitive*.
   Paul **ran into** his girlfriend at the library.
   He **looked at** her in surprise.

3. Some verbs can be either intransitive or transitive.
   I usually **wake up** at 7:00.
   Then I **wake up** my brother. (Then I **wake** my brother **up.**)

10 Interaction

PROCEDURE
1. Refer to General Guidelines for Interaction, page x.
2. Demonstrate a Circle Practice using the first question with a small group of students in front of the class. One student asks that question to all others in the group. When a student answers *Yes, I do/did*, other students in the group ask for more information.
3. Recap the activity by sharing experiences as a class.

Workbook: *page 18, exercise F*

11 Reentry

PROCEDURE
1. Refer to General Guidelines for Reentry, page x.
2. Go over the explanation of intransitive and transitive phrasal verbs in the box. Have students write sentences on the board using the other phrasal verbs in the lists. Ask them to show which verbs are transitive in their sentences.
3. Model the stress on the phrasal verbs and have students repeat.
4. Have students complete the exercise paragraphs individually or in pairs and review answers with the whole class.
5. Ask students if they can find a new phrasal verb in the paragraphs (My luck *ran out* for the day!). Can they tell whether it is transitive or intransitive? Can they paraphrase its meaning?

Answers: **1.** woke up **2.** get up **3.** looked at **4.** ran into **5.** looking for **6.** sat down **7.** stood up **8.** came back.

LANGUAGE NOTES

1. Phrasal verbs (PVs) can be intransitive (never take an object), transitive, or used both ways. Understanding these terms can help students know which are probably separable in the next Practices.
2. Intransitive phrasal verbs never have an object so they are always inseparable. Most transitive PVs are separable. There are relatively few PVs like *look at, look for,* and *run into* that are transitive and inseparable.
3. When phrasal verbs have idiomatic meanings, as they usually do, the stress is on the second word in the phrase, for example: *come back, get up, watch out, put up with, look forward to,* etc. In *look at* and *look for,* whose meanings are not truly idiomatic, the stress is on the main verb. However, in the idiomatic expression *look out!* (Be careful!), we stress the particle.

12 Presentation

PROCEDURE

1. Refer to General Guidelines for Presentation, page x.
2. Using the pictures (or a sweater and ridiculously large pants) demonstrate the meaning of the phrasal verbs. Practice the conversations with real clothing if possible.

LANGUAGE NOTE

The noun object of a separable phrasal verb can be used in two positions, separating or not separating the verb. Pronoun objects always separate the separable phrasal verb.

Complete the paragraphs with the correct form of one of the phrasal verbs from page 45. Do not use the same phrasal verb twice. Two of the verbs in the chart are not used.

A Lucky Day

When I (1) _____ this morning, I had a feeling that today was going to be a good day. As usual I didn't (2) _____ immediately. I just lay there in bed and enjoyed the peace of the morning for a few minutes.

After breakfast I (3) _____ my list of things to do and decided to go shopping. I had a couple of gifts to buy and some letters to take to the post office, so I headed downtown. At the post office I had my first lucky event. I (4) _____ a friend who wanted to go shopping with me. We had more good luck downtown. We found everything we were (5) _____ very quickly, so we decided to go to a museum to see a new exhibit. After about an hour at the exhibit, we realized we were quite tired, so we (6) _____ on a bench to rest. When I (7) _____ to go, I saw a ten-dollar bill on the floor — just enough for us to have lunch. At the restaurant my friend and I both ordered fish. A few minutes later the waitress (8) _____ and said, "Sorry, we're out of fish." With that, my luck ran out for the day!

12 Presentation

Asking for opinions on clothes

	Separable phrasal verbs with nouns	Separable phrasal verbs with pronouns
	1. Try the sweater **on.** ⟶ **Try on** the sweater. ⟶	**Try** it **on.** (not possible)
	**2. Put** the pants **back.** ⟶ **Put back** the pants. ⟶	**Put** them **back.** (not possible)

A
> A: What do you think of this shirt?
> B: It's nice. Why don't you **try it on?**

B
> A: What do you think of these pants?
> B: They're awful. **Put them back.**

13 Pronunciation 📼

Repeat these sentences.

1. Try the shorts on.

   Try them on.

2. Put the skirt back.

   Put it back.

14 Practice

Ask a classmate for his or her honest opinion of each of the items of clothing below. Follow the conversation models in *12*.

1.

2.

3.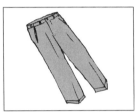

4.

5.

6.

7.

8.

9.

10.

11.

12.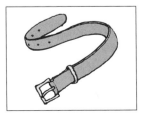

13 Pronunciation

PROCEDURE
1. Refer to General Guidelines for Pronunciation, page x.
2. Write the following sentences on the board and ask students to use dots to mark the stress. *Please pick the book up. Please pick it up. / Please put your books away. Please put them away.*

LANGUAGE NOTE
The major stress in declarative sentences usually falls on the last word, which is a preposition in this case. Since we have taught students that prepositions do not usually have secondary or primary stress, students sometimes stress the main verb in these sentences rather than the final word. There is no problem when the phrasal verb is not separated because the stress falls naturally on a noun (*Try on the shorts*). Be sure students do not stress the object pronouns *it* and *them* in these sentences.

14 Practice

1. Refer to General Guidelines for Practice, page x.
2. Put the conversation models from Presentation 12 on the board. Do items 1 and 2 with the whole class.

Answers: Answers will vary depending on a student's opinion of the clothing pictured, but will follow model A or B in Presentation 12.

> **Workbook: *pages 18–19, exercise G***

15 Reentry

PROCEDURE
1. Refer to General Guidelines for Reentry, page x.
2. Have a student read each sentence and paraphrase the underlined expression. Encourage students to look at the paraphrases in the box only if necessary.
3. Have students repeat the separable phrasal verb for stress practice if needed.

Answers: **1.** telephone again **2.** return **3.** return **4.** use, wear **5.** remove **6.** take from the floor **7.** put in a cabinet, store **8.** discard, throw in the garbage **9.** started something working **10.** stopping something **11.** increase the volume **12.** decrease the volume

16 Practice

PROCEDURE
1. Refer to General Guidelines for Practice, page x.
2. Pair students. Have them take turns reading the numbered questions and comments. Together have them write one or more appropriate responses using PV's, separating the verb with a pronoun if possible.
3. Recap the Practice with the class. Say any one of the items 1-10. Students give as many appropriate responses as possible.

Possible answers: **1.** Can you take them back to the library for me? / They're old. I don't want them. Throw them away. **2.** Shall I turn it up? / Do you want me to turn it up? **3.** Why don't you take it off? **4.** I threw it out. / I put it away in the closet. **5.** Are you asking me to turn it down? / Shall I turn it down? **6.** Let me turn up the volume. **7.** Well, let's turn them off. **8.** Yes. You can put it away. **9.** Is he/she going to call (me) back? **10.** No, I gave it back to you last Friday.

Variation: Make this Practice into a game in which teams get a point for logical and appropriate responses to each question or statement. If responses are written, several teams can compete at once. If responses are oral, have two teams. Alternate the opportunity to answer first. Then continue accepting responses and giving points until no team can think of a different response.

15 Reentry

Phrasal verbs

Read each sentence. Choose the correct synonym for the underlined phrasal verb from the box. You can use a synonym more than once.

decrease the volume	start something working
discard, throw in the garbage	stop something
increase the volume	take from the floor
put in a cabinet, store	telephone again
remove	use, wear
return	

1. Mary called. She's going to <u>call</u> you <u>back</u> at 4:00.
2. I believe you borrowed my calculator. Did you <u>give</u> it <u>back</u>?
3. This book is overdue at the library. Can you <u>take</u> it <u>back</u>?
4. Here's your coat. <u>Put</u> it <u>on</u> and let's go.
5. If the shoes hurt you, <u>take</u> them <u>off</u>.
6. When you drop things, please <u>pick</u> them <u>up</u>.
7. If you're not using the tools, please <u>put</u> them <u>away</u>.
8. These sneakers are in terrible condition. You can <u>throw</u> them <u>away</u>.
9. We really don't need that light. Who <u>turned</u> it <u>on</u>?
10. We're not watching the TV. How about <u>turning</u> it <u>off</u>?
11. I can't hear the radio. Please <u>turn</u> it <u>up</u>.
12. The TV is too loud. Please <u>turn</u> it <u>down</u>.

16 Practice

Read the sentences. Respond with a question, comment, or suggestion using one of the phrasal verbs in *11* or *15*. Sometimes more than one is possible.

1. What should I do with these books?
2. I can't hear the TV. It's too low.
3. This ring is bothering me.
4. What did you do with yesterday's newspaper?
5. That radio is too loud.
6. This program looks good, but I can't hear it.
7. I don't think we need these lights.
8. Are you finished with the iron?
9. Your boss called you.
10. Do you still have my English book?

17 Listening 🔊

Copy the answer format five times on your paper and number them from 1-5.

SALESPERSON:	____ polite	____ rude
CUSTOMER:	____ polite	____ rude
PROBLEM:	_____	

First Listening

Listen to the five conversations to see if the speakers sound polite or rude. Check the correct responses.

Second Listening

Listen to the conversations again. This time listen for the problem and write what you think it is.

18 Interaction

Work with a partner. Imagine you are in a clothing store. One of you is looking for something to wear on a special occasion. Use the questions to plan your conversation. Then write it together. Practice it and role play it for your class.

Planning Questions

1. What is the special occasion?
2. When is it?
3. What pieces of clothing are you looking for?
4. How much money do you have to spend?
5. Will you find what you are looking for or decide to keep looking?

Useful language:

CLERK	CUSTOMER
May I help you?	I'd like to see ____ .
What color would you like?	Can you show me ____ ?
Here's a / Here are some ____ in your size.	Do you have ____ in size ____ ?
	Do you have ____ in a lighter / darker color?
Would you like to try ____ on?	
The fitting rooms are ____ .	
How does it / do they fit?	Where can I try ____ on?
	No, you can put ____ back.
How do you like ____ ?	I'll take ____ .

■ EXPANSION ACTIVITY: Class dictionary of phrasal verbs

1. Have students watch for phrasal verbs in outside reading, copy the verb and its context, and bring it to present to the class. (If you are in the U.S., students can listen for phrasal verbs in conversations too, but expect only a very general context.)
2. Have students write the phrasal verbs they bring in on the board with the context. Discuss the meaning and paraphrase if possible.
3. Have students suggest comments or questions to which they can respond using the new phrasal verb.
4. Have students choose the best example. The person who brought the verb writes it on a file card with the comment or question and response chosen as best. Keep all cards in a box and review from time to time.
5. After a number of new phrasal verbs have been added to the class file or dictionary, have a game in which teams compete (see *Variation* in #16) to see which can respond correctly to the most comments or questions.

17 Listening

PROCEDURE
1. Refer to General Guidelines for Listening, page x.
2. Play the tape or read the script for the Listening. The tape includes the directions on page 49.
3. If you are reading the script: For the First Listening, give students 5 seconds after each conversation to say if the speakers sound polite or rude. For the Second Listening, give students 10 seconds after each conversation to write the problem.
4. For script and answers, see page 197.

18 Interaction

PROCEDURE
Refer to General Guidelines for Interaction, page x.

■ EXPANSION ACTIVITY 3: Going shopping (page 190)

19 Writing

1. Refer to General Guidelines for Writing, page xi.
2. Follow the steps outlined in parts A, B, and C. Have students make a final edited copy of their paragraphs if you like.

20 Reading

1. Refer to General Guidelines for Reading, page x.
2. For the Second Reading, have students form small groups. Read instruction 1. Ask for an example of a suggestion (*barter, trade things*). Circulate and help with list-making if needed.
3. Have groups compare their suggestions and agree on a list to be ranked.
4. Read instruction 2. Be sure students do this step alone.
5. Read instruction 3. Students work together and rank the suggestions from best to least best.
6. Put group rankings on the board. Discuss reasons for any disagreements.
7. Have students look for two new idiomatic expressions (*shop around, burns a hole in my pocket* and try to guess their meaning.
8. Give students an opportunity to react to the reading in a personal way. Consider using some of the discussion questions in *Reacting to the Reading* on page 52.

19 Writing

A. **Work with a partner. Tell your partner something that happened to you in a store. Use these questions as a guide:**

1. When and where did this happen?
2. Were you alone or with someone else?
3. Why did you go to the store and who did you talk with?
4. What happened? Were you happy or angry about it?

B. **As you listen to your partner's story, take notes to help you remember the important ideas. If necessary, ask questions about what you did not understand after he or she finishes talking.**

C. **From your notes write a paragraph about what happened to your partner in the store. Exchange papers. Read your partner's paragraph and offer your partner suggestions if his or her paragraph is unclear.**

20 Reading

Before You Read

1. Does your local newspaper have an interview column? Who is usually interviewed in this column?

2. Are you good with money? Are you careful or careless with it? Do you save some of your money every month or spend it all?

First Reading

Read the questions below. Then read the interview responses to find the answers.

1. What does **barter** mean? What kinds of things does Mary Peterson barter for?

2. What's the problem with buying things that are cheap?

3. Why doesn't Bob Brown worry about how much he spends?

4. What magazine can help you make ends meet? What does it do for you?

5. Why doesn't Sandra Diaz buy much on credit?

6. What information do you need to be able to do comparison-shopping?

Today's Questions

How do you make ends meet? What do you do to get the most for your money?

Mary Peterson, homemaker, Riverview

I barter. I trade things I don't use for things I want. Sometimes I barter my skills, too. For example, I sew for my neighbor, and she babysits for my kids. So, we both win.

Pedro Silva, post office employee, Winfield

I look for quality. I can't always afford the best, but I buy the best I can afford. When you buy something cheap, you think you're saving money, but actually you're wasting it. Cheap items don't last long.

Bob Brown, government employee, Westlake

Make ends meet? I can't! I always owe someone money. Money burns a hole in my pocket, and credit's great! Maybe I should be more careful, but life's too short and I have a lot of fun.

Victoria Chen, businesswoman, Winfield

We do things for ourselves. We make all our own small repairs; we fix our cars ourselves. We also read *Value* magazine before we make any big purchases. They test products and give you the facts so you can decide what to buy and what not to buy.

Sandra Diaz, police officer, Winfield

First of all, I don't buy much on credit. I save my money until I can afford what I want. That way I don't have to pay interest. Then I have two questions I always ask myself: Do you need this or just want it? Is it worth the price?

Henry Lee, retired teacher, Middlesex

I shop around. I compare prices. You know, you can't really save money if you buy the first thing you see. Of course, I'm lucky. I'm retired and I have the time to do that. It must be very hard for young people — you know, both working, with kids and all. Maybe they don't have the time to comparison-shop.

LANGUAGE NOTE

Cheap has two meanings, not expensive and of poor quality. For this reason, when someone wants to be sure the meaning is clear, he/she says *inexpensive* for *not costing much money* rather than *cheap*.

Possible answers: First Reading: **1.** exchange, or trade one thing for another; She sews for a neighbor who babysits for her. **2.** Cheap things aren't durable; they don't last. **3.** He says "life's too short." He wants to enjoy life. He has credit so he uses it. **4.** *Value* magazine; The company that publishes *Value* tests products and gives people information about how good they are. **5.** She doesn't like to pay the interest charges. **6.** You have to compare prices from different stores. Getting that information takes time.

Possible answers: Second Reading: **1.** List: a. barter or trade things/skills b. buy quality c. do things for yourself d. read a consumer magazine e. don't buy on credit (don't spend money on interest) f. ask yourself if you really need things g. compare prices.

Reacting to the Reading: Discussion Questions
1. How do children learn to handle money correctly?
2. How does a credit card work?
3. What is credit good for? What are the dangers of having credit cards?

■ EXPANSION ACTIVITY: Learning about credit
1. Bring credit card brochures and applications to class. Have students read them.
2. Talk about the information requested and how credit cards work.
3. Have pairs of students fill out an application together, giving imaginary information where needed.

21 Final Activity

PROCEDURE
1. Refer to General Guidelines for Final Activity, page xi.
2. Have groups write out five possible questions and select one.
3. The student who needs the least practice speaking English should be the interviewer. The other students write their answers to the question. Have students consult with each other so there is variety in their answers.
4. After students practice, call one group at a time to the front. Interviewers interview their group members and then turn to the class for impromptu answers to their questions.

Workbook: *page 19, exercises H, I*

Second Reading

1. Work in a small group. Make a list of the suggestions the six people in the reading give for how to economize and get more for your money. Each group member must make a copy of the list.

2. Work alone and think about each suggestion. Which will save the most money? Number the suggestions 1, 2, 3, etc. Number 1 should be the best in your opinion.

3. Work as a group. Talk about the importance of each suggestion and try to agree on which should be number 1, 2, 3, etc. Report your group ranking to the class.

21 Final Activity

A. Work in a group of four or five students. Make a list of several questions you might ask in a TV street interview, and choose one of them. One member of the group is the interviewer. The others prepare their personal responses to the question.

B. Demonstrate answers to your interview question for the class. Then interview three or four members of your class.

UNIT 4

COMMUNICATION	GRAMMAR
Talking about things that have happened recently ▪ Things in the kitchen and the living room ▪ Locating things in a room ▪ Verifying facts and opinions	Present perfect statements (irregular verbs) ▪ Prepositions: *in front of*, *in back of*, etc. ▪ Tag questions with *do* and *does*
	SKILLS
	Listening to landlord and tenant conversations ▪ Writing a descriptive paragraph ▪ Reading about recycling

A New Apartment

When Cristina and Gino got back from their honeymoon, they moved into Gino's apartment. They were quite comfortable there for a while, but recently they have had problems with the plumbing. They have spoken to the landlady, but she hasn't done anything. Two weeks ago, they started looking for a better place to live. They have seen many apartments, but they haven't found anything they like.

Just yesterday, Gino was talking to a friend at work who told him about a neighbor of his with an apartment for rent. Gino called the owners and made an appointment to see the place.

Gino and Cristina arrived a few minutes ago to see the apartment. They have met the landlord, and he is showing them the apartment.

CRISTINA: The kitchen is wonderful, isn't it, Gino? Look at all the cabinets and drawers.

GINO: The counter space couldn't be better, and I really like the work area in the middle. The cabinets aren't in the best condition, but I can refinish them myself. The appliances are furnished, aren't they, Mr. Smith?

MR. SMITH: No. This is an unfurnished apartment. The stove and the refrigerator belong to the present tenant.

Useful materials: floor plans and interior and exterior pictures of houses and apartments; pictures showing lots of things in different positions (a crowded desk); pictures of environmental problems; five interesting objects, for example, a cigar box, a yo-yo, a toy dog, a calculator, and a pair of scissors

A New Apartment

PROCEDURE
Refer to General Guidelines for Opener, page ix.

COMPREHENSION QUESTIONS

Now listen to these sentences. Say *Yes, that's right*, *No, that's wrong*, or *I don't know. Maybe.*

1. Cristina and Gino are living in Cristina's old apartment. *No, that's wrong.*
2. The plumbing in their apartment is in good condition. *No, that's wrong.*
3. They are looking for a new apartment. *Yes, that's right.*
4. They went to see an apartment yesterday. *I don't know. Maybe.*
5. Gino learned about this apartment from a friend. *Yes, that's right.*

Now answer these questions.

6. Do Gino and Cristina both like the kitchen? *Yes, they do.*
7. Is the kitchen in perfect condition? *No, it isn't.*
8. What does Cristina think about the bedrooms? *They aren't very big.*
9. How much is the rent? *$500 a month.*
10. When can they move in? *On the first of next month.*

DISCUSSION QUESTIONS

1. Who is more enthusiastic about the apartment, Cristina or Gino? Refer to lines in the conversation when you answer.
2. What do you think convinces Gino and Cristina to take the apartment?
3. What would you look for in an apartment?

Hon is short for *Honey*, a common term of endearment, especially for one's spouse.

CULTURAL NOTES
1. Many houses and apartments built in the U.S. in recent years have an open area that serves as both living room and dining room.
2. Most landlords require tenants to pay a security deposit equal to a month's rent and to sign a lease.

1 Vocabulary in Context

PROCEDURE
1. Refer to General Guidelines for Vocabulary in Context, page ix.
2. Have students work alone or in pairs on Parts A and B. Check answers with the whole class.

Answers: **A.** 1. landlord, landlady 2. unfurnished 3. rent 4. tenant 5. vacant 6. lease 7. sign 8. security deposit **B.** 1. is perfect, the best 2. paint, put a new finish on 3. large, great 4. quite, rather, pretty 5. space 6. Sometime before the last day of the month. 7. We can't find a better one.

> **Workbook: *page 20, exercise A***

CRISTINA: What do you think, hon? The bedrooms aren't very big.
GINO: No, but there are two of them, and they have great closets. The living room/dining room area is tremendous. There's room for the couch under those windows, and my recliner can go right here.
CRISTINA: You like this place, don't you?
GINO: I sure do. Do you like it?
CRISTINA: It's kind of cute. I guess I could see us living here.
GINO: It's definitely the best place we've seen so far. Excuse me, Mr. Smith. What did you say the rent was?
MR. SMITH: $500 a month. If you decide to take it, I'd like an extra month's rent as a security deposit.
CRISTINA: And when will the apartment be vacant?
MR. SMITH: By the end of the month. You can move in on the first.
GINO: We can't beat it, Cris.
CRISTINA: I agree. Let's take it.
GINO: We'll take it, Mr. Smith. Do you want us to sign a lease?
MR. SMITH: Yes. I always require a one-year lease. Let's go back to the house. I'd like you to meet my wife.

1 Vocabulary in Context 🔲

A. Use words from the conversation and introduction, pages 53-54, to complete the definitions.

1. The owner of the house or apartment you rent is called your _____ or _____ .
2. An apartment that is rented with no furniture is a/an _____ apartment.
3. The money you pay to live in someone else's apartment or house is called _____ .
4. A person who pays rent to live in a house or apartment is called a/an _____ .
5. If an apartment is empty, we say it is _____ .
6. A/An _____ is a rental contract.
7. When you rent an apartment, you usually have to _____ a lease for one year.
8. When you sign the lease, you usually pay two months' rent, one for the first month and one as a/an _____ to make sure you pay the last month's rent and leave the place in good condition.

B. The following underlined words and expressions appear in the conversation on pages 53-54. What do they mean? You can check the context in the story.

1. couldn't be better
2. refinish
3. tremendous
4. It's kind of cute.
5. There's room for
6. By the end of the month.
7. We can't beat it.

2 Reentry

Simple past vs. past continuous

Complete the following paragraph about Gino and Cristina's situation with the simple past or the past continuous tense of one of the verbs in the box.

agree	go	sleep
begin	have	spend
come back	have to	talk
find	make	tell
get up	shop	

Gino and Cristina had a wonderful time on their honeymoon in Europe. They (1) _____ a few days with Gino's family in Italy, and they (2) _____ to Paris, too.

A couple of weeks after they (3) _____ , they (4) _____ to have problems with the plumbing in their apartment. One night while they (5) _____ , a pipe broke in the kitchen. When Cristina (6) _____ in the morning, she (7) _____ a pool of water on the kitchen floor.

Two weeks later, they (8) _____ a problem while Cristina (9) _____ at the new mall with Gloria, and Gino was still at work. This time a pipe burst in the bathroom under the sink. The second incident (10) _____ them decide that they (11) _____ find a better place.

Last Monday afternoon, Gino (12) _____ to a friend at work who (13) _____ him about a vacant apartment in his neighborhood. Gino (14) _____ Cristina about the place, and she (15) _____ they should call the owner right away for an appointment.

2 Reentry

PROCEDURE
1. Refer to General Guidelines for Reentry, page x.
2. Have students complete the paragraphs individually or in pairs. Then check answers with the whole class.

Answers: **1.** spent **2.** went **3.** came back **4.** began **5.** were sleeping **6.** got up **7.** found **8.** had **9.** was shopping **10.** made **11.** had to **12.** talked **13.** told **14.** told **15.** agreed

Workbook: *page 21, exercise B*

3 Presentation

PROCEDURE

1. Refer to General Guidelines for Presentation, page ix.
2. Students learned the part participle of *be* in *Book 3*. Write *Base*, *Past*, and *Past Participle* on the board. Review the past participle of *be* by asking students to fill in the first two columns (*be* and *was/were*). Then write *I have/haven't ___ sick recently*. Ask for the word that goes in the blank and write *been* in the third column.
3. Have students read model sentences 1 and 2 and write a rule for forming the present perfect, *have/has* + past participle.
4. To expand the Presentation, put the following statements on the board. Have students identify the complete verb in each. To show that the present perfect is an indefinite past, ask when each thing happened. Students won't be able to tell you.
   a. Cristina and Gino have found a new apartment.
   b. I have lost my wallet.
   c. I have seen the movie *Three Men and a Baby*.
   d. Most students have done their homework.
   e. Your teacher has spoken to the principal.

LANGUAGE NOTE

Some students have problems with *have had* and *has had* because they look like two main verbs in a row. Using other present perfect verbs as models, show that the first *have* is the auxiliary and the second is the main verb.

3 Presentation

Talking about things that have happened recently

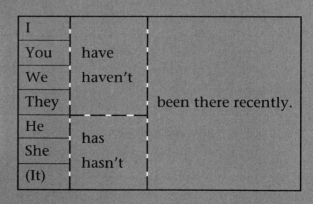

Principal parts of some irregular verbs			
	Base	**Past**	**Past Participle**
Same simple past and past participle form	feel	felt	felt
	find	found	found
	have	had	had
	lose	lost	lost
	meet	met	met
Different simple past and past participle form	be	was/were	been
	do	did	done
	eat	ate	eaten
	go	went	gone
	see	saw	seen
	speak	spoke	spoken
	take	took	taken

Use the **present perfect** to talk about the indefinite past — a period of time that began in the past and continues to the present. Use adverbs of time such as: **so far, recently,** and **lately.**

I		
You	have	
We	haven't	
They		been there recently.
He	has	
She	hasn't	
(It)		

1. Gino and Cristina **have had** problems with their apartment **recently.**

2. They **have spoken** to the landlady, but **so far** she **hasn't done** anything.

3. Cristina **has seen** many apartments **lately,** but she **hasn't found** anything she likes.

4 Practice

Complete the sentences with the correct form of the verb in parentheses to show that something has or hasn't happened in the indefinite past.

1. Sam is looking for a better car. He _____ (see) a lot of cars recently, but he _____ (not / find) anything he can afford.

2. Liz works for the telephone company. She _____ (have) problems with a co-worker recently. She _____ (speak) to her boss, but the boss _____ (not / do) anything to try to solve the problems.

3. Tom and Adela are working very hard. They _____ (not / take) a vacation recently. They _____ (be) too busy and, besides, they _____ (not / have) the money.

4. Toshio Ito doesn't live in Winfield, but he _____ (be) to Winfield several times recently. He _____ (meet) friends of the Logans, and he _____ (feel) very welcome there.

5. Some of the teachers at Winfield High School think they are too heavy, so they _____ (be) on a diet recently. They _____ (eat) a lot of salad, but they _____ (not / eat) much ice cream. They _____ (lose) quite a bit of weight.

6. Joyce is usually healthy, but she _____ (be) sick recently. She _____ (not / feel) well, so she _____ (not / do) her homework. She _____ (not / go) to school, so she _____ (not / take) any exams.

5 Practice

Work with a partner. Read the situation and talk about what the people have or haven't done recently. Use the verbs in parentheses.

1. Gloria got sick two days ago, and she is still sick. (go, feel, take, go, do)

2. Liz had an argument with her boyfriend Dave a week ago. They still aren't talking to each other. (speak, go out, be angry/upset, see)

3. Howard and Elinor Young are working very hard these days. (have, be, feel, go, eat)

4. Tom has been very forgetful lately. (lose, find)

5. Lisa and Joyce's class has taken three trips recently. (be/go to, see, meet)

4 Practice

PROCEDURE
1. Refer to General Guidelines for Practice, page x.
2. Do with the whole class.

Answers: **1.** has seen, hasn't found **2.** has had, has spoken, hasn't done **3.** haven't taken, have been, haven't had **4.** has been, has met, has felt **5.** have been, have eaten, haven't eaten, have lost **6.** has been, hasn't felt, hasn't done, hasn't gone, hasn't taken

5 Practice

PROCEDURE
1. Refer to General Guidelines for Practice, page x.
2. Before students begin work with a partner, have them give affirmative and negative examples for #1.
3. After students work with a partner, have them compare their sentences with those of another pair or discuss with the whole class.

Possible answers: **1.** She hasn't gone to school. She hasn't felt well. She has taken some aspirin, but she hasn't gone to the doctor. She hasn't done any homework. **2.** They haven't spoken to each other in days. They haven't gone out either. They have been very angry/upset with each other. They haven't seen each other for a week. **3.** They haven't had time to go to the movies. They have been very busy. They have felt very tired at the end of a day. They have gone to bed late every night. They have eaten in a restaurant more than usual. **4.** He has lost his keys twice. Fortunately he has found them both time. **5.** The class has been/gone to Washington, but they haven't met the President. They have seen the White House though.

■ EXPANSION ACTIVITY: What I have/haven't done today
Have students write a paragraph about things they have and haven't done today or this week using some of the verbs in the top box on page 56. Students might begin with: *Today has been a _____ day. I have done a lot of things that I wanted to do. / I haven't done anything I wanted to do.*

6 Interaction

PROCEDURE

1. Refer to General Guidelines for Interaction, page x.
2. After pair practice, have the class share experiences and opinions on these topics.

Optional: Have students do the activity in a small group or have partners select one item and survey the class and report the results to the class.

> **Workbook: *page 22, exercises C, D***

7 Vocabulary in Context

PROCEDURE

1. Refer to General Guidelines for Vocabulary in Context, page ix.
2. After presenting the vocabulary, have students practice in pairs. One student points to something in one of the pictures and asks for confirmation from the other. For example: A: *This is the oven isn't it?* B: *No, it isn't. That's the stove.*

6 Interaction

Talk with a partner about things you have and haven't done.

> places you have / haven't been
> A: I've been to ____New York____ . What about you?
> B: I haven't been to ____New York____ , but I've been
> to ____Washington____ .
> I've been to ____New York____ , too.

1. places you have / haven't been
2. movies you have / haven't seen
3. things you have lost, and have / haven't found
4. people you have / haven't met
5. classes you have / haven't taken

7 Vocabulary in Context

Things in the kitchen and the living room

1. cabinet
2. counter
3. drawer
4. sink
5. refrigerator
6. freezer
7. stove
8. oven
9. large appliances = stove and refrigerator
10. small appliances = toaster, blender

11. couch/sofa
12. recliner
13. armchair
14. coffee table
15. end tables
16. rug
17. lamp
18. bookcase

8 Practice

Complete the sentences with the new vocabulary on page 58. Use each word only once.

The Kitchen

1. When you get home from the store, you put the groceries on the _____ or the kitchen table.
2. Then you put things away in the _____ above the counter or in the _____ where they stay cold.
3. The silverware — the knives, forks, and spoons — often go in a _____ just under the countertop.
4. Before eating fruit and vegetables, you should wash them in the _____ .
5. The refrigerator and the _____ are the biggest appliances in a kitchen.
6. If you want to bake bread, you will use the _____ in your stove.

The Living Room

7. In a living room, several people can sit on the _____ .
8. Some people like to relax in a chair that goes back. It's called a _____ .
9. Living room tables have different names. If they go at the ends of the couch, they are called _____ .
10. The table that goes in front of the couch is called a _____ . There is sometimes a _____ on the floor, too.

9 Presentation

Locating things in a room

In many kitchens, things are positioned in this way:

1. The sink is **under** a window.

2. Some cabinets are **above** a counter.

3. A table might be **in the** | **middle** | **of** the room.
   | **center** |

above	= higher than
below	= lower than
over	= directly above
under	= directly below

8 Practice

PROCEDURE
Refer to General Guidelines for Practice, page x.

Answers: 1. counter 2. cabinets, refrigerator 3. drawer 4. sink 5. stove 6. oven 7. couch/sofa 8. recliner 9. end tables 10. coffee table, rug.

■ EXPANSION ACTIVITY: Interior decorator

1. Have students imagine that they are interior decorators. With the class brainstorm a list of potential clients, e.g., a computer business establishing a new office; a young, artistic couple with no children; a couple with six kids, etc.
2. Form groups of three or four students. Each group chooses a client and plans one room for them in their house/apartment/office. Students find or draw pictures of the furnishings for the room and make a poster to show to the clients.
3. Then groups role play a situation in which the interior decorators present their ideas to the clients (the class). Clients can approve the selection or criticize it.

9 Presentation

PROCEDURE
Refer to General Guidelines for Presentation, page ix.

LANGUAGE NOTE
Like prepositions in general, *above, below, over,* and *under* are often used idiomatically. The definitions in the box are generally true for spacial relationship only. *Over* and *under* can also mean *more than* and *less than* (overage, underage), but so can *above* and *below* (above average and below average). We say *above* and *below* *zero,* but we can say both *over/under* and *above/below* other temperatures.

10 Practice

PROCEDURE
1. Refer to General Guidelines for Practice, page x.
2. Do the activity in small groups or with the whole class. See how many sentences students can make using a given preposition before changing to a new one.

Variation: Make this Practice into a game. Form teams of about four members. Ask a question with one preposition. Give teams one minute to write all the examples they can see in the room. Change the preposition and repeat. The team with the most correct sentences wins. To play the game orally, form two teams. Alternate the opportunity to answer first. Then continue accepting responses and giving points until no team can think of a different response.

■ EXPANSION ACTIVITY 4A: Drawing floor plans (page 190)
■ EXPANSION ACTIVITY 4B: Describing actions (page 190)

11 Interaction

PROCEDURE
Note: You will need one floor plan and one set of statements A, B, C, and D found on page 172 in the student's book for every four students.

1. Refer to General Guidelines for Interaction, page x.
2. Have each group choose a leader and a secretary. The leader's job is to direct the cooperative effort, supervising turn taking, etc. The secretary completes the floor plan for the group.

Answer: Have students compare their floor plans with those of classmates or with yours.

12 Listening

PROCEDURE
1. Refer to General Guidelines for Listening, page x.
2. Play the tape or read the script for the Listening. The tape includes the directions on page 61.
3. *If reading the script:* Give students 10 seconds to draw in furniture and appliances before reading another room description.

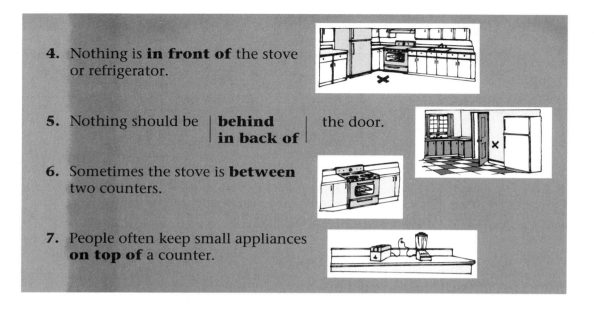

4. Nothing is **in front of** the stove or refrigerator.

5. Nothing should be | **behind** **in back of** | the door.

6. Sometimes the stove is **between** two counters.

7. People often keep small appliances **on top of** a counter.

10 Practice

Talk with your classmates about the positions of things in your classroom or in pictures that you bring to class. Use the prepositions in *9*, as well as *near*, *next to*, and *across from*.

> under
>
> A: Is there anything in this room that is **under** something else?
> B: Yes, there is. My books are **under** my seat.

11 Interaction

Work in a group of four students. Make a copy of the floor plan for the first floor of the Logans' new house. Room 1 is the kitchen, 2 is the dining room, 3 is the living room, and 4 is a study/guest room. Your teacher will give each group member some information about where the furniture and appliances are located in the house. Share your information and complete the floor plan.

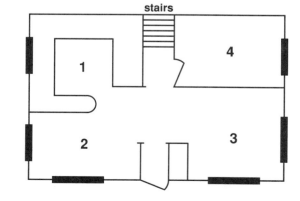

12 Listening 📼

Make another copy of the floor plan. The Logans' neighbors, the Polinskys, have an identical house, but their furniture and appliances are organized differently. Listen to the descriptions of their rooms and draw in their furniture and appliances.

13 Writing

A. Talk with your partner about what makes a nice room. Is it the furniture? The light? The atmosphere? Write down some ideas.

B. Now write a paragraph describing a room you really like. It can be a room in your home or in a public place. Make notes about the details you will include. Use the topics below as a guide. Begin your paragraph with the details and end with a summary statement about why you like the room or its general atmosphere.

1. Location, size, color, use of room (if not clear from name)
2. Number and location of doors, windows
3. Major furniture or objects in the room and their location
4. Smaller details about the room
5. Conclusion: why you like the room; the general atmosphere of the room

C. Now read your partner's paragraph. Talk about whether or not you like the room he or she described in the paragraph. Are your partner's ideas about a nice room similar to yours?

14 Reentry

Tag questions

Work with a partner. Write five statements with tag questions to check information or the meaning of words in the opening story on pages 53-54. Use *be* in the present or past tense. Then ask other classmates to confirm your ideas or definitions.

> A: A lease is a rental contract, isn't it?
> B: Yes, it is.

> A: The cabinets were in good condition, weren't they?
> B: No, they weren't, but Gino can refinish them.

Script

1. In the Polinskys' study/guest room, there is a long bookcase with a TV on it on the right wall as you go in the door. Across from the TV, there's a sofa with a bed inside for guests to use. There's a desk under the window with bookcases on both sides.
2. In the living room, the couch is on the back wall across from the front window. There's one end table with a lamp on it at the left side of the couch as you are looking at it. There's no rug on the floor, but there is a coffee table in front of the couch with a plant on it. There are two big armchairs, one in front of each window. There's a small table at the right side of each chair.
3. The dining room is the same as the Logans', except the Polinskys' has four stools.
4. In the kitchen, the sink is in the middle of the back counter. The stove is under the window. There is nothing in front of the curved counter. The refrigerator is in the middle of the right wall across from the stove. There's a washing machine next to it on the dining room side.

Answer: Have students compare their drawings with those of classmates or with yours.

13 Writing

PROCEDURE
1. Refer to General Guidelines for Writing, page xi.
2. Write the prepositions in Presentation 9 on the board and encourage students to use them.

> Workbook: *page 23, exercises E, F*

14 Reentry

PROCEDURE
1. Refer to General Guidelines for Reentry, page x.
2. Refer to Language Notes for Presentation 9, page 29 for information on tag questions.

Possible questions: 1. The apartment isn't perfect, is it? 2. The bedrooms weren't very big, were they? 3. The counter space was good, wasn't it?

15 Presentation

PROCEDURE
1. Refer to General Guidelines for Presentation, page ix.
2. Refer to Language Notes for Presentation 9, page 29 for information on tag questions.

16 Practice

PROCEDURE
1. Refer to General Guidelines for Practice, page x.
2. Have students work in pairs.

Answers for tag questions: **1.** doesn't it? **2.** do you? **3.** don't they? **4.** does it? **5.** don't you? **6.** don't we? **7.** do you? **8.** don't you? **9.** does it? **10.** don't we?

17 Practice

PROCEDURE
1. Refer to General Guidelines for Practice, page x.
2. Brainstorm possible verbs other than *look* and *have* and write them on the board. (For example: *need, smell*)

Possible answers: **good apartment**: This place has character, doesn't it? We don't have to do anything to this place, do we? **bad apartment**: This place needs a lots of repairs, doesn't it? This room doesn't smell good, does it?

■ EXPANSION ACTIVITY 4C: Checking information in a short talk (page 190)
■ EXPANSION ACTIVITY 4D: You ____, don't you? (page 190)

Workbook: *page 24, exercise G*

18 Listening

PROCEDURE
1. Refer to General Guidelines for Listening, page x.
2. Play the tape or read the script for the Listening. The tape includes the directions on page 63.
3. *If reading the script*: For the First Listening give students 15 seconds to complete the answer format. For the Second Listening give students 20 seconds

15 Presentation 🔲

Verifying facts and opinions

To verify facts and opinions in a present tense statement, use tag questions with **do** and **does.**

A
A: This apartment doesn't look very good, **does it?**
B: | No, it doesn't. I don't like it. | (expected response)
   | Yes, it does. | (unexpected response)

B
A: The owners don't require a lease, **do they?**
B: | No, they don't. | (expected response)
   | Oh, yes, they do. | (unexpected response)

C
CRISTINA: You like this place, **don't you?**
GINO: I sure do. It's terrific!

D
A: The apartment has three bedrooms, **doesn't it?**
B: No, it doesn't. Only two.

16 Practice

Add a tag question to each statement and check the information with a classmate who plays the role of the landlord or landlady. Give expected or unexpected responses.

1. The plumbing works OK.
2. You don't have problems with the plumbing.
3. The appliances belong to the present tenant.
4. The rent doesn't include gas and electricity.
5. You require a lease.
6. We have to sign a lease.
7. You don't have any other apartments.
8. You take checks.
9. The ceiling doesn't leak.
10. We have to pay a security deposit.

17 Practice

Work with a partner. Imagine you are in one of the apartments in the pictures. You can't see the whole apartment in the picture, but you can imagine what the rest of it is like. Take turns and comment first on the good apartment, then on the bad one. Be sure to use tag questions.

good apartment
A: The stove looks brand new, doesn't it?
B: It sure does. Not a scratch on it.

bad apartment
A: This place doesn't have much light, does it?
B: It sure doesn't. It's like night in here.

18 Listening 🎵

Copy this answer format three times on your paper. Number them 1, 2, and 3.

TOPIC OF THE CONVERSATION: _____
PROBLEM: _____ NO PROBLEM: _____

First Listening

Listen for the general idea of the conversations and complete the answer format.

Second Listening

Number your paper from 1-9. Listen to the conversations again and write *T* (True), *F* (False), or *NG* (Not Given) for each statement.

Conversation 1
1. The landlady has to get a painter to paint the apartment.
2. The tenant is happy to help the landlady.
3. The landlady paid for the paint.

to respond to the statements for each conversation.

Script

Conversation 1

TENANT: Thanks for the paint, Mrs. Soto. I plan to paint the apartment this weekend.

LANDLADY: You're welcome, John. It's a pleasure to have a good tenant like you. If you weren't going to paint your apartment, I would have to pay a painter.

TENANT: I wouldn't want you to do that. You've done a lot of things for me and the rent is reasonable. The least I can do is paint the place if you pay for the paint.

Conversation 2

TENANT: Mr. West, I'm sorry to have to mention it again, but the refrigerator isn't cooling well at all. You said you would fix it.

LANDLORD: Mrs. Inglewood, I'm looking for a repairman. Just give me time.

TENANT: I have given you time. This is the third time I've asked you to do something about it. The darn refrigerator is costing me money. Food is going bad.

LANDLORD: OK. I'll take care of it today or tomorrow.

Conversation 3

TENANT: Mr. Bartlett, could I talk to you for a minute?

LANDLORD: How about tomorrow? I'm in a hurry right now.

TENANT: It'll just take a minute. My husband and I would like to know why you are you raising the rent. We really don't think that this apartment is worth $450.

LANDLORD: Mrs. Steinman, as you know, everything is getting more expensive these days. That includes repairs on apartments and taxes. It's impossible for me not to raise the rent.

TENANT: Would you consider only $425 a month instead of $450?

LANDLORD: Sorry. I can't do that. $450 for an apartment is very reasonable these days.

Answers: First Listening: **Conversation 1**: Topic: painting the apartment; No problem **Conversation 2**: Topic: Fixing the refrigerator; Problem **Conversation 3**: Topic: the rent or cost of the apartment; Problem

Answers: Second Listening: **1.** F **2.** T **3.** T **4.** T **5.** NG **6.** T **7.** F **8.** T **9.** F

PROCEDURE

1. Refer to General Guidelines for Reading, page x.
2. Have students take the test and do the "First Reading" task with a partner. Check the answers with the whole class.
3. Before students do the "Second Reading" part A activity (page 66) in small groups, demonstrate on the board that when we take notes we do not copy whole sentences.
4. Check the "Second Reading" task. List the evidence students give you on the board. Use these lists as suggested in the Expansion Activity "Illustrating ideas with facts" that follows on page 65.
5. Have students do part B in their groups.
6. Use some of the discussion questions suggested in "Reacting to the Reading" on page 65.

Answers: First Reading: **1.** a. trash, garbage, waste b. Burn it. Bury it. Recycle it. **2.** a. place we can dump trash/the dump b. (in Answer 8) factory (in Answer 9) living things like trees, flowers c. dirt, ground, earth d. (in Answer 5) decomposable, decomposes naturally e. (in Answer 4) a poisonous liquid that filters into the ground water f. (in Answer 9) soil made from decomposing plants g. (in Answer 5) the opposite of *float*, go down under the water h. (in Answer 10) a period with no rain, infer from parallel position to *water*.

Possible answers: Second Reading: **1.** garbage truck example in Answer 1; one third of landfills will soon be full in Answer 2, etc. **2.** Answer 2: 80% in landfills. **3.** Answers 4, 5, and 7. **4.** Implied in Answer 10, we have recycled in emergencies but not when there is no emergency; also suggested in Answer 5, garbage is thrown from ships; in Answer 6, only 10% of American garbage is recycled; and in Answer 8 that people must do special work to recycle. **5.** In Answer 8: metals, glass, plastic; in Answer 9: burnable things can be 'recycled' into electricity and biodegradable garbage can become compost. Recycling of water might be mentioned in relation to Answer 10.

Conversation 2
4. The refrigerator belongs to the landlord.
5. The refrigerator is new.
6. The tenant has spoken to the landlord about the problem before.

Conversation 3
7. The tenant rents a house.
8. The tenant could pay $425.
9. The landlord agrees to $425 for the rent.

19 Reading

Before You Read

1. Do you throw away all of your trash or do you recycle some of it?
2. How much trash do you think you throw away each week?

First Reading

Work with a partner. Take the test at the beginning of the article to see how much you know about trash. Answer *true* or *false*, and then read the answers for the details. Talk with your partner about difficult words in the reading and complete this vocabulary exercise.

1. In the true/false statements, find
   a. three words for what we throw away
   b. three ways to handle what we throw away

2. Check the reading and give definitions or paraphrases for these words:
   a. landfill
   b. plant *(two meanings)*
   c. soil
   d. biodegradable
   e. leachate
   f. compost
   g. sink
   h. drought

Test Your Knowledge of Trash

How much do you know about what you throw away every day?

T F **1.** Americans throw away a lot of garbage every year.

T F **2.** In the United States, more trash is burned than is buried in landfills or recycled.

T F **3.** Dumping or burying trash in landfills is expensive.

T F **4.** If they are not built correctly, landfills can be dangerous to people.

T F **5.** People dump a lot of garbage in the oceans, too.

T F **6.** The United States recycles about 50% of its trash.

T F **7.** What we throw away decays or decomposes fast and cannot hurt people.

T F **8.** In modern waste management, machines do everything. People don't touch the trash.

T F **9.** A recycling plant can produce electricity and soil to grow plants in.

T F **10.** Recycling is a new idea.

ANSWERS

1. *True*. The typical American throws away about 1,300 lbs. (590 kg.) of garbage a year. About 84 lbs. (38 kg.) of it are plastic. For the nation as a whole, this means 160 million tons of waste a year, or enough to make a chain of 10-ton garbage trucks halfway to the moon.

2. *False*. Approximately 80% of all U.S. trash ends up in one of about 6,000 landfills across the country. Before the middle of the 1990s, one-third of these landfills will be full.

3. *True*. It is most expensive where land costs a lot. In the northeastern part of the United States, cities can pay up to $135 to dump one ton of garbage in a landfill.

4. *True*. Decaying garbage generates methane gas, so landfills must have proper ventilation or they explode in fire. Rain and snow on garbage creates leachate, a poisonous liquid that filters into the groundwater if landfills do not have adequate drainage.

5. *True*. Fishermen, ships of all kinds, and offshore oil and gas drilling operations dump tons of garbage in the oceans, including tons of plastic containers that are not biodegradable and do not sink. They come floating up on the world's beaches, sometimes bringing dead marine life with them.

6. *False*. In the early 1990s, Japan recycled about 50% of its trash; the U.S. only about 10%, according to estimates of the U.S. Environmental Protection Agency.

7. *False*. Archeologists and students from the University of Arizona, under the direction of William Rathje, are digging up old landfills. Landfills, contrary to what most of us believe, preserve things very well. Some food and yard waste does decompose, of course, but 75% of our trash has the same weight, volume, and form after forty years. You can even read the newspapers, which Rathje has found make up 16% of our buried trash. Furthermore, these archeologists calculate, 1% of our garbage is hazardous waste such as the toxic chemicals sulfuric acid, mercuric oxide, and lead in batteries and other electrical supplies.

8. *False*. When people put out the garbage, they must separate the recyclable from the non-recyclable materials. At a Rhode Island recycling plant, the system handles the metals and the glass, but people must separate the plastic by hand.

9. *True*. In some recycling plants, everything that is not recycled is burned to produce electric power. In Florida, there is a private recycling business that is changing garbage into compost, which is the best soil and very good for growing plants.

10. *False*. In emergencies like droughts and wars, people have recycled all kinds of materials and have been very careful about how much water, gasoline, and electricity they used. Today we are in another kind of emergency. We must protect ourselves and our planet Earth, so governments are passing laws to bring back the old habit of recycling.

Reacting to the Reading: Discussion Questions

1. How is trash handled in your community? Are people in your community careful about how much trash they make? Do they recycle things? Is there an official government position on recycling?
2. Do you have more up-to-date information on recycling than what is presented in this article?
3. What other dangers to our planet do you know about? Can you make a short talk (alone or with a partner) about another danger?

■ EXPANSION ACTIVITY: Illustrating ideas with facts

1. Have students write a paragraph to illustrate any of the following topic sentences with evidence they have found in the reading.
   a. Garbage is a serious problem in the United States.
   b. Of the three ways to handle garbage, dumping is the most common.
   c. The trash we throw away is dangerous.
   d. Recycling our trash will help us in three/four ways.
2. If possible, have students find other facts to support their main ideas in current periodicals. Teach them to give the source of their information in parentheses after they use it. For example, (*Value*, June 1990, pp. 13-14).
3. Have students prepare an environmental awareness bulletin board, including their paragraphs and pictures from magazines and newspapers.

■ EXPANSION ACTIVITY: Describing an apartment that you would like

1. As preparation for the Final Activity, review the ways to modify nouns: single word and compound word modifiers precede the nouns they modify; phrases and relative clauses follow the nouns they modify.
2. Have students talk about the apartment they would like using this model:
   A: I hear that you are looking for a new apartment.
   B: Right.
   A: What kind of place are you looking for?
   B: I'd like a/an ____ apartment.
      I'd like an apartment with/near ____.
      I'd like an apartment that ____.
      I'd like a landlord/landlady who ____.
3. Have students talk about the roommate they would like using this model:
   A: I hear that you are looking for someone to share your apartment.
   B: Right. I can't afford to live alone.
   A: What kind of person are you looking for?
   B: I'd like someone who ____.

20 Final Activity

PROCEDURE
Refer to General Guidelines for Final Activity, page xi.

■ EXPANSION ACTIVITY: Having rental problems
1. Review the conversations in Listening 18.
2. Have students work in groups of three.
3. Give students these planning questions for a role play in which a tenant complains to the landlord/landlady or vice versa.

Planning Questions:
• Who has a complaint, landlord/landlady or tenants? What is it?
• How will the complaint be made, politely or impolitely? What will the reaction be?
• What is the result of the conversation? Are the tenants going to move? Is the landlord/landlady going to evict the tenants? Are the repairs going to be made?

Workbook: *page 25, exercise H*

Second Reading

A. **Read the test answers again and find the following:**

1. evidence that garbage is a big problem in the United States
2. evidence that dumping trash is the most common way to handle it
3. evidence that the trash we throw away can be dangerous
4. evidence that it is not easy to get people to recycle
5. evidence of what we should recycle and how recycling will help us

B. **Discuss this question in your group. Then read the answer on page 173.**

What do you think can be made from each of these items — old plastic bottles, tires, newspapers, and glass?

20 Final Activity

A. **Form a group of three. Two of you share an apartment and are looking for a better place. The third person is the landlord or landlady of an apartment that you are thinking about renting. Use these questions to help you plan your conversation.**

1. What's wrong with your present apartment?
2. What kind of apartment are you looking for?
3. Describe the apartment you are considering. Does it have what you want? If not, what's wrong with it?
4. What kind of people are the landlord/landlady and the possible tenants? Polite? Rude? Old? Young?
5. Are you going to take the apartment or not? If not, why not?

B. **Write a conversation in which you visit an apartment you are considering renting. Discuss the advantages and/or disadvantages of the apartment. Ask the landlord/landlady for information. Decide whether or not to take the place. Practice the conversation and role play it for your class.**

Useful language:

TENANTS			LANDLORD/LANDLADY
It	has	____ .	I require ____ .
	doesn't have		Appliances are / aren't furnished.
I'd rather have ____ .			
It's too ____ .			If you decide to take it, ____ .
It isn't ____ enough.			I don't want any ____ in my
This has the	best	____ .	apartment.
	worst		

UNIT 5

COMMUNICATION
Explaining what's wrong ▪ Offering to help ▪ Talking about what you have and haven't done ▪ Talking about the very recent past

GRAMMAR
Present perfect tense of regular and irregular verbs ▪ Present perfect: *yes/no* questions and short answers ▪ Simple past vs. present perfect ▪ *Just* with simple past

SKILLS
Writing a letter while on a trip ▪ Listening to a conversation ▪ Reading about an organization

On the Road

Gino Leone has been in Buffalo on business. On his way home to Winfield, he passes a couple of young men standing at the side of the road. Something is wrong with their car, so he stops to see if he can help.

GINO: Can I give you a lift to the next garage?

TONY: Thanks. We'd really appreciate it.

GINO: Hop in . . . My name's Gino Leone.

TONY: Nice to meet you, Gino. I'm Tony Perez.

JOE: And I'm Joe Brennan.

GINO: Nice to meet you both. What's wrong with your car?

JOE: Well, we don't know exactly, but it looks like something's wrong with the electrical system.

TONY: You wouldn't believe it. We've had problems off and on all the way from California.

GINO: California? You've come a long way. How long have you been on the road?

TONY: Since April. We've stayed with friends, and we've camped out when the weather's been warm enough. We've really seen a lot of the country!

GINO: I guess you have. It sounds like you've had a great trip!

JOE: Yes, it has been great, but now we've got the car to worry about. I hope we have enough money to fix it.

Useful materials: magazine pictures of things that have gone wrong; pictures of people doing different things; a U.S. map

On the Road

PROCEDURE
Refer to General Guidelines for Opener, page ix.

COMPREHENSION QUESTIONS

Now answer these questions.
1. Where is Gino going to take Tony and Joe? *To a garage.*
2. What's the problem with Joe and Tony's car? *Something's wrong with the electrical system.*
3. Has the trip been easy for Joe and Tony? *No, it hasn't. They have had problems off and on all the way.*
4. When did they leave California? *In April.*
5. Do Joe and Tony have enough money to fix their car? *Maybe. They hope they do.*

Now listen to these sentences. Say *Yes, that's right*, *No, that's wrong*, or *I don't know. Maybe.*
6. Joe and Tony will be happy to ask their parents for money. *No, that's wrong.*
7. It will be easy for Joe and Tony to find a job in a fast food restaurant. *I don't know. Maybe.*
8. Joe and Tony have worked in fast food restaurants before. *I don't know. Maybe.*
9. The people at the garage can help Joe and Tony immediately. *No, that's wrong.*
10. Gino has eaten breakfast, but Joe and Tony haven't. *No, that's wrong.*

DISCUSSION QUESTIONS
1. Would you pick up these two young men if you were Gino?
2. Which would you do if you had all the money you needed on a trip—stay with friends, camp out, or stay in hotels?
3. When Gino says, "I'll treat you", he means he will pay. Would you treat a stranger to a meal like Gino does? Why or why not? Under what circumstances?

1. *Can I give you a lift?* and *Hop in* are very informal expressions. More formal alternatives are *Can I give you a ride?* and *Get in.*
2. *I'll treat you* or *My treat* are ways to say that you will pay the bill.

CULTURAL NOTE

Americans don't usually treat strangers to meals. In this case, Gino knows Tony and Joe are having bad luck and, being a nice person, he offers to pay.

1 Vocabulary in Context

PROCEDURE

1. Refer to General Guidelines for Vocabulary in Context, page ix.
2. Have students work individually or in pairs. Check the exercise with the whole class.

Answers: 1. the problem/wrong 2. on the road 3. a lift 4. on his way 5. Something's wrong 6. a couple of 7. Any chance 8. come a long way 9. folks 10. off and on

GINO: What will you do if you don't?

TONY: I guess we could ask our folks for help, but I sure don't want to do that.

JOE: What's the job situation like around here? Any chance we could find a job in a fast food restaurant?

GINO: Maybe . . . Here's the gas station. Check and see if they can help you. I'll wait here.

JOE: They just sent the tow truck out. It'll be half an hour.

GINO: Have you guys eaten breakfast yet?

TONY: No, we haven't, but . . .

GINO: I haven't either. Come on. I'll treat you. There's a good place across the highway.

1 Vocabulary in Context 🔲

Find another way to say the underlined idea. Use a word or expression from the conversation or the introduction (pages 67-68).

1. What's <u>the matter</u> with your car?

2. Joe and Tony have been <u>traveling</u> for several months.

3. Can I give you <u>a ride</u>?

4. Gino is <u>going</u> home to Winfield.

5. <u>There's a problem</u> with the electrical system.

6. Gino saw <u>two</u> young men standing at the side of the road.

7. <u>Is there a possibility</u> we could find a job here?

8. You've <u>traveled far</u>.

9. Tony's and Joe's <u>parents</u> live in California.

10. We've had problems <u>occasionally</u> during the trip.

Explaining what's wrong; offering to help

A

A: Car problems, eh? What's the matter?
B: The car won't start.
A: Maybe I can figure out what's wrong.
B: Thanks. I'd sure appreciate that.

B

A: What's wrong with the TV?
B: I don't know. It just went off.
A: Let me take a look.
B: Great.

C

Other car problems:

We've got a flat tire.

We ran out of gas.

Something's wrong with the steering.

Other household problems:

The sink is clogged.

A pipe is leaking.

The radio won't work.

A: You look kind of upset. What's the matter?
B: It's my math assignment. I'm stuck. I just can't do it.
A: Let me see. Maybe I can help.
B: I sure hope so.

2 Presentation

PROCEDURE
1. Refer to General Guidelines for Presentation, page ix.
2. Have students guess the meaning of *stuck* (*can't do it, can't continue*).

■ EXPANSION ACTIVITY: Talking about what's wrong
1. Add practice before the Interaction in the following way. Have students find pictures that suggest something has gone wrong; for example, a child who has spilled his food, broken down vehicles, angry couples, etc.
2. Have students take the roles of people in the pictures, write conversations like those in Presentation 2, and role play them for the class.

3 Interaction

1. Refer to General Guidelines for Interaction, page x.
2. You may want to brainstorm situations with the whole class.

> Workbook: *page 26, exercise A*

4 Presentation

1. Refer to General Guidelines for Presentation, page ix.
2. To expand the Presentation, put the following verbs on the board and have students make statements about what they have or haven't done this week in class: *study, enjoy, listen to, talk about/to,* etc.

---

3 Interaction

Work with a partner. Discuss and write down three or four situations in which a person might have a problem that another person could help with, maybe at school, at home, on the road, or in some other public place. Choose one situation and write a conversation that begins as suggested below. Continue the conversation until the problem is resolved. Practice it and role play it for the class.

A:	Open the conversation by asking what's wrong.
B:	Explain the problem.
A:	Offer to help.
B:	Express appreciation.

4 Presentation

Talking about what you have and haven't done

> To talk about what you have and haven't done sometime in the past, use the present perfect tense.

Principal parts of regular verbs

Base	Past	Past Participle*	
stay	stayed	stayed	/d/
camp	camped	camped	/t/
visit	visited	visited	/id/

* Same pronunciation as the simple past tense.

Tony and Joe have been on the road since April.

1. They **have visited** big cities and small towns.
2. Joe **has liked** the big cities.
3. Tony **has enjoyed** the small towns.
4. They **haven't called** home very much.
5. Tony **hasn't talked** to his parents very often.

5 Pronunciation 🔊

Pronounce these sentences.

1. I've never been to Alaska.
2. You've come a long way.
3. He's seen a lot of the country.
4. She's traveled quite a bit this summer.
5. It's been a difficult trip.
6. We've stayed with friends.
7. They've camped out.

Contractions:	
I've	= I have
You've	= You have
He's	= He has
She's	= She has
It's	= It has
We've	= We have
They've	= They have

6 Practice

A. Complete the sentences with the present perfect of one of the verbs in the box. Use the affirmative or negative, whichever makes sense. There may be more than one correct answer. You don't have to use all of the verbs.

call	miss	stay	walk
camp	prepare	talk	wash
cook	rain	visit	watch

Since April . . .

1. Tony and Joe _____ many interesting places.
2. They _____ in Yellowstone National Park.
3. Joe _____ most of the meals, since he likes to cook.
4. Tony _____ the dishes.
5. They _____ in hotels.
6. They _____ much TV lately.
7. They _____ miles and miles in the woods.
8. Fortunately, they have had good weather. It _____ much.
9. Tony _____ to his folks occasionally.
10. Apparently Joe _____ his mom and dad because he _____ them only once since he left.

B. Continue talking with a partner about things Tony and Joe have or haven't done on their trip. Write ten sentences and share them with your classmates. You might want to use some of the verbs in the box below.

attend	listen	look for
collect	live with	rent
learn to	live without	use

5 Pronunciation

Focus: Contractions of the auxiliary verbs *have* and *has* with subject pronouns

PROCEDURE
1. Refer to General Guidelines for Pronunciation, page x.
2. Have students explain the contractions in these sentences: *He's studying.* (He is) *He's studied all day.* (He has) *It's nice to meet you.* (It is) *It's been nice to see you.* (It has) Then dictate sentences and have students write them without contractions, for example: *We've studied Units 1 to 4. Gino's visited Boston recently. Gino has visited Boston recently. We have studied Units 1 to 4.*

Note: When the main verb after *has* begins with *s* and after *have* begins with *v*, the difference between the present perfect and the simple past is difficult to distinguish. For example, *Gino's stopped to pick up Joe and Tony.* sounds like *Gino stopped to pick up Joe and Tony. I've visited* sounds like *I visited.* To give students a clue to write present perfect verbs, include *recently* or *lately* in dictations.

6 Practice

PROCEDURE
1. Refer to General Guidelines for Practice, page x.
2. Have students work individually or in pairs. Check answers with the whole class. Encourage students to use contractions with the pronouns.

Answers: **A.** 1. have visited 2. 've camped 3. has cooked/prepared 4. has washed 5. haven't stayed 6. haven't watched 7. 've walked 8. hasn't rained 9. has talked 10. hasn't missed, 's called.
B. Answers will vary, for example: They've lived with bugs at campgrounds. They've learned to depend on themselves. They haven't used a razor very much. They've rented a canoe and traveled down rivers.

Workbook: *page 27, exercise B*

7 Presentation

PROCEDURE

1. Refer to General Guidelines for Presentation, page ix.
2. Review irregular past participles from page 56 before introducing the new ones. Write the base form of verbs on the board and have teams compete to see which can write the most correct sentences about things that have happened recently in class.

8 Practice

PROCEDURE

1. Refer to General Guidelines for Practice, page x.
2. Have students complete the paragraphs individually or in pairs. Check answers with the whole class.

Answers: **1.** left **2.** have had **3.** have driven **4.** have done **5.** haven't spent **6.** haven't eaten **7.** haven't stayed **8.** have slept **9.** has written **10.** hasn't sent **11.** called **12.** haven't gotten **13.** have had **14.** has broken down **15.** have bought **16.** wrote

■ EXPANSION ACTIVITY: Past participle tic tac toe

1. Draw a tic tac toe diagram on the board (two vertical lines crossed by two horizontal lines, forming nine equal squares). In each square put the base form of a verb whose past participle you want students to practice. Put in one or two regular verbs.
2. Divide the class in two teams or play several rounds with smaller teams. One team is the *X's* and the other the *O's*. Flip a coin to see who begins.
3. Team members confer and choose a square where they want to try to put their symbol. To get the *X* or *O*, the team must use the past participle of the verb correctly in a sentence within 15 seconds. If they can't, the turn passes to the other team who can try the same square or a different one. You can require sentences about what has happened in class, to *Intercom 2000* characters, in your town, etc. The first team to get three *X's* or three *O's* in a row wins.

7 Presentation

Present perfect statements with more irregular verbs

Principal parts of more irregular verbs			
	Base	**Past**	**Past Participle**
Same simple past and past participle form	buy leave send sleep spend	bought left sent slept spent	bought left sent slept spent
Different simple past and past participle form	break (down) drive get write	broke drove got wrote	broken driven gotten written

8 Practice

Complete the paragraphs with the present perfect or simple past of the verb in parentheses. Use the affirmative or negative, whichever makes sense.

Tony Perez and Joe Brennan are on a trip across the United States. They (1) _____ (leave) California a couple of months ago and are near New York City now. So far, they (2) _____ (have) a great time on their trip. They (3) _____ (drive) thousands of miles, and they (4) _____ (do) many interesting things, but they (5) _____ (spend) a lot of money. They (6) _____ (eat) in many restaurants, and they (7) _____ (stay) in any hotels or motels. They (8) _____ (sleep) many nights under the stars.

Tony (9) _____ (write) a few letters to his family and friends, but Joe (10) _____ (send) even a postcard. He (11) _____ (call) his parents on their anniversary, but they (12) _____ (get) any mail.

Tony and Joe (13) _____ (have) car problems along the way. Their poor old car (14) _____ (break down) several times, most recently on the way to New York. They (15) _____ (buy) a lot of oil because the engine has been burning a lot of it. They're out of money, and just yesterday Tony (16) _____ (write) to his parents for help.

9 Practice

Complete this letter that Tony wrote to his parents with the correct tense and form of one of these verbs: *get, have, help, meet, spend, walk, want, write.* **Use the affirmative or negative, whichever makes sense. You can use a verb twice.**

> *Dear Mom and Dad,*
>
> *Thanks for your letter. Sorry I _____ or called recently. We _____ a great time so there's not much time to write. Last weekend we _____ to Canada . . . across the bridge at Niagara Falls, that is.*
>
> *I hope you're all fine. Joe and I are doing OK, but the car isn't. We _____ a lot of problems recently. A few days ago it left us stranded on the way to New York. We _____ our last dime yesterday getting the electrical system fixed.*
>
> *Not all the news is bad, though. A couple of days ago we _____ a man named Gino Leone, and he _____ us find part-time jobs in a little town called Winfield, near NYC. Unfortunately, we _____ our first paychecks yet. I _____ to ask you for money, but you said you would help if we got desperate. Well, we're desperate. So please send $200 ASAP, care of the Roma Restaurant, Winfield, New York 11500.*
>
> *Thanks a million! I'll call soon.*
>
> *Love,*
> *Tony*

10 Writing

A. Imagine that you are traveling in some area of your country or in some other country in the world. You have been there for a while, and you will be staying there for a few more days. Make some notes about things you have done so far and what you plan to do before you return home.

B. Now write a letter to your English-speaking friends telling them some of the following things: *where you have been, what you have done and seen, where you have stayed, what you have eaten, what you have bought, how much you have spent.* You can also mention your plans for the rest of your stay.

C. Now share your letter with your classmates. When you read it, use the word ZING instead of the name of the city or country. Can your classmates guess where you are writing from?

9 Practice

PROCEDURE
1. Refer to General Guidelines for Practice, page x.
2. Have students work individually. Check the exercise with the whole class.

Answers: haven't written; have had; walked; have had; spent; met; helped; haven't gotten; didn't want

Workbook: *page 28, exercise C*

10 Writing

PROCEDURE
1. Refer to General Guidelines for Writing, page xi.
2. Have students do part A individually or brainstorm ideas with the whole class.

Option for part C: Have students write their letters using ZING in place of the name of the city or country. Put the letters on the wall. Pair students and have them read the letters and list their guesses for the places. The pair that guesses the most places correctly is the winner.

11 Presentation

PROCEDURE
1. Refer to General Guidelines for Presentation, page ix.
2. To expand the Presentation, put a few more verbs on the board, such as: *see, make, go to, eat*. Have students ask and answer yes/no questions about Tony and Joe's trip using the verbs.

12 Practice

PROCEDURE
1. Refer to General Guidelines for Practice, page x.
2. Do the activity in pairs or with the whole class.

Answers: **1.** A: Have you seen a movie recently? B: Yes, I have./No, I haven't. **2.** A: Have Joe and Tony been in Hawaii recently? B: No, they haven't. **3.** A: Has it rained today? B: Yes, it has./No, it hasn't. **4.** A: Has Sekila seen her family recently? B: No, she hasn't. **5.** A: Have Cristina and Gino been in Italy recently? B: Yes, they have. (On their honeymoon.) **6.** A: Have you bought anything today? B: Yes, I have./No, I haven't. **7.** A: Has Joe and Tony's car broken down recently? B: Yes, it has. **8.** A: Have you watched TV today? B: Yes, I have./No, I haven't. **9.** A: Has Tony written a letter recently? B: Yes, he has. **10.** A: Has it snowed this week? B: Yes, it has./ No, it hasn't.

13 Interaction

PROCEDURE
1. Refer to General Guidelines for Interaction, page x.
2. After students prepare their papers, demonstrate the activity with #1.
3. To end the activity, have students tell you interesting anecdotes they heard from their classmates. They don't have to give you names.

■ EXPANSION ACTIVITY: How have you been lately?
1. Have students write 5-10 interview questions using past participles from Presentations 4 and 7 and Practice 6 or any other past participles they ask you for. The questions should be like those in Interaction 13. For example, *Have you gone anywhere interesting lately?*
2. Have students work in pairs and interview each other, using these questions.

11 Presentation

Present perfect: *yes/no* questions and short answers

Questions

Have	I you we they	been to NY? been to NY?
Has	he she	
Has	it	rained today?

Short answers

Yes,	I you we they	have.	No,	I you we they	haven't.
Yes,	he she	has.	No,	he she	hasn't.
Yes,	it	has.	No,	it	hasn't.

A
A: Has Tony written to his parents recently?
B: Yes, he has.
A: Has Joe called his folks lately?
B: No, he hasn't.

B
A: Have Joe and Tony been on the road recently?
B: Yes, they have.
A: Have they been in California lately?
B: No, they haven't.

12 Practice

Practice with a partner. Ask questions about what has happened lately using the cues. Give short answers and offer more information, if possible.

1. you / see a movie / recently
2. Joe and Tony / be / in Hawaii recently
3. rain / today

4. Sekila / see her family recently
5. Cristina and Gino / be in Italy recently
6. you / buy anything today
7. Joe and Tony's car / break down recently
8. you / watch TV today
9. Tony / write a letter recently
10. snow / this week

13 Interaction

Copy #1-8 on your paper, leaving about five lines between items. Talk to as many students as possible in your class and try to find a person who has done each of these things recently. Write the person's name on your paper. Ask him or her other questions (*where, when, why*, etc.) to get more specific information. Make notes so you can tell your classmates what you have learned.

1. see a bad movie
2. stay up all night
3. have a fight with someone
4. lose an important possession
5. read a good book, story, or article
6. be embarrassed
7. do something secretly
8. break something

14 Presentation

Talking about the very recent past

To emphasize that something happened very recently, use:
was/were + **just**   OR   **just** + simple past

A   Gino was in Buffalo very recently.
    Gino **was just** in Buffalo.

B   A: Does Gino know Joe and Tony?
    B: Not really. He **just met** them.

3. After students interview each other, have them write a paragraph about their partner's life recently, based on the information obtained in the interview.
4. Have students read their papers aloud; other members of the class can ask additional questions of the person who was written about.

■ EXPANSION ACTIVITY: Where have they been?
1. Put a United States map on the wall and give students time to study it. (Ideally each pair of students should have a map.)
2. Talk with students about where Joe and Tony started from and where they are now. Then ask them to study their maps and decide on ten places Joe and Tony have visited in their trip across the country. They should mark the route on the map if possible or list the places on their papers.
3. Write this model question on the board and suggest that many questions should begin this way: *Have Joe and Tony _____?*
4. Have two pairs sit together and take turns asking questions to find out if Joe and Tony have visited the same places on their two maps. Students should draw the route of the other pair on their map or list the places on their route next to their own.

Workbook: *pages 28–29, exercise D*

14 Presentation

PROCEDURE
1. Refer to General Guidelines for Presentation, page ix.
2. To expand the Presentation, use a few magazine pictures and have students tell you what just happened. For example, someone waiting for a cab, *Her plane/train just arrived.* If you prefer, describe a situation and ask students to tell you what just happened. *A student has an exam in his hands. He is smiling.* (He just got an A on the exam.)

15 Practice

PROCEDURE
1. Refer to General Guidelines for Practice, page x.
2. Have students work in pairs and share their responses.

Possible answers: **1.** No. It just broke down. **2.** No. The garage just sent it out. **3.** No. They just left. **4.** I just did it. **5.** Sorry. I just lent it to Ana. **6.** Yes. Sam just told me. **7.** Sorry. I just gave it to a friend. **8.** Yes. I just got a letter. **9.** Yes. I just saw her yesterday. **10.** OK, but I'm not very hungry. I just ate. **11.** Yes, but I just found it. **12.** Yes. I just talked to her last week.

■ EXPANSION ACTIVITY 5A: What did they just do? (page 190)

> **Workbook:** *page 29, exercise E*

16 Listening

PROCEDURE
1. Refer to General Guidelines for Listening, page x.
2. Play the tape or read the script for the Listening. The tape includes the directions on pages 76-77.
3. If reading the script, give students 45 seconds to answer the questions after each listening.

Script

BRAD: I really appreciate the ride to Florida, Jim.

JIM: Glad to have the company. Besides I'd do anything for your dad.

BRAD: Yeah, he's pretty great, isn't he? And it's great of you to take me to Orlando. Dad says you don't usually go there.

JIM: Well, my usual route is Tampa and Miami, but Orlando's not really that much out of the way. Do you have friends in Orlando?

BRAD: Yeah. And my roommate and some other friends from college are going to be there, too.

JIM: Are you going to Disney World?

BRAD: Well, maybe...but probably only Epcot Center. They've got terrific computer exhibits and stuff like that. But honestly, what I really want is some sun and sand.

JIM: The best you can do in Orlando is a pool, but I guess your friends have a car, right?

BRAD: You bet! It's not too far to the ocean, is it?

JIM: No, about an hour by car. How long will you be staying?

15 Practice

Think of a response to each question using *just* to mean very recently. Use the verbs in the box or your own ideas.

1. Is Joe and Tony's car working?
2. Is the tow truck available?
3. Are the Logans here?
4. It's time to do your homework.
5. Can I borrow your book?
6. Have you heard that Ed had another accident?
7. Can I read today's paper?
8. Have you heard from your brother lately?
9. Have you seen your best friend lately?
10. Let's get some breakfast.
11. I heard you lost your English book.
12. Have you called your sister recently?

Useful vocabulary:
be
break down
do
eat
find
get a letter
give
leave
lend
see
send . . . out
talk
tell

16 Listening

Brad Linderman, a college sophomore, is on his way to Florida in Jim Barker's truck.

Map of Florida showing Tallahassee, Jacksonville, St. Augustine, Orlando, Tampa, Fort Lauderdale, Miami, and Key West.

First Listening

Number your paper from 1-10. Listen for the main ideas and answer questions 1-5.

1. What is Jim's usual route in Florida?
2. What city is Brad going to?
3. What does Brad want to do in Florida?
4. What does Jim offer to do for Brad?
5. At the end of the conversation, where are they going to stop?

Second Listening

Listen again and find answers to questions 6-10, if possible. If the information is not given, write *NG*.

6. How did Brad meet Jim?
7. What does Jim carry in his truck?
8. Where do you think Brad lives? What makes you think so?
9. How long will they be in Florida?
10. How does Jim feel about traveling alone? What does he say and do to give this idea?

17 Reading

Before You Read

1. What are some of the least expensive places to stay in your country when you are traveling?
2. Is there a big difference in price between the expensive and inexpensive places to stay in your country?
3. What kind of accommodations would be best for students?

First Reading

Work with a partner. Student 1 reads the first half of the brochure ("Discovering Hostels," page 78) and Student 2 reads the second half of the brochure beginning with "How Do Hostels Work?," page 79. Student 1 then asks Student 2 the questions in A, and Student 2 asks Student 1 the questions in B.

A. Student 1 asks Student 2 these questions:

1. Who can use AYH hostels?
2. What rules and regulations should you expect at AYH hostels?
3. What do you have to bring with you?
4. Where can you get an AYH membership and what do you get with it? How much do memberships cost?

B. Student 2 asks Student 1 these questions:

1. What is a hostel? What accommodations can you expect?
2. Where are AYH hostels located?
3. How much do they cost per night?
4. Why do hostels cost so little per night?

BRAD: Just a week. It's my spring vacation.

JIM: Would you like me to pick you up on my way back north, a week from Sunday?

BRAD: Could you really? That'd be fantastic!

JIM: Sure. I'm really glad to have a passenger. It gets lonesome on the road, all by myself. You hungry?

BRAD: Yeah. I haven't had anything to eat since breakfast.

JIM: Good, I'll treat you to lunch. There's a great little restaurant just up the road. It has the best hamburgers.

BRAD: Gee, thanks a lot.

JIM: My pleasure.

Answers for the First and Second Listening: **1.** Tampa and Miami **2.** Orlando **3.** He wants to visit Epcot Center, but what he really wants is some sun and sand. **4.** To pick him up on his way back north next week. **5.** At a restaurant for lunch. **6.** Brad's father and Jim are friends. **7.** NG **8.** At a college. He mentions a roommate and college friends. **9.** NG, but it is a little more than a week. **10.** It gets lonesome alone. He is glad to have a passenger.

17 Reading

PROCEDURE

1. Refer to General Guidelines for Reading, page x.
2. Pair students. One is #1, the other #2. Have all students number their papers A. 1-4 and B. 1-4, leaving plenty of space for answers.
3. Have all #1s sit on one side of the room; #2s on the other.
4. Have #1s read the first half of the brochure silently and answer the questions in B. The #2s read the second half and answer the questions in A.
5. Have all #1s discuss and agree on the answers to B; #2s do the same for A.
6. Have students return to their partners and ask their partners for information about the part of the brochure they did not read. The #1s ask #2s for the answers to A. The #2s ask #1s for the answers to B.
7. Reform the whole class with #1s on one side and #2s on the other. Discuss the questions in A, asking #1s for the answers. The #2s should comment only if #1s cannot. Discuss the answers to questions in B with #2s.

8. *Optional/Second Reading:* Assign the complete
   brochure for homework. Students should write
   questions about anything they did not understand.
   The next day answer students' questions about
   the reading and have a class discussion on the
   advantages and disadvantages of hostels.
9. Have partners do part C together. Then have them
   sit with another pair and do part D.
10. Use some of the discussion questions suggested in
    "Reacting to the Reading" below.

Answers to Parts A and B: **A.** **1.** Travelers of all ages,
but you must be a member of AYH or IYHF. **2.** See top
of page 79, e.g., No alcohol, no illegal drugs, no pets.
Restricted smoking. **3.** Membership card or money
to pay for one. Student #1 can add that you have to
bring sheets. **4.** At most AYH hostels or from the
address given. You get card, handbook and subscription
to *Knapsack* magazine. Cost: $10 for youths and senior
citizens; $25 for adults; $30 for families. Temporary
memberships: $2-$3 per night. **B.** **1.** Low-cost place
for travelers to stay. Separate dormitory-style bedrooms
and bathrooms for males and females; common living
room, dining room, and kitchen. **2.** In many
different places like a lighthouse, a high-rise building,
or a battleship. **3.** $5-$13. **4.** Hostelers/travelers
provide their own personal items, clean up after
themselves, and do general chores.

Answers for Part C: **1.** yes **2.** 20 **3.** #7: Fullerton
Hacienda, yes **4.** no **5.** #9

Reacting to the Reading: Discussion Questions
1. What would you like or not like about staying in
   an AYH hostel?
2. If you had an IYHF card, what countries would you
   like to visit and why?

■ EXPANSION ACTIVITY 5B: In a hostel common room (page 191)

Discovering AYH Hostels

Travel can be exciting, educational . . . and expensive. Why pay more for high-priced hotels when American Youth Hostels offer some of the least expensive and most dynamic travel facilities anywhere? AYH is a non-profit organization that provides travelers with clean, comfortable, safe, overnight accommodations for $5-$13 a night.

But hostels are more than low-cost accommodations. Some are really different. As an AYH member, you can stay at a lighthouse on the California coast, a high-rise in the nation's capital, even on board a World War II battleship in Massachusetts. And you'll have plenty of choices. There are more than 200 hostels in the U.S. and 5,000 in more than 70 other countries.

What is a hostel?

Hostels are dormitory-style accommodations with separate bedrooms and bathrooms for males and females. The center of the hostel is the common room where hostelers of all ages meet and make new friends. Hostels typically provide a self-service kitchen and dining area, too. Some hostels even provide extras like private family rooms, laundry facilities, and bicycle storage.

Simplicity is the rule at hostels. Beds come with a blanket and pillow. Kitchens are equipped with pots and pans, dishes, and utensils, but travelers provide their own personal items like towels, sheets, and food. Hostelers always clean up after themselves and help with general chores, which is why AYH is able to keep its overnight fees so attractively low.

	Hostel/Location	Phone #	Capacity	Open Year-round; open dates	Wheelchair Accessible	Family Rooms	Special Notes
	ALASKA						
1	Anchorage Int'l AYH-Hostel 700 H St./#2; Anchorage, AK 99501	907/276-3635	72	yes	yes	yes	Gateway to Alaska; historic tour
2	Delta Int'l Hostel Box 971; Delta Junction, AK 99737	907/895-5074	10	6/1-9/1	no	no	End of Alaska/Canadian Hwy., near wilderness
3	Juneau Int'l AYH Hostel 614 Harris St.; Juneau, AK 99801	907/586-9559	40	yes	yes	yes	Hiking trails, State capital museum
	ARIZONA						
4	Flagstaff Int'l AYH-Hostel 23 N. Leroux; Flagstaff, AZ 86001	602/774-2731	60	yes	no	yes	Historic bldg.; tours, car rentals; museums
5	Grand Canyon Int'l AYH-Hostel P.O. Box 270; Grand Canyon, AZ 86023	602/638-9018	20	yes	no	no	Grand Canyon Nat'l Park, space limited
6	Valley of the Sun Int'l AYH-Hostel 1026 N. Ninth St.; Phoenix, AZ 85006	602/262-9439	36	yes	no	yes	Park, theater, Heard Museum tours, nature hikes
	CALIFORNIA						
7	Fullerton Hacienda AYH-Hostel 1700 N. Harbor Blvd.; Fullerton, CA 92635	714/738-3721	15	yes call	yes	no	Disneyland & Knotts Berry Farm Park, 5 miles
8	Eel River Redwoods AYH-Hostel 70400 Highway 101; Leggett, CA 95455	707/925-6469	36	5/1-10/29	no	yes	Giant redwoods, hiking, swimming, bikes, sauna
9	Hidden Villa Ranch AYH-Hostel 26870 Moody Rd.; Los Altos Hills, CA 94022	415/941-6407	29	9/1-6/1	no	no	Hostel on 1,650-acre farm/wilderness preserve

How do hostels work?

No two hostels are alike, but they all share the same basic customs and rules.

- Hostels are typically closed during the day. Hostelers check in each evening around 5 PM, and check out in the morning. Day use is available at some hostels.
- Three consecutive nights is the maximum stay at a hostel.
- Alcohol and illegal drugs are prohibited on hostel property.
- Smoking is restricted to designated areas or may be prohibited completely in the hostel building.
- Pets of guests are not permitted on hostel property.

Every hostel is supervised by a resident hostel manager who ensures the hostel's smooth operation. Hostel managers are knowledgeable about their locale and are happy to provide visitors with information.

Hostel users must be AYH or IYHF members. Memberships are available for purchase at most AYH hostels, ranging from $10 for youths and senior citizens, to $25 for adults and $30 for families. Many hostels also offer temporary memberships at $2-$3 per night.

Who can join?

Don't let the name fool you. AYH welcomes bicyclists, hikers, and travelers of all ages, from the young to the young at heart. Your membership includes:

- AYH MEMBERSHIP CARD
- THE AYH HANDBOOK, a guide to more than 200 hostels in the United States.
- A SUBSCRIPTION TO *Knapsack*, the travel magazine of American Youth Hostels

For more information write to:

American Youth Hostels
Travel Store
P.O. Box 37613
Washington, DC 20013-7613

Going overseas?

AYH is a member of the International Youth Hostel Federation (IYHF), which means your AYH membership card is valid at more than 5,000 hostels worldwide. For a complete listing of international hostels, consult the IYHF Handbook, available from your local AYH council or the AYH Travel Store.

PROCEDURE
1. Refer to General Guidelines for Final Activity, page xi.
2. The *Traveler's Aid Society*, which has offices in airports, and railroad and bus stations in most large American cities, helps travelers solve their problems. The organization is supported by contributions to the United Way campaign and private donations.

Workbook: *page 30, exercises F, G*

C. **Now work together and answer these questions about the hostels in the chart on page 78.**

1. Does the hostel in Juneau, Alaska, have family accommodations?
2. How many people can stay at the Grand Canyon Hostel?
3. Which hostel is near Disneyland? Is it open all year?
4. Is hostel #8 open in December?
5. Which hostel is on a farm?

D. **Talk with another pair in your class about the hostels in the chart. Ask and answer questions like the following:**

1. Which hostel sounds the best/nicest/most interesting to you and why?
2. Which is the nearest to ____ /the farthest from ____ ?

18 | **Final Activity**

Form a group of three or four students. Two of you are traveling in the United States. The other one or two of you are going to offer help to the travelers when something goes wrong. As a group, brainstorm answers to the following questions:

- What means of transportation are the travelers using?
- For that means of transportation, make a list of the problems the travelers could have. Also make a list of general things that could go wrong; for example, someone could get sick.

Now use these questions to help you plan and role play a call or request for help. The travelers should explain the problem clearly. The people who are going to help should ask questions and then offer help in some way. Practice your role play before presenting it to the class, but do not write out the exact words you are going to use.

1. What kind of transportation are you using?
2. Where did you start? Where are you at the moment? What is your final destination?
3. What goes wrong during your trip? What kind of help do you need?
4. Who are you going to contact for help? You might call the police or the parents of an American friend. Perhaps your parents gave you the name of someone to contact in an emergency. There is also an organization called the *Traveler's Aid Society* that is located in many cities across the country.

UNIT 6

COMMUNICATION
Talking about likes and dislikes ▪ Making comparisons ▪ Discussing advantages and disadvantages; giving reasons

GRAMMAR
Information questions in the present perfect ▪ Questions with *how long*; answers with *since* and *for* ▪ Gerunds as subjects of verbs ▪

Too many, too much, not enough + countable/noncountable noun ▪ *As many/ much* + countable/noncountable noun + *as*

SKILLS
Listening to short interviews ▪ Reading about an invention ▪ Writing about a problem

Meeting an Old Friend

Cristina was in New York City recently to update the information on her visa. While she was waiting for the train back to Winfield, she saw a young woman who looked familiar. She hesitated a moment, and then said . . .

CRISTINA: Excuse me. Aren't you Diane Keenan?

DIANE: Yes . . .

CRISTINA: I'm Cristina Silva.

DIANE: Cristina! Of course! What are *you* doing here?

CRISTINA: I live here . . . that is, I live in Winfield. I'm on my way home. And you? Where are you going?

DIANE: I just got in from Connecticut. I was visiting a friend for the weekend. How have you been? How long have you been in the States?

CRISTINA: For about three years. I came to visit a relative and stayed. I'm studying art history at Winfield Community College, and I just got married.

DIANE: That's wonderful. Congratulations!

CRISTINA: Thanks. How long have you been back in the States?

DIANE: Since 1988. I worked and traveled in South America for a while, but eventually I got homesick.

CRISTINA: I guess traveling and living by yourself can get kind of lonely.

DIANE: Yeah, it sure can. So how do you like living in Winfield? It's a lot smaller than Bogota!

CRISTINA: Oh, I love it. The people are friendly, and you don't have as many problems as in a big city. Are you going to stay in New York?

DIANE: Yes, I am. Everybody thinks I'm crazy, but I enjoy living in big cities. There are so many different things to do . . . so much culture. I could go to the theater every night if I could afford it.

Useful materials: pictures of people doing different activities; pictures showing scenes of life in big cities, suburbs, small towns, and the country

Meeting an Old Friend

PROCEDURE
Refer to General Guidelines for Opener, page ix.

COMPREHENSION QUESTIONS
Now answer these questions.
1. Why did Cristina go to New York? *To update the information on her visa.*
2. Where was Cristina going when she ran into Diane? *Back to Winfield.*
3. Where was Diane last weekend? *She was visiting a friend in Connecticut.*
4. When did Cristina come to the United States? *Three years ago.*
5. Why does Cristina like living in Winfield? *The people are friendly. There aren't many problems.*
6. Has Cristina always lived in a small town. *No, she hasn't. She lived in Bogota, the capital of Colombia.*
7. Why does Diane like living in New York City? *There is a lot to do. There is a lot of culture.*
8. Can Diane afford to go to the theater every night? *No, she can't.*
9. What doesn't Cristina like about big cities now? *They are too crowded. There's too much noise. The rents are high.*
10. When are Cristina and Diane going to see each other again? *Probably the next time Cristina comes into New York City.*

DISCUSSION QUESTIONS
1. What things do people talk about when they haven't seen each other for a long time? Which things do Cristina and Diane talk about?
2. Which is better—to have friends who like the same things as you or friends who like different things? Why?
3. Which do you prefer—a small town or a big city? Why?

1 Vocabulary in Context

PROCEDURE
1. Refer to General Guidelines for Vocabulary in Context, page ix.
2. Have students do the exercises individually or in pairs. Check answers with the whole class.

Answers: **A. 1.** familiar **2.** get into **3.** relative **4.** Eventually **5.** homesick **6.** by yourself **7.** Suburbs **8.** too crowded **B. 1.** quite, rather **2.** I prefer (an emphatic expression); any time **3.** I agree! (emphatic expression) **4.** decide to do something different **5.** Inform/Call me **6.** anticipate with pleasure/be happy thinking about

Workbook: *page 31, exercise A*

CRISTINA: Give me the suburbs or the country any day. Big cities are too crowded, and there's too much noise. Besides, rents are cheaper outside the city.

DIANE: You can say that again! Maybe if I visit you in Winfield, I'll change my mind.

CRISTINA: You just might, and you're always invited. Listen, Diane, it's time for my train, but let me give you my phone number.

DIANE: OK, and here's mine. Let me know if you're coming into the city. We can have lunch or something.

CRISTINA: Fine. I'll look forward to that. It's been great seeing you again. And give me a call sometime.

1 Vocabulary in Context

A. Find words and expressions in Cristina and Diane's conversation and the introduction that complete these definitions.

1. Someone who is recognizable or known to you is _____ .
2. _____ is a two-word verb meaning to *arrive*.
3. A/an _____ is a person in your family.
4. _____ means *in the end*.
5. When you feel _____ , you miss your family and/or country.
6. If you do something _____ , you do it alone.
7. _____ are residential areas outside of a city.
8. When there are too many people and cars in a city, it is _____ .

B. What do these expressions from the conversation mean? Check the context and give a paraphrase.

1. You get <u>kind of</u> lonely.
2. <u>Give me</u> the suburbs <u>any day</u>.
3. <u>You can say that again</u>!
4. Maybe I'll <u>change my mind</u>.
5. <u>Let me know</u> if you're coming into the city.
6. I'll <u>look forward to</u> that.

2 Presentation 📼

Information questions in the present perfect

A
A: What have Gino and Cristina done recently?
B: They've been to Italy on their honeymoon.
C: They've also rented a new apartment.

B
A: Where has Diane been recently?
B: She's been in Connecticut.
A: Why did she go there?
B: To visit a friend.

3 Practice

The *Intercom 2000* characters have been various places and done various things lately. Ask a partner where they have been. Look at the chart for answers and then guess why they went there.

Gino	to Buffalo to the new landlord's house to the library
Cristina	to Ray's Unpainted Furniture to the doctor
Gino and Cristina	to their new apartment
Bob	to the police station to his counselor's office at school
Elinor	to Columbia University in New York City to see Joyce's teacher
Joyce and Lisa	to the sporting goods store to the doctor to Winfield Community College

A: Where has Gino been recently?
B: He's been to the library.
A: Why do you | suppose | he went to the library?
       | think |
B: Maybe to get some information on how to refinish cabinets.

2 Presentation

PROCEDURE
1. Refer to General Guidelines for Presentation, page ix.
2. Before beginning this Presentation, you might want to review Wh-question formation with other compound verb phrases. For example, write cues like these on the board: *Bob is working at home. What?* (What is he doing?) *Bob can do many things. What?* (What can he do?)
3. To expand the Presentation, put cues like the following on the board: *Who/see recently? What/buy recently? Who/talk to recently? What/read recently?* Have students ask and answer questions.

3 Practice

PROCEDURE
1. Refer to General Guidelines for Practice, page x.
2. Read the instructions and have students study the chart. Ask a few yes/no questions to be sure students can find the information they need. (*Has Gino been to the police station?/Have Joyce and Lisa been to the doctor?*)

Answers: Conversations will follow the model. Information for *B's* first response comes from the chart. Second responses will vary.

Workbook: *page 31, exercise B*

4 Presentation

PROCEDURE
1. Refer to General Guidelines for Presentation, page ix.
2. Call students' attention to the present tense verbs in statements A and B (*It's December. Gino and Cristina are married.* and relate them to the line marked *now* in the diagram. Call attention to the past tenses verbs in A and B (*They got married two months ago.*), and relate them to 1989 in the diagram.
3. Ask students to explain when to use *since* and when to use *for*. Then go over the explanation in the box and demonstrate with reference to the diagram.

5 Practice

PROCEDURE
1. Refer to General Guidelines for Practice, page x.
2. Do the Practice as a whole class practice if you choose.

6 Interaction

PROCEDURE
1. Refer to General Guidelines for Interaction, page x.
2. After students read the instructions and situations A and B, have them read the Useful language and tell you which comments are useful in which situation.

---

4 Presentation

Asking and answering questions about length of time

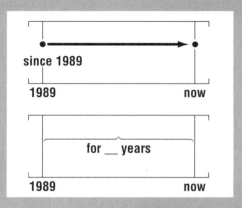

Use **since** or **for** with the present perfect to answer how long a present situation has been true.
- Use **since** with a *point* in time: 1988, March, Monday, 10:00 AM
- Use **for** with a *period* of time: 3 years, 2 hours, a day

A It's December. Gino and Cristina are married. They got married two months ago.

> A: How long have Gino and Cristina been married?
> B: They've been married **since October.**
>   They've been married **for two months.**

B Cristina lives in Winfield. She came to Winfield in 1987.

> A: How long has Cristina lived in Winfield?
> B: She's lived in Winfield **since 1987.**
>   She's lived in Winfield **for three years.**

5 Practice

Work with two other students. One student asks the questions; the other two students answer the questions, using *since* and *for*.

> A: How long have you been in class today?
> B: I've been in class for half an hour.
> C: That means you've been in class since 9:00.

1. How long have you lived in (your city or town)?
2. How long have you been a student?
3. How long have you studied English?
4. How long has your teacher worked in your school?
5. How long has your mother/father lived in (your city)?
6. How long has your mother/father worked for (name of company)?

7. How long have you known (teacher, student)?
8. How long have you had your (pen, watch, bike)?
9. How long have you studied at (name of school)?
10. How long have you played the (instrument)?

6 Interaction

Work with a partner. Read situations A and B below and select one. Write a conversation following the instructions. Practice it and role play it for the class.

A. You are friends who haven't seen each other for a while.

B. You are foreign students studying in the United States. You meet at a party.

Useful language:
Where have you been?
I haven't seen you | since | ____ .
| for |
It's been a long time.
How have you been?
I just got back from out of town.
How long have you been ____ ?
Have you | seen | ____ yet?
| gone to |

7 Presentation

Gerunds as subjects of verbs

The **-ing** form of the verb is called a *gerund* when it is used as a noun. The *gerund* is often the subject of the sentence.	A: Do you like to travel by yourself? B: Not really. **Traveling by yourself** can be lonely.

■ EXPANSION ACTIVITY: How long has it been?

1. Use the chalkboard to record student answers to the following questions, which you write on the left:
   1. How long have you lived in this city?
   2. How long have you been a student here?
   3. How long have you known your teacher?
   4. How long have you had *Intercom 2000, Book 4*?
   5. How long have you studied English?
   6. How long have you been at school today?
2. Along the top of the board, put students' names, and have each student write in his/her answers.
3. When the data is all in the chart, have students work in pairs to copy the data for each question, calculate an average for the class, and write sentences to summarize the findings. For example, *The students in this class have lived in this city an average of ____ years.*
4. Have the best summary statements written on the board. Those sentences can then be used for a dictation the next day.

Optional: In large classes, do this Expansion in small groups, and have groups report and compare results.

> Workbook: *page 32, exercise C*

7 Presentation

PROCEDURE

1. Refer to General Guidelines for Presentation, page ix.
2. Prepare students for the use of *verb + -ing* as the subject of a sentence by writing the following on the board: ____ *is fun*. Have students suggest ways to complete the sentence (*Basketball is fun.*) and write them under the blank. Write the words *eat ice cream* on the board. Then suggest a completion like *Eating ice cream is fun*. Write *Eating ice cream* under the blank. Have students suggest other completions using verbs + *-ing*.

LANGUAGE NOTES

1. An infinitive (*To eat*) can also be used as the subject of a sentence (*To eat ice cream is fun*), but is more formal and rare in conversation.
2. *Like* can also be followed by the gerund. (See Presentation 10.)

8 Practice

PROCEDURE
1. Refer to General Guidelines for Practice, page x.
2. Do the Practice in small groups or with the whole class. Have students take turns asking the questions.
3. If done in small groups, have students summarize the class's reasons for liking and not liking the activities.

Possible answers for Student B's second sentence:
1. Playing solitaire is fun when you are alone.
2. Reading the newspaper keeps you up-to-date.
3. Going jogging is too hard. I'd rather walk.
4. Listening to the radio while studying helps me. I like to study with soft music.   **5.** Watching a lot of TV is bad for me because I don't study enough.   **6.** Eating a lot of candy is bad for my teeth.   **7.** Gossiping isn't good because you can hurt other people's feelings.   **8.** Smoking is bad for your health.

9 Interaction

PROCEDURE
1. Refer to General Guidelines for Interaction, page x.
2. Have students copy the form. If they leave the extra space suggested, they can write information about more than one person who likes and dislikes the activity.

■ EXPANSION ACTIVITY: Living in the city is exciting!
1. Give each student fifteen index cards or slips of paper. On the board write the following adjectives: *expensive, boring, lonely, exciting, fun, easy, hard, interesting, tiring, healthy, annoying, confusing, frightening, nerve-wracking, relaxing.*
2. Have students write one adjective on the back of each slip of paper. On the other side they write a sentence that starts with a verb + *-ing* as a subject, and for which the adjective on the other side is a completion. For example, if the adjective is *relaxing,* a student might write: *Listening to soft music is ____.* Tell students to make their sentences as informative as possible without completing the sentence with the adjective.
3. Students work with a partner and hold up their cards, one at a time, showing the partner the sentence with the blank. If the partner guesses the adjective on the back correctly, he/she gets one point. Fifteen is a perfect score. The winner is the person who writes the best sentences so that his/her partner can correctly guess the most.

8 Practice

Talk with your classmates about the reasons they like or don't like each activity. Follow the model in *7*.

1. play solitaire
2. read the newspaper
3. go jogging
4. listen to the radio while studying
5. watch a lot of TV
6. eat a lot of candy
7. gossip
8. smoke

Useful vocabulary:

solitaire: a card game played by one person alone
gossip: to talk about other people

9 Interaction

A. **Copy the following list of activities on your paper. Leave about five lines between items. Talk to your classmates and try to find at least one person who likes and one who doesn't like each activity. Ask them why they like or don't like the activity. Write names, *yes* or *no*, and reasons on your paper. Do not write the name of a classmate in more than one activity.**

> jog
> A: Do you like to jog?
> B: | Yes, I do. **Jogging** is fun.   It's good exercise, too.
> | No, I don't. **Jogging** makes you hot and tired.

	Name	Yes/No	Reason
1. eat alone			
2. exercise			
3. study at night			
4. write in English			
5. tell jokes or stories			
6. go camping			
7. sew			
8. watch horror movies			

B. **With the class, share your reason for liking/not liking each activity. Then take a vote to find out which is the favorite activity and which is the least favorite.**

10 Presentation 📟

Talking about likes and dislikes

The gerund is often used to talk about likes and dislikes.

A: Do you like **studying** by yourself?
B: Yes, I do. I | love | **studying** by myself. Do you?
               | enjoy |
A: No, I don't. I | don't like | **studying** by myself.
                  | dislike |
                  | don't enjoy |
                  | hate |
   I prefer **studying** with at least one other person. If I have a problem, my friend can sometimes help me.

11 Practice

Work with a partner. Ask and answer questions using gerunds after verbs. Give your own opinions.

Cristina / enjoy / drive long distances
A: Does Cristina enjoy driving long distances?
B: No, she doesn't. She hates driving more than two hours because she doesn't like sitting in one place.

1. Lisa and Joyce / like / play indoors a lot

2. Elinor / like / work at night

3. most people / enjoy / be on a diet

4. Bob / enjoy / watch a lot of TV

5. Sam / like / work long hours

6. Logans / like / live in their new house

7. Adela / like / study late at night

8. Youngs / enjoy / have a big house

9. Cristina / prefer / live in a small town

10. Diane Keenan / enjoy / live in New York City

Variation: Have partners write sentences together and compete against another pair.

Workbook: *page 33, exercise D*

10 Presentation

PROCEDURE
1. Refer to General Guidelines for Presentation, page ix.
2. Write the verbs in the Presentation on the board: *like, love, enjoy, dislike, hate, prefer.*
3. Have students make sentences about themselves using these verbs. Encourage new activities such as *reading in English* or *listening to rock music.*

LANGUAGE NOTE
The verbs *like, love, hate* and *prefer* can also be completed with an infinitive. *Enjoy* and *dislike* use the gerund only.

11 Practice

PROCEDURE
Refer to General Guidelines for Practice, page x.

Answers: Student A's questions are: **1.** Do Lisa and Joyce like playing indoors a lot? **2.** Does Elinor like working at night? **3.** Do most people enjoy being on a diet? **4.** Does Bob enjoy watching a lot of TV? **5.** Does Sam like working long hours? **6.** Do the Logans like living in their new house? **7.** Does Adela like studying late at night? **8.** Do the Youngs enjoy having a big house? **9.** Does Cristina prefer living in a small town? **10.** Does Diane Keenan enjoy living in New York City? Student B's answers to questions will vary. Encourage students to use *like, dislike, enjoy,* and *prefer* with a gerund.

12 Interaction

PROCEDURE
1. Refer to General Guidelines for Interaction, page x.
2. Give students time to complete the chart with information about themselves for #1-6. Help them add two situations of their own for #7 and #8.

Workbook: *page 33, exercise E*

13 Reentry

PROCEDURE
1. Refer to General Guidelines for Reentry, page x.
2. After doing 1-3, have students suggest other people or activities, for example: *singer a* and *singer b, men* and *women*.

12 Interaction

Complete the chart with information about yourself. Complete #7 and #8 with your own ideas. Then talk with a classmate. Ask and answer questions about what you enjoy doing most in the different situations. As you talk, complete the information about your classmate.

When	I enjoy...	My partner enjoys...
1. rainy days	*reading*	
2. sunny days		
3. early in the morning		
4. before going to bed		
5. after eating		
6. not feeling well		
7.		
8.		

13 Reentry

Making comparisons using *too* + adjective/adjective + *enough*

Divide the class into two teams. Team A will defend one opinion; team B will defend another. A member of one team begins with a comment using *too* + adjective or adjective + *enough*. Someone from the other side must respond to it. For #4 and #5, choose your own people or activities.

> **Team A:** hockey   **Team B:** baseball
>
> A: Baseball is not exciting enough.
> B: That's not true. It's very exciting when you understand the game well and get to know the players. Besides, hockey is too rough.

Team A	Team B
1. classical music	rock and roll
2. movies	plays
3. Americans	another nationality
4.	
5.	

14 Presentation

Discussing advantages and disadvantages; giving reasons

Comparing with Nouns		
	Countable	**Noncountable**
Excessive	too many cars	too much noise
Insufficient	not enough people	not enough time
Equal	as many problems as	as much crime as

a big city

a small town

the suburbs

the country

A

> A: I don't like big cities. There is **too much traffic.**
> B: I don't like the country. There are **too many bugs.**

B

> A: I don't like big cities. There is**n't enough peace and quiet.**
> B: I don't like small towns. There are**n't enough libraries and museums.**

C

> A: I prefer small towns because they don't have **as much traffic as** big cities.
> B: I prefer big cities because they don't have **as many bugs as** the country.

14 Presentation

PROCEDURE
1. Refer to General Guidelines for Presentation, page ix.
2. Before beginning this Presentation, review the difference between *countable* and *noncountable* nouns.
3. Talk about the pictures and the advantages and disadvantages of living in each place.
4. To expand the Presentation, have students make comments using other nouns. (See the box on p. 90.) Work first with model A, then B, and finally C.

CULTURAL NOTE
According to estimates of the U.S. Census Bureau, about 25% of Americans lived in rural areas in 1988. According to their definition, rural areas include small towns. Therefore, about 75% lived in urban areas that include suburbs.

15 Practice

PROCEDURE

Refer to General Guidelines for Practice, page x.

Answers: Answers follow the models in *14*, for example:

A city: There are too many parking problems.
country: There's too much grass to cut.

B suburbs: There aren't enough factories.
small towns: There aren't enough things to do.

C I prefer small towns because there aren't as many robberies as in big cities.
I prefer big cities because there aren't as many mosquitoes as in the country.

> **Workbook: *page 34, exercise F***

16 Listening

PROCEDURE

1. Refer to General Guidelines for Listening, page x.
2. Play the tape or read the script for the Listening. The tape includes the directions on pages 90-91.
3. *If reading the script:* In the First Listening, give students 10 seconds to decide which question was asked.

Script

1. Oh, yes, life in the suburbs is great! I can drive everywhere and my kids have nice places to play. My husband likes commuting into the city for work, but I'm glad I don't have to. I have a nice part-time job just 10 minutes from our house. I take the kids to school in the morning and drive to work. I'm home when the kids are home in the afternoon.

2. Well, I haven't lived here very long. In fact I just arrived about a month ago. But one thing I noticed right away is that it's hard to get to places if you don't have a car. In my country, you can get anywhere on a train or bus. And there were stores in my neighborhood. Now I have to ask my neighbor for a ride to the shopping mall when he goes there. I guess I'm going to have to get a car. Also, there's not too much to do on the weekends out here. Life can get pretty boring.

3. Yes, because it's too quiet out here! No, I'm serious. I miss the noise, the crowds, the restaurants that are open all night. I know some people love the sound of crickets and animals, but they bother me.

15 Practice

Talk with a small group of your classmates about the advantages and disadvantages of big cities, suburbs, small towns, or the country. First practice following model A in *14*, then model B, and finally model C.

> **Useful vocabulary:**
>
> | | | |
> |---|---|---|
> | open space | pollution | sunlight |
> | noise | theaters | trees and grass |
> | bugs | grass to cut | things to do |
> | cars | emergency services | tree-lined streets |
> | traffic | medical care | factories |
> | robberies | big buildings | sports/athletic events |
> | crime | parking problems | |
> | pressure, stress | garbage in the streets | |

16 Listening

Number your paper from 1-5. A reporter, Jack Walker, has interviewed people who live in different areas for his new radio talk show, *Changing Times*.

First Listening

Listen to the people's answers and decide which question you think Jack asked.

1. **a.** Where would you like to live?
   b. Would you like to move to the suburbs?
   c. Do you enjoy living in the suburbs?

2. **a.** What are some of the disadvantages of living in the suburbs?
   b. What do you like about life in the suburbs?
   c. Do your kids like life in the suburbs?

3. **a.** Would you rather live in New York City or Winfield?
   b. Are you thinking about moving back into the city?
   c. Why do you want to move into the city?

4. **a.** Is life in the big city better than life in a small town?
   b. Which is better, life in the city or in a small town?
   c. What is the biggest advantage to living in a small town?

5. **a.** Do you think it is an advantage or disadvantage to live in a small town?
   b. What do you think is the biggest disadvantage to small town life?
   c. Why don't you like big city life?

Second Listening

Listen again to each conversation and talk with your classmates about what you learned about each person. What kind of person is he or she? What does he or she like and not like? Would you choose him or her for a friend? Why? Why not?

17 Reading

Before You Read

1. Do you have good public transportation where you live?
2. What do you think transportation will be like in the twenty-first century?
3. What would you do if you were caught in a traffic jam and had to wait a long time for the traffic to move?
4. Do you know how a magnet works? What is magnetic attraction and repulsion?

First Reading

Skim the article about *maglev* and find answers to these questions.

1. What is maglev? What is it like?
2. How does maglev move?
3. Who invented it? Who designed and built it?

Maglev: A LESSON IN PROBLEM-SOLVING

1 You are sitting in a huge, motionless traffic jam waiting to cross the Bronx-Whitestone Bridge connecting Long Island and New York City. It's Friday night. You are tired and see no hope of getting home quickly. What do you do? Do you say some not-so-nice things under your breath, honk your horn in frustration, read the newspaper, listen to music, or look at the problem caused by so many cars and think, "There must be a better way"?

2 Dr. James R. Powell, a scientist at Brookhaven National Laboratories in New York, found himself in that very situation in 1960. He thought about the problem that faced him,

and the idea came to him that magnetism could be used to make a better mass transportation vehicle, a sort of flying train. It would look like an airplane fuselage without wings.

Magnetism would lift it slightly off a rail or track and propel it forward on a cushion of air at speeds up to 310 miles per hour. Running short and medium distances in and between cities, it would get many cars off the road.

They keep me awake. I guess I have to give myself time to adjust. I've only been here a week, but I just might move back.

4. In a small town, for sure. In the city you pay higher taxes, and what do you get? Dirt, crime, and noise! Here you have trees and you can hear the birds singing. But most important, we're a community; we know each other and we watch out for each other. We have good schools and good recreational areas nearby. Of course, I wish there were better places to shop, but when I really want to, I can drive to a big shopping mall about an hour from here.

5. Well, for me it's the lack of privacy. Out here everybody knows everything you're doing. You can't do anything in this town without somebody knowing it. I was born in a middle-sized city. Then I moved to a really big city where I lived for 30 years. But life got too expensive and as I got older I thought I would like the peace and quiet of a small town. You get peace and quiet from nature, but I can't get used to the way people talk about each other. I don't like all the gossip.

Answers: First Listening: **1.** c **2.** a **3.** b **4.** b **5.** b
Possible answers: Second Listening: **1.** mother of small children with part-time job near home; husband commutes to the city for work; likes to be with her children; **2.** new in town; has come from another country that has good mass transportation; independent; not too happy to ask for rides; is considering buying a car **3.** once lived in a big city and misses it; not a nature-lover; realistic; knows she needs time to adjust **4.** doesn't like to pay taxes for nothing; a nature-lover; likes to share with neighbors; likes to shop **5.** has lived in cities most of the time; likes privacy; doesn't like to gossip; doesn't have much money

17 Reading

PROCEDURE
Refer to General Guidelines for Reading, page x.

Answers: First Reading: **1.** a mass transportation vehicle; like a flying train **2.** Magnetism lifts it slightly off a track or rail and propels it on a cushion of air. It moves very fast, up to 310 miles per hour. **3.** Dr. James R. Powell invented it. Powell and a colleague, Dr. Gordon T. Danby, presented the idea at an engineering conference. Dr. Henry H. Kolm directed the design and building of a scale model at M.I.T.

Answers: Second Reading: **1.** Powell got the idea when he was stuck in a traffic jam. **2.** A guideway is a track or rail on which maglev runs. The Japanese guideway is like a cradle; the train sits *in* it. The German guideway is a rail; the train runs *on* it. The German train has sides that hook around the rail it runs on. The Japanese train does not. It looks somewhat like a loaf of French bread. **3.** Maglev is fast and quiet because there is no friction between wheels and rails. It is safe because it has a back-up power system that will stop the train smoothly if the main power fails. **4.** Because our transportation problems are worse than ever now. Highways and airports are overcrowded. **5.** Over short and medium distances, maglev will be faster. We won't have the traffic problems of cars or the long trips to and from airports. It will cost less than building new roads and airports, especially because of the high price of land. **6.** Instead of complaining about problems, we can think about ways to solve them. New ways of doing things cost money. If we want benefits in the future, we must invest time and money now.

Reacting to the Reading: Discussion Questions

1. If you want to be an inventor, what do you have to be able to do?
2. What kind of inventions would be useful for you? Complete this sentence: *I would like a machine/tool that ____.*
3. Have you ever invented anything or solved a difficult problem? Tell about your experience.
4. What do you think are some of the most important inventions in the history of man? What did each make possible?

■ EXPANSION ACTIVITY 6: How maglev works (page 191)

3 Powell and a colleague, Dr. Gordon T. Danby, presented the idea for maglev at an engineering conference in 1966, and it was well-received. Research and development began at the Massachusetts Institute of Technology (M.I.T.) in Cambridge under the direction of Dr. Henry H. Kolm, and by 1974 he had a scale model of the vehicle that he called Magneplane. Unfortunately, in February of 1975, all U.S. government money for research and development of maglev was cut off, and without it, there was no future for the new technology in the United States. Fortunately, there was both interest and funding in Germany and Japan, and maglev is a reality today. There are slower-moving maglevs in the Birmingham, England, airport and in Japan. Prototypes of high-speed commercial vehicles are being tested in Germany and Japan. A high-speed maglev should be running from Hanover to Hamburg, a distance of 95 miles, by the mid-1990s. Japan is working on high-speed trains from Tokyo to Narita International Airport (30 miles) and from Tokyo to Osaka (350 miles).

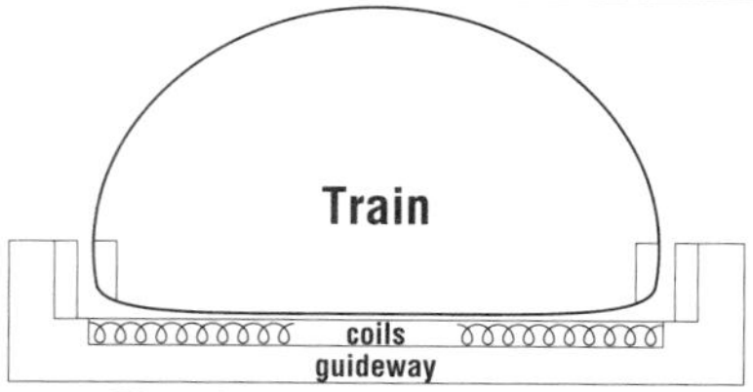

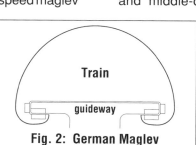

Fig. 1: Japanese Maglev

Fig. 2: German Maglev

4 What does maglev look like? Japanese engineers designed a vehicle that runs in a cradle-like track or guideway (*See Fig. 1*). The German engineers designed one that hooks around a rail-like guideway (*See Fig. 2*). Magnetic attraction and repulsion pull and push maglev forward. To stop the trains, the magnetic forces are reversed, much like airplanes are stopped by reversing the force of the engines. Both types of maglev are quiet, fast, and safe. Since maglev rides on air, there is no friction between wheels and rails to make noise or to slow it down. If the external power fails, there is a battery-operated system on the train itself that takes over and brings the cars to a smooth stop.

5 Since 1960 our traffic problems have gotten worse, not better, and we need an alternative like maglev more than ever. Not only are highways over-crowded but they are very expensive, and in many parts of the world there is no land available to build more. In the last half of the twentieth century, we have depended on airplanes for most medium and long distance travel, but airports take up space, most are far from cities, and the airspace above them is overcrowded. Air travelers often spend more time getting from home to airport A and from airport B to their destination than flying from city to city.

6 So maglev could be the answer to our problems. It could become the typical short- and middle-distance mass transportation system of the twenty-first century. If it does, we will enjoy many benefits. We will ride in safe, fast, quiet trains between cities up to about 500 miles apart in less time than it takes to fly if you include the time for ground transportation. We will conserve precious land because maglev can be built where railroads ran, down the middle of existing super-highways or elevated above existing streets and roads. And we will probably save money, too. According to a German estimate, a mile of two-way track will cost about nine million dollars (1990 estimate) whereas a mile of interstate highway costs about 25 million dollars in the United States.

7 So next time you find yourself in a difficult situation, remember this story of maglev. If you look closely at the problem that you face, you may be the one to find the solution.

Second Reading

In a small group, talk about the answers to these questions.

1. Where did the idea for maglev come from?

2. What is a guideway? How are the Japanese and German guideways different? How do the trains look different?

3. Why is maglev fast, quiet, and safe?

4. Why is maglev more important in the 1990s than ever before?

5. What advantages does maglev have over cars and airplanes?

6. What lesson or lessons can be learned from maglev?

18 Writing

A. Talk with a partner about problems in your area. List three or four you could write about.

B. Work independently. Choose one of the ideas and write a paragraph about the problem, using the following suggestions.

• Describe the problem in detail so it is clear to someone who doesn't live where you do.

• Tell how long the problem has existed, how it affects people, and what has been done to try to solve it.

• Suggest a possible solution to the problem.

C. Share your paragraph with a classmate who may have some suggestions for you.

19 Final Activity

Class Debate

A. Form four groups of student debate teams. Each team supports the advantages of living in one of the following: big cities, the suburbs, small towns, or the country. Meet in your group and discuss why people would rather live in the area your group represents.

18 Writing

PROCEDURE
Refer to General Guidelines for Writing, page xi.

■ EXPANSION ACTIVITY: Proposal writing
1. Tell students to imagine that a rich businessperson is going to give money to local communities to help them solve their problems. To be eligible for this money, the community must write a proposal that must include the following:
   a. description of the community and inhabitants
   b. statement of the problem or need
   c. objective of the project; what they would do with the money they are given
   d. expected results; how the lives of people in the community will be different when this project is completed
2. Form groups of four to eight students. Each group decides what it wants to propose and makes general plans for each of the four parts.
3. Students divide the writing of the rough draft among themselves, one or two students per section.
4. Groups then meet to read and make improvements on the drafts and prepare a final copy of the proposal.
5. Groups then share their ideas with the class in a brief panel presentation.

19 Final Activity

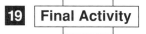

PROCEDURE
1. Refer to General Guidelines for Final Activity, page xi.
2. Talk with students about what a debate is. Write the statement to be debated on the board.
3. Form groups and have students plan their comments about the good things in their area and the bad things in other areas. Have each person write out two comments, he or she wants to make.
4. Review the ways to agree and disagree in the box. Make statements such as the following and ask students to respond with one of the comments: *Big cities are ugly. I love big cities. There's nothing to do in small towns. Suburbs are boring. I don't like the country. It's too quiet. Cities need more parks and green areas. In small towns, your neighbors know everything you do.*

■ EXPANSION ACTIVITY: Let's go back!

1. Have students work in pairs or small groups to create a role play in which roommates find they disagree about the apartment they moved into a couple of months ago. Maybe they moved from a city to a small town or from the country to a big city. One or more of the roommates thinks that they should move back to where they came from. The other or others argue to stay where they are.

2. Brainstorm planning questions with the class before group work.

Workbook: *page 35, exercise G*

Planning Questions:

Be ready to defend the good things in your area.

• What makes life good in your area?

• What is easy/nice to do in your area?

• What can you do there that you can't do in other areas?

Be ready to comment on the bad things in other areas.

• What is there too much/many of in other areas?

• What isn't there enough of in other areas?

B. After you have finished planning, sit together as a class. The students who have prepared to defend rural and small town life will sit on one side of the room and the students who have prepared to defend big city and suburban life on the other. Debate the truth of the following statement. Your teacher can decide which half of the class presents better arguments.

It is better to live in the country or a small town than in a big city or the suburbs.

> **Useful language:**
>
> *Ways to agree*
>   You're right.
>   You can say that again.
>   So do I.
>   I do, too.
>
> *Ways to agree with limitations*
>   You're right, but _____ .
>   I agree with you, but _____ .
>   I agree in part, but don't forget that _____ .
>
> *Ways to disagree*
>   I don't agree with you because _____ .
>   That's not true. The truth is _____ .
>   Neither do I.
>   I don't either.

UNIT 7

COMMUNICATION
Talking about shapes and traffic signs ▪ Stating and evaluating alternatives ▪ Making decisions

GRAMMAR
Already and *yet* with the present perfect ▪ *Will/might* + *have to/be able to* + verb ▪ *Could* in alternatives

SKILLS
Listening to problems ▪ Writing about a group decision ▪ Reading a poem

Making a Decision

Howard Young has just picked up his daughter, Liz, at work. Earlier in the week Liz accepted a new job as a ticket agent with Worldwide Airlines in New York City. Several months ago she applied for a job as a flight attendant, but was offered a job as a ticket agent instead.

LIZ: Sorry to keep you waiting, Dad.

HOWARD: That's OK. It gave me time to read the paper . . . and think.

LIZ: And think about what?

HOWARD: Oh . . . nothing really . . . it's really none of my business.

LIZ: Dad, what are you talking about?

HOWARD: Well . . . Liz, let me get to the point. Your mother and I know you're an adult, but we can't help worrying about you, especially with your decision to live alone in the City.

LIZ: Mmmm . . . I've thought about it a long time, Dad. I'm sure this is what I want to do. In some ways I'd like to stay in Winfield, but I would hate commuting every day. Dave commutes and he hates it . . . Watch out, Dad. You can't go that way.

Useful materials: a state driver's manual; newsprint and markers

Making a Decision

PROCEDURE
Refer to General Guidelines for Opener, page ix.

COMPREHENSION QUESTIONS

Now answer these questions.
1. What has happened in Liz's life recently? *She has a new job.*
2. Did Liz get out of work on time? *No, she didn't. She was a little late.*
3. What did Howard Young do while he was waiting for Liz? *He read the paper and thought about some things.*
4. Where does Liz want to live? *In an apartment in New York City.*
5. How do her parents feel about her decision? *They are worried because she wants to live alone in New York City.*

Now listen to these sentences. Say *Yes, that's right, No, that's wrong*, or *I don't know. Maybe.*
6. Dave is Liz's boyfriend. *I don't know. Maybe.*
7. Howard knows the streets of Winfield perfectly. *No, that's wrong.*
8. Liz is also worried about living alone in New York City. *No, that's wrong.*
9. Liz is going to stay with a friend while she looks for an apartment. *Yes, that's right.*
10. Howard thinks Liz won't have enough money for rent and for fun if she lives alone. *Yes, that's right.*

DISCUSSION QUESTIONS
1. Do you think that Howard Young knows how to communicate well with his daughter? Give examples to support your opinion.
2. What are some advantages and disadvantages of living alone? Of having a roommate?
3. Liz says she wants to live in New York City because she doesn't want to commute. What other reasons could she have?

Rents in New York City (Manhattan) are very high. A studio apartment might cost Liz $700-800 a month without utilities.

1 Vocabulary in Context

PROCEDURE

1. Refer to General Guidelines for Vocabulary in Context, page ix.
2. Have students do Parts A and B individually or in pairs. Check answers to the exercises with the whole class.

Answers: **A. 1.** decided **2.** decision **3.** opportunity **4.** accepted **5.** commute **6.** lots of **7.** salary **8.** left over **B. 1.** b **2.** e **3.** h **4.** i **5.** g **6.** f **7.** c **8.** a **9.** d **10.** g

■ EXPANSION ACTIVITY: Reflexive pronoun reentry

1. Ask students for examples using the expression *by* + ____*self* and write them on the board. Ask for a paraphrase of the meaning (*alone or without help*).
2. Have students complete these sentences with *by* and the correct pronoun.
   a. When Bob gets his permanent driver's license, he will be able to drive ____.
   b. Sometimes Gloria likes to study with her friends; sometimes she likes to study ____.
   c. It's dangerous to leave small children at home ____.
   d. A sentence is a complete idea. It can stand ____.
   e. We don't need help. We can do this ____.
   f. Sometimes my friends don't understand why I like to work ____.
   g. You and Dan will have to go to the movies ____. I can't go.
   h. After college, Sam wants to live ____.
   i. ...Joyce is very independent. She likes to do most things ____.
   j. Human babies are dependent creatures. They can't survive ____.
   k. The pine tree stood at the back of the yard ____.
   l. Don't be so lazy, Jimmy. You'll have to solve the problem ____.

HOWARD: Since when? What's going on in this town?

LIZ: Dad, they changed that to a one-way street months ago.

HOWARD: Really? What did they do that for? . . . Now where were we?

LIZ: I was telling you that I don't want to commute.

HOWARD: Yes. Well . . . the new job is a good opportunity, but . . . well . . . we just don't like the idea of your living by yourself in New York City.

LIZ: Oh, Dad! Lots of women live alone in the city. Besides, I can stay with Sue until I find a place of my own. I've already talked to her and she says it's fine.

HOWARD: Have you checked the rents in New York yet? If you live alone, you'll have to spend almost every penny of your salary on rent. You won't have much left over for fun.

LIZ: Oh, Dad. Please don't be so negative. I know apartments are expensive, but I'll be making good money. I think I'll be able to afford a small place in a nice neighborhood that's fairly close to the ticket office.

HOWARD: Well . . . I hope you're right.

1 Vocabulary in Context 🖷

A. Complete the paragraph with the following words from Liz and Howard's conversation. Use each word only once. Use the verbs in their correct forms.

accept	commute	decide	opportunity
lots of	left over	decision	salary

   Liz has just (1) ____ to change jobs. It really wasn't a very hard (2) ____ because she was getting tired of living at home, and she wanted a/an (3) ____ to do something different. She (4) ____ a job with Worldwide Airlines in New York City last week, which means she has to move to the City or (5) ____ from Winfield. Her parents aren't very happy about her living alone in New York, but she says (6) ____ women do and she sees no problem. She says her (7) ____ will be big enough to pay her rent, and that she will also have some money (8) ____ for fun.

B. Check the conversation and its introduction, and match each item with its use or paraphrase. Two items have the same answer.

1. <u>Sorry</u> to keep you waiting.
2. It's <u>none of my business</u>.
3. Let me <u>get to the point</u>.
4. <u>We can't help</u> worrying about you.
5. <u>Mmmm . . .</u>
6. <u>In some ways, . . .</u>
7. <u>Watch out!</u>
8. <u>What</u> did they do that <u>for</u>?
9. <u>Now where were we?</u>
10. <u>Well . . .</u>

a. why
b. a way to begin an apology
c. Be careful!
d. What were we talking about?
e. I shouldn't be interested.
f. For some reasons, . . .
g. indicates person is thinking
h. Here's my main thought/idea.
i. It's impossible not to . . .

2 Vocabulary in Context

Shapes and traffic signs

This sign is a **circle.** It's **round.**

This sign is a **rectangle.** It's **rectangular.**

This sign is a **triangle.** It's **triangular.**

This sign is a **square.** It's **square.**

This sign is an **octagon.** It's **octagonal.** It has eight sides.

This sign is a **pentagon.** It's **pentagonal.** It has five sides.

This sign is a **diamond.**

■ EXPANSION ACTIVITY: Alone or by yourself?

1. Assign students to small groups and have them find out how many people in their group would rather do these things by themselves and how many with other people.
2. After the count is taken they should talk about and write down the reasons some people prefer to do these things alone or with another person.

   a. study
   b. clean the house
   c. cook
   d. run
   e. listen to music
   f. watch TV
   g. live

Workbook: *page 36, exercise A*

2 Vocabulary in Context

PROCEDURE
1. Refer to General Guidelines for Vocabulary in Context, page ix.
2. Have students provide descriptions for signs H-N like those given for A-G. Encourage them to talk about the shapes within the signs too.

■ EXPANSION ACTIVITY: I'm thinking of something round

1. To give students more practice in using the vocabulary of shapes, play a guessing game in which one student thinks of an object in the room or in pictures on the wall and gives clues using shapes or lines. For example, *I'm thinking of something square.* The student who guesses correctly thinks of the next object.
2. Teach new vocabulary as necessary, for example, *oval* or *curve. I'm thinking of something that has a beautiful curve.* (a guitar)

3 Practice

PROCEDURE
Refer to General Guidelines for Practice, page x.

Possible answers: Sign H is a diamond. It warns people that a pedestrian crossing is nearby. Sign I is a rectangle. It tells drivers to keep to the right. Sign J is a rectangle. It tells drivers that they cannot make a U-turn. Sign K is a square. It tells drivers that they cannot park in this area. Sign L is a diamond. It warns people to watch out for handicapped people. Sign M is a triangle. It tells drivers that they must not pass. Sign N is a square. It says that you cannot turn left at this street.

■ EXPANSION ACTIVITY: Making road signs

1. Send away for a driver's manual for one or more of the states of the United States. Write to:
   > State Department of Motor Vehicles
   > Capital City, State, USA
2. Have students make different signs using colored paper, markers, and newsprint or poster board.
3. Place the signs in the chalk tray and write a letter above each.
4. Make statements about the shape or purpose of the sign. You can also say something that we might hear from people in a car or on the sidewalk such as: *Slow down. You're going ten miles over the speed limit.* Students write the letter of the sign they think you are referring to.

Variation: Have students make the statements.

4 Interaction

PROCEDURE
1. Refer to General Guidelines for Interaction, page x.
2. Give students time to prepare their drawings (possibly as homework). Have them sign the drawings and hide them inside a file folder or magazine.
3. Have students tell a partner or the whole class what to draw.

■ EXPANSION ACTIVITY 7A: Learning to drive (page 191)

> Workbook: *page 37, exercise B*

3 Practice

Work with a partner. Talk about signs H-N above, and write two sentences to describe the shape of the sign and its purpose.

> Sign L is a diamond. It warns people that a crossing for handicapped people is nearby.

4 Interaction

Review the prepositions of place in *Unit 4*, pages 59-60, and in the *Useful vocabulary* box here. Draw shapes in different positions on your paper. Give your classmates instructions to help them draw the shapes you drew. Now show them your drawings. Did you communicate well? Could they follow your instructions?

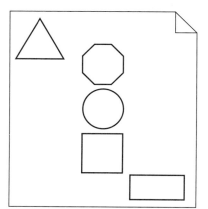

> **Useful vocabulary:**
>
> in the top right corner
> in the bottom left corner

> Draw a circle in the center of the paper. Draw a triangle in the top left corner. Draw a rectangle in the bottom right corner. Draw an octagon above the circle. Draw a square below the circle.

5 Presentation 📼

Already and *yet* with the present perfect

> **Already** and **yet** refer to a time *before now*.
> - Use **already** in affirmative statements after **have/has** and before the main verb.
> - Use **yet** at the end of negative and interrogative statements.

A Liz has **already** accepted the job with Worldwide Airlines.

B She has **already** talked to Sue, but she hasn't moved into Sue's apartment **yet.**

C
> A: Has Liz left the telephone company **yet?**
> B: Yes, she has. She has **already** left the phone company, but she hasn't started her new job **yet.**

D
> A: Has Liz moved to New York City **yet?**
> B: No, **not yet.**

6 Practice

When Liz found out that she got the job with Worldwide Airlines, she made a list of things to do. She has checked off the things that she has already done.

> *Things to do . . .*
> ✓ *talk to Sue*
>   *start looking for an apartment*
> ✓ *make medical and dental appointments*
> ✓ *go to the doctor*
>   *go to the dentist*
> ✓ *buy some new clothes*
>   *pack my things*
>   *take change of address card to Post Office*
> ✓ *fill out forms at WA*
>   *pick up uniforms*
> ✓ *call Dave*

A. **Make sentences about the things that Liz has already done and those things that she hasn't done yet. (Follow models A and B in *5*.)**

B. **Repeat the exercise, asking and answering questions following models C and D in *5*.**

---

5 Presentation

PROCEDURE
1. Refer to General Guidelines for Presentation, page ix.
2. After reading or playing the tape for the sentences, ask for a paraphrase of *already* and *yet*. If necessary, refer to the explanation in the box.
3. To expand the Presentation, ask students for sentences about things they have already done today and things they haven't done yet, but will do before they go to bed tonight.

6 Practice

PROCEDURE
1. Refer to General Guidelines for Practice, page x.
2. Read the instructions and give students time to study Liz's list. Ask a few yes/no questions to be sure they can find the information they need. (*Has Liz _____?*)
3. Students can do part A individually or with a partner. Check answers with the whole class.
4. Do part B as a whole class or pair practice.

Answers: **A.** Liz has already talked to Sue / made medical and dental appointments / gone to the doctor / bought some new clothes / filled out forms at Worldwide Airlines / called Dave. She hasn't started looking for an apartment yet / gone to the dentist yet / packed her things yet / taken a change of address card to the Post Office yet / picked up her uniforms yet. **B.** Conversation follows models C and D.

7 Interaction

PROCEDURE
1. Refer to General Guidelines for Interaction, page x.
2. Summaries will be similar to the following:
   I talked with ____. At the beginning of the week, he/she said he/she had to ____, ___, etc. It's now Friday. He/She has done three of these things. He/She has ____. He/She hasn't ____ yet.

■ EXPANSION ACTIVITY: Just checking up on you
1. Write this sentence on the board: *Have you ____ yet?*
2. Brainstorm situations in which people check up on chores that other people have to do (for example, parents and children, promises people make you, bosses checking on employees, etc.)
3. Give students 10 minutes to plan a mini-role play (nothing written out) in which someone checks up on what another person was supposed to do. The situation can work out in different ways, for example: everything is OK, there is one chore the person tries to avoid by changing the subject, or the person can be very forgetful and have done nothing.

> Workbook: *pages 37-39, exercises C, D, E*

8 Presentation

PROCEDURE
1. Refer to General Guidelines for Presentation, page ix.
2. To expand the Presentation, suggest it is the end of the day and it is raining very hard. It is time to go home, and you don't have a car. Have students suggest alternatives and give an advantage or disadvantage for each using *will/might have to/be able to.*

LANGUAGE NOTE
Alternatives are possibilities. *Could* is the auxiliary we use most often to state them. *Might* is sometimes used.

7 Interaction

List five things that you want to be sure to do this week. Put your name on your list and turn it in to your teacher. Later in the week, take the list your teacher gives you. Talk to the person who wrote it and find out if he or she has done everything on the list. Write sentences summarizing what your partner has and hasn't done this week.

> A: Have you _____ yet?
> B: Yes. I've already done that.
>   No, not yet. But thanks for reminding me.

8 Presentation

Stating and evaluating alternatives

> To state alternatives, use **could** + *verb*. To talk about their advantages and disadvantages, use:
>
> | **will** | + | **have to** | + verb |
> | **might** | | **be able to** | |

1. Liz is now working for Worldwide Airlines in New York City. Where should she live?

   ALTERNATIVE 1: She **could** live at home in Winfield and commute to work.

   ALTERNATIVE 2: She **could** find a roommate and share an apartment in New York.

   ALTERNATIVE 3: She **could** find a small apartment in New York and live alone.

2. ADVANTAGES AND DISADVANTAGES

   A: Living alone is a good idea. If she lives alone, she **will be able to** decorate her apartment the way she likes.

   B: Right. She **won't have to** pick up her things if she doesn't want to.

   C: Yes, but if she lives alone, she **will have to** spend all her salary on rent. She **might not be able to** enjoy life in New York.

9 Practice

Complete the following sentences. Use the *Useful vocabulary* for ideas.

> **Useful vocabulary:**
>
> | | | | |
> |---|---|---|---|
> | buy | economize on | listen to | save |
> | clean | go (out) | pay for | spend |
> | commute | go to | pay rent | take (classes) |
> | eat | help | | |

ALTERNATIVE 1: Living in Winfield is a good/bad idea.

1. If Liz lives in Winfield,
    she will be able to ____ .
    she won't have to ____ .
    she will have to ____ .
    she won't be able to ____ .

ALTERNATIVE 2: Getting a roommate is a good/bad idea.

2. If Liz gets a roommate,
    she ____ have to ____ .
    she ____ be able to ____ .

ALTERNATIVE 3: Living alone is a good/bad idea.

3. If Liz lives alone,
    she might have to ____ .
    she will be able to ____ .
    she might not be able to ____ .
    she won't have to ____ .

10 Practice

Work with a partner or in a small group. Read the situation and talk about the advantages and disadvantages of each alternative suggested. For each alternative, try to use:

- will/might have to; won't/might not have to
- will/might be able to; won't/might not be able to

SITUATION 1: The class is planning a party for this weekend. It could be at the beach or it could be at the school. The weather forecast is for rain.

1. If the party is at the beach, ____ .
2. If it's at the school, ____ .

9 Practice

PROCEDURE

1. Refer to General Guidelines for Practice, page x.
2. Have students work with a partner or in a small group and write out the completed sentences.
3. Check the exercise with the whole class. After students give their ideas, ask them to state whether they gave a pro (for) or a con (against) sentence.

Possible answers: **1.** she will be able to save money on rent/won't have to pay rent/will have to commute/won't be able to go to the theater as often. **2.** she will have to eat her roommate's cooking sometimes/will be able to economize on rent. **3.** she might have to eat a lot of bread and butter/will be able to spend more quiet evenings/might not be able to go to the movies much/won't have to listen to her roommate's kind of music.

10 Practice

PROCEDURE

1. Refer to General Guidelines for Practice, page x.
2. Have students keep a written record of their ideas using *will/might/won't/might not + have to/be able to,* but tell them to have a normal discussion.
3. Recap as a class. First call for sentences using *will/might/won't/might not + have to/be able to.* Then have the class agree on what people should do in each case.

Possible answers: Situation 1: **1.** we will be able to go swimming. / we will have to have another place in case of rain. **2.** we will be able to stay later at the school than at the beach. / we might have to pay for the use of the building. / we won't have to make a map.

Possible answers (continued): **Situation 2: 1.** he might be able to buy medicines at a discount. / he might have to do work on weekends. **2.** he might be able to work in the emergency room. / he will have to be careful or he might get sick. **3.** he won't be able to rest. / the kids will keep him running. **Situation 3: 1.** Mark will be able to quit his job. / Peggy will have to commute to work at the hospital. **2.** Sally will be able to swim easily. **3.** they might not be able to afford a horse for Ricky. **4.** he will have to be careful or he might have an accident.

■ EXPANSION ACTIVITY 7B: Listing in order of priority (page 191)

> **Workbook:** *pages 39-40, exercises F, G, H*

11 Reentry

PROCEDURE

Refer to General Guidelines for Reentry, page x.

Possible answers: **1.** I would have it at a beach where they have a place to go to in case of rain. **2.** I would work at the hospital because I want to be a doctor some day. **3.** If I were Sally, I wouldn't want to move far from Winfield. I would want to stay on the swim team.

> **Workbook:** *page 41, exercises I, J*

12 Listening

PROCEDURE
1. Refer to General Guidelines for Listening, page x.
2. Play the tape or read the script for the Listening. The tape includes the directions on pages 102-103 and the example.
3. If reading the script: For the First Listening give students 10 seconds to write the decision or problem. For the Second Listening, give students 20 seconds to write the alternatives and check one.
4. For script and answers see page 198.

SITUATION 2: Ted is thinking of getting a summer job. He could work at a drugstore, he could work at the hospital, or he could work at a day camp with young children.

1. If he works at the drugstore, _____ .
2. If he works at the hospital, _____ .
3. If he works at the camp, _____ .

SITUATION 3: Mark and Peggy Jones, friends of the Logans, are thinking of moving to a small farm about 25 miles from Winfield. Mark wants to quit working in an office. Peggy will have to continue working at the Winfield Hospital where she is a nurse. They have two children. Ricky is 12 and has always wanted a horse. Sally is 10 and loves to swim. She is on the junior swim team at the Winfield pool.

1. If the Jones move to the farm, they / Mark / Peggy / Ricky / Sally _____ .
2. If they don't move to the farm, _____ .
3. If Mark quits working, _____ .
4. If Ricky gets a horse, _____ .

11 Reentry

Telling what you would do

Talk with a partner about what you would do if you were each of the people in *10*.

> If I were Ricky, I would be happy to move to the farm because there would be a place for my horse.

1. If I were in charge of the class party, _____ .
2. If I were Ted, _____ .
3. If I were Mark / Peggy / Ricky / Sally, _____ .

12 Listening

Look at the answer box at the top of page 103. Copy this box five times on a sheet of paper. Number them from 1-5. Listen to the conversations. In each conversation the people have to make a decision or solve a problem.

First Listening
Write what the people have to decide.

Second Listening

Write the alternatives they have and check the one they choose. Listen to the example.

DECISION/PROBLEM:	*what to do Saturday*	
ALTERNATIVES:	*clean house*	✓ *go to beach*

13 Interaction

Work in a group and practice your decision-making skills. Choose one of the two situations. Follow these steps in your discussion.

1. State the alternatives.
2. Discuss the advantages and disadvantages of each alternative.
3. Decide what you should do. State what you would like to do and give your reasons. Take a vote if necessary.

SITUATION A: Your class is going to have a party.
DECISION 1: Decide where you should have it.
DECISION 2: Decide what time of day to have it.
DECISION 3: Decide what food and music to have.

SITUATION B: Your class wants to take a trip together.
DECISION 1: Decide where you should go.
DECISION 2: Decide what transportation to use.
DECISION 3: Decide when to go.

14 Writing

A. **Review the decisions your group made in *13*.**

B. **Write a short report about the decisions. Follow this model.**

PARAGRAPH 1: **Introduction**
Mention the general topic of your discussion and the individual decisions your group had to make.

PARAGRAPH 2: **Body**
Present the alternatives for the first decision. Tell what you decided and why.

13 Interaction

PROCEDURE
1. Refer to General Guidelines for Interaction, page x.
2. Use these decisions for practice if you have other real decisions that the class can discuss and make.
3. One situation could be done first with the whole class, the other in small groups.
4. Have students take notes on the alternatives the group thinks of and the reasons they are good or bad for use in Writing 14.

14 Writing

PROCEDURE
1. Refer to General Guidelines for Writing, page xi.
2. Have students review and check their notes with other group members before writing their reports.
3. Have the class share experiences using these questions: *Was it easy to make the decisions? Did everyone in the group agree? How did you decide when there were problems?*

Optional: Have pairs of students, or each group, work together to produce one report. One way to divide the work in a group is to have two students write the first draft, two others read and suggest changes to the group, and two others edit and produce the final copy.

15 Reading

PROCEDURE
1. Refer to General Guidelines for Reading, page x.
2. Have students read about the life of Robert Frost and use some or all of these questions as a comprehension check:
   a. Where and when was Frost born?
   b. Why did his family leave California and return to New England?
   c. How much formal education did he have?
   d. Was farming Frost's greatest interest?
   e. Where did Frost teach?
   f. Where was Frost's poetry first published?
   g. How long was the family in England?
   h. What changed in his life when he returned to the United States?
   i. ...What prizes and honors did he receive?
3. Read the poem or play the tape twice.
4. Discuss answers to the "First Reading" questions and answer students' questions about the language of the poem.
5. Read the poem or play the tape again before doing the "Second Reading" task.
6. It is not necessary to insist on complete understanding of this poem. Listening to the beauty of the language is enjoyable and valuable.
7. Use some of the discussion questions suggested in *Reacting to the Reading* on page 105.

PARAGRAPH 3: **Body**
Mention the alternatives for the second decision. Tell what you decided and why.

PARAGRAPH 4: **Body**
Mention the alternatives for the third decision. Tell what you decided and why.

PARAGRAPH 5: **Conclusion**
Make a final comment on the discussion. Was it easy to make the decisions? Did everyone in the group agree?

C. Now share your report with the other group members. Ask them to read your paper and to offer suggestions for improving your writing. Make the improvements, and give your teacher your final draft.

15 Reading

Before You Read

1. Have you ever read any poems in English?
2. What are poems like? How are they different from prose writing (stories and essays)? Are poems like any other art form?
3. Have you ever read any poems by Robert Frost? If so, what do you know about Frost or his poetry?

First read about Robert Frost, who wrote the poem you are going to read. Find out when and where he lived and what his life was like.

The American poet, Robert Lee Frost (1874-1963), was born in San Francisco, California. When Frost was eleven, his father died and his mother took the family back to the home of his father's parents in Lawrence, Massachusetts. Frost lived most of the rest of his life in New England — in Massachusetts, Vermont, and New Hampshire.

After high school, Frost attended Dartmouth and Harvard colleges, but he wasn't satisfied with his academic experiences, and left college to work. He married a high school classmate, Elinor White, and worked at different jobs in Lawrence for a while. Finally Robert and Elinor settled on a chicken farm in Derry, New Hampshire, the first of their many rural homes.

Frost worked at farming, but he preferred walking in the woods, searching for rare flowers, and writing poetry. Often the farm chores went undone. His family grew and when he was offered a teaching job at the Pinkerton Academy in Derry, he accepted, happy to have a steady salary. He later spent many years teaching at Amherst College in Amherst, Massachusetts.

In his early years as a poet, Frost's work was not well-accepted by critics in the United States. He wrote poems that were based on the reality of the rural life he knew. He stated his ideas about life clearly and quite simply but often with a great deal of irony. American critics preferred poetry that was complex in image and thought. In 1912 he took his family to England where poets were writing more realistic poetry and there his first two collections, *A Boy's Will* and *North of Boston*, were published.

When he returned to America three years later, things changed. *North of Boston* was published in the United States, and he became known and loved by many people at home. He won four Pulitzer Prizes for poetry (1924, 1931, 1937, and 1943), and the United States Senate honored him on both his 75th and 85th birthdays. In 1961 he wrote a poem for the inauguration of President John F. Kennedy and recited it at the ceremony.

Robert Frost died in Boston on January 29, 1963.

First Reading

Read the poem silently as your teacher or the reader on the tape reads it aloud. Then try to answer these questions.

1. Where is the poet?
2. Describe the road he is walking along.
3. What decision does he have to make?
4. What is the condition of each road?
5. Which road does he take and why?

The Road Not Taken

Two roads diverged° in a yellow wood,°
And sorry I could not travel both
And be one traveler, long° I stood
And looked down one as far as I could
To where it bent° in the undergrowth;°

Then took the other, as just as fair,°
And having perhaps the better claim,°
Because it was grassy and wanted wear;°
Though° as for that the passing there
Had worn° them really about the same,

And both that morning equally lay
In leaves no step had trodden° black.
Oh, I kept the first for another day!
Yet knowing how way° leads on to way,
I doubted° if I should° ever come back.

I shall be telling this with a sigh°
Somewhere ages and ages° hence:°
Two roads diverged in a wood, and I —
I took the one less traveled by,
And that has made all the difference.

went in different directions / woods, forest

for a long time

turned / low plants, bushes

pretty
reason to take it
wasn't used
But
used

beaten down by stepping on

road
was not sure / would

a sound people make when tired or not too happy
long periods of time / in the future

Possible answers: First Reading: **1.** in the woods **2.** It was shaped like a Y. **3.** which branch of the Y to take **4.** Both were pretty, one was grassier and wasn't used, but almost the same number of people have taken each road in the past. **5.** Not the first one he looks at in stanza 1, the other one. Not the one that goes into the bushes.

Possible answers: Second Reading: **A. 1.** "Sorry I could not travel both and be one traveler" **2.** "long I stood" **3.** "And both that morning equally lay / In leaves no step had trodden black." **4.** "Oh, I kept the first for another day!" **B. 1.** We sometimes say we will do things, but life surprises us and changes our plans. One decision can change your life. **2.** Possibly a grandchild. He might sigh because he realizes life didn't permit him to take the other way. **3.** *Possible answer:* Taking the road that fewer people take makes all the difference (good or bad). Maybe it is better to go the way fewer people go. Maybe it is better to stick with the crowd. Life is ambiguous like these lines.

Reacting to the Reading: Discussion Questions

1. What have been easy or difficult decisions that you have had to make in your life? Talk about them.
2. Are you trying to make a decision at the moment? Talk about it.
3. What have you learned about how to make decisions?

■ EXPANSION ACTIVITY: Memorizing poems

1. Make a folder with a selection of short, simple poems that you find in anthologies or contemporary magazines.
2. Put the poems where students can read them and select one to memorize.
3. Help students with pronunciation and meaning, and have them recite the poem for the class.
4. Do not discourage students from selecting the same poem. You can illustrate that different interpretations are always possible.

PROCEDURE

1. Refer to General Guidelines for Final Activity, page xi.
2. Have students read the situation silently. Answer questions about things they do not understand.
3. Form groups and have students brainstorm as many alternatives as possible and then evaluate them.
4. Have a class discussion of the alternatives and what groups think Mara and Robert should do.

Variation: Have group members take notes on their discussion and prepare a written report including the alternatives, their decision, and their reasons.

■ EXPANSION ACTIVITY: Writing about a problem

1. Have students write a paragraph to describe a problem they know about. They can use the Final Activity as a model or write a letter to an advice columnist.
2. Select a few of the best paragraphs, make copies, and give to students in small groups to discuss.
3. If you prefer, give students these situations for decision-making.

Situation 1: Mary has done quite well in high school. She has a B average, and she has participated in sports and other activities. She is a senior and has been thinking about what to do next year. Her parents, who are both college graduates, want her to go to college. Mary doesn't know what she wants to do in the future. Her parents say college is the place to find out. Mary says she has decided to get a job at a fast food restaurant for a while. Her parents are very upset and say that she can't live at home if she is not in college. She won't be able to live alone on her pay from the restaurant.

Situation 2: Steve is the youngest of three brothers. He's 16 and he wants to get a part-time job. His grades are average, and his parents aren't happy because they know he could get better grades if he tried harder. His parents don't want him to get a job because they are afraid that his grades will get worse.

Workbook: *page 42, exercises K, L, M*

Second Reading

A.   Read the poem again and find evidence in the poem of the following ideas:

1. The poet wants to take both roads.

2. It is not easy for the poet to decide.

3. The poet is the first person to come this way on this day.

4. The poet plans to come this way again.

B.   Discuss answers to these questions with your classmates.

1. What is the poet saying about life in the last three lines of stanza three?

2. Who do you think the poet might be telling this incident to in the future? Why might he tell it with a sigh?

3. What does the poet mean when he writes, "I took the one less traveled by, And that has made all the difference"?

16 | Final Activity

Form a group of three or four students. Read the situation. Using *could + verb*, talk about the alternatives Mara and Robert have. Then talk about the advantages and disadvantages of each alternative. Decide what you believe they should do and why. After your group discussion, compare the alternatives and decisions of your group with the alternatives and decisions of other groups.

SITUATION: Mara and Robert are elderly people who live on a very small pension. They don't have to worry about medical expenses because they can go to a government clinic. They have to pay for their rent, food, clothing, and other necessities from their pension money. They almost never buy anything that they don't absolutely need — no luxuries of any kind. They don't go to the movies or enjoy other entertainment that costs money. They need all their money for food and household necessities and, even then, they sometimes go to bed hungry.

When Mara and Robert go to the grocery store, they are often tempted to steal small items of food or other necessities. They haven't stolen anything yet, but they are close to doing so. They cannot see any alternatives. What should they do?

COMMUNICATION
Emphasizing continuing or repeated action • Talking about situations and their results • Telling and reacting to news • Talking about the duration of situations

GRAMMAR
Present perfect continuous • Present perfect vs. present perfect continuous •

Result clauses with *so . . . that, such (a/an) . . . that* • Time clauses with *until*

SKILLS
Listening to a telephone conversation • Reading a personal essay • Writing about a relationship with a friend or family member

News From Winfield

Liz Young started working at Worldwide Airlines three weeks ago. She is staying with her friend, Sue, until she can find a place of her own. She's been so busy with work and looking for an apartment that she hasn't called her folks in over a week.

ELINOR: Hello.
LIZ: Hi, Mom.
ELINOR: Liz! Where have you been? I've been trying to call you, but you're never home.
LIZ: Oh, Mom, I've been so busy, but I'm fine. Guess what?
ELINOR: You've found an apartment.
LIZ: Right . . . well, not exactly. I've found a roommate, a friend of Sue's. New York is such an expensive city that I just can't afford to live alone. Now all we have to do is find an apartment.

ELINOR: Liz, that's the best news I've heard in a long time. Your dad's going to be relieved, too. Who's your new roommate? What's she like?
LIZ: Her name is Nilda Rosado. She works at Macy's. She's really nice. I think we're going to get along fine.
ELINOR: And how's the job? How do you like New York?
LIZ: The job's fine and I'm getting used to New York, but it's really noisy compared to Winfield. How's everybody at home?
ELINOR: We're fine, honey. Everybody's busy, as usual. The guys are rebuilding the engine of the old car. It's been a big job. They started working on it two weeks ago, and they still haven't finished.
LIZ: What's the news from the rest of Winfield?

Useful materials: pictures of people doing different things; pictures from which results can be inferred

News From Winfield

PROCEDURE
Refer to General Guidelines for Opener, page ix.

COMPREHENSION QUESTIONS

Now answer these questions.
1. How long has Liz been living at Sue's place? *For three weeks.*
2. Why hasn't Elinor found Liz at home when she calls? *Liz is very busy with her job and looking for an apartment.*
3. Has Liz found her own apartment? *No, she hasn't. She has found a roommate.*
4. Why has Liz decided to live with Nilda Rosado? *She can't afford to live alone. It's too expensive.*
5. What difference does Liz notice between Winfield and New York City? *New York is noisier.*
6. Are the Logans going to move to Texas for sure? *It's not sure right now. They might be moving.*
7. What opportunity does Tom have? *To have a partnership in a travel agency.*
8. Which of the children is happy about the move? *Bob.*
9. Why is Cristina a little worried about Gino? *He's having problems with his boss.*
10. When will Liz and Elinor see each other? *This weekend.*

DISCUSSION QUESTIONS
1. Who do you think is working on the old car? Why?
2. Why do you think that Sam isn't sure he wants to leave Winfield?
3. If you were Tom or Adela, would you move to Texas? Why or why not?
4. Why are people very busy when they move to a new city or change jobs? What do they have to do?
5. What qualities make a person easy to live with?

LANGUAGE NOTE
Having a *partnership* means Tom will be part owner of the agency.

1 Vocabulary in Context

PROCEDURE

Refer to General Guidelines for Vocabulary in Context, page ix.

Answers: **1.** over **2.** be relieved **3.** get along with **4.** get used to **5.** kidding **6.** the rest of **7.** boss **8.** the type **9.** catch up on **10.** miss.

2 Presentation

PROCEDURE

1. Refer to General Guidelines for Presentation, page ix.
2. Ask students to show you what changes when the continuous form is used instead of the present perfect.

ELINOR: You won't believe it, but the Logans might be moving to Texas.

LIZ: NO! You're kidding! Texas? Why Texas?

ELINOR: Tom has a friend in Dallas who offered him a partnership in his travel agency there.

LIZ: Wow! What an opportunity! What do the rest of them think about the move?

ELINOR: Bob's already talking about going to the University of Texas, but Lisa's having trouble getting used to the idea. Sam's not sure he wants to leave Winfield.

LIZ: I can understand that. Any news from Gino and Cristina?

ELINOR: I saw Cristina the other day. She didn't say much, but she's a little worried about Gino. I guess he's been having problems with his boss at the Roma.

LIZ: That's incredible. Gino's not the type to have problems with anyone.

ELINOR: I really don't understand it all. You'll have to talk to them.

LIZ: Well, I'm coming home this weekend, so I can catch up on all the details.

ELINOR: Wonderful! It'll be good to see you. We miss you a lot.

LIZ: Me, too, Mom. See you Friday.

1 Vocabulary in Context

Find words or expressions in Liz and Elinor's conversation and its introduction that have the same meaning as the following words or expressions.

1. more than a

2. feel less worried

3. be friends, have a good relationship

4. begin to know and feel comfortable with

5. joking

6. the others

7. supervisor, the person you work for

8. the kind of person

9. learn what has happened recently

10. feel lonely without

2 Presentation 📼

Emphasizing continuing or repeated action

> Like the present perfect, the *present perfect continuous* is used to describe actions or situations that began in the past and have been continuing up to the present.
>
> The *present perfect continuous*, however, emphasizes the continuing or repeated nature of an action, more than the present perfect does.

1. PRESENT PERFECT: I have tried to call you many times today.
   PRESENT PERFECT CONTINUOUS: I **have been trying** to call you today.

2. PRESENT PERFECT: Gino hasn't worked overtime lately.
   PRESENT PERFECT CONTINUOUS: Gino **hasn't been working** overtime lately.

3. PRESENT PERFECT: I have lived here for ten years.
   PRESENT PERFECT CONTINUOUS: I **have been living** here for ten years.

3 Practice

A. **Change the emphasis in these sentences to continuing action.**

1. Bob has gotten a lot of exercise recently.
2. Gino and Cristina have worked on their new apartment recently.
3. Gloria and Bob have not played much tennis lately.
4. Adela has had headaches recently.
5. Sam hasn't looked for a car lately.
6. I have read the newspaper every day recently.
7. Things have changed very fast recently.
8. Liz has not lived in Winfield recently.

B. **Talk to a classmate about things that you, members of your family, your landlord/landlady, or your class have/haven't been doing lately. Use the present perfect continuous of verbs such as:** *study, practice, fix, build, make, paint, think about, play, plan.*

3 Practice

PROCEDURE
1. Refer to General Guidelines for Practice, page x.
2. Do Part A as a whole class.
3. Pair students for Part B. Have students tell their partners about five different people/situations and write five sentences.

Answers: **A. 1.** has been getting **2.** have been working **3.** have not been playing **4.** has been having **5.** hasn't been looking for **6.** have been reading **7.** have been changing **8.** has not been living. **B.** Answers will vary.

■ EXPANSION ACTIVITY: Henri's been busy!
1. Copy this information about Henri on the board. Henri still does all the things in his list of important dates.

   Henri's important dates (written on his 21st birthday)
   First spoke: one year old (since)
   First walked: one year old (since)
   First drew a picture: two years old (since)
   First argued with his parents: five years old (for)
   First skied: nine years old (for)
   First drove a car: sixteen years old (for)
   First went to a nightclub: nineteen years old (since)

2. Have students write sentences about Henri using the present perfect continuous with *for* or *since*.
3. Discuss the sentences and have students make corrections.

Answers: Henry has been speaking since he was one year old. He has been walking since he was one year old, too. He's been drawing pictures since he was two years old. He's been arguing with his parents for sixteen years. He's been skiing for twelve years. He's been driving (a car) for five years. He's been going to nightclubs since he was nineteen years old.

Workbook: *page 43, exercises A, B*

4 Presentation

PROCEDURE
1. Refer to General Guidelines for Presentation, page ix.
2. To expand the Presentation, put statements like the following on the board. Ask students to tell you if the actions are distinct/countable or continuing, and if they are complete or incomplete.
   a. We have been cleaning the classroom all day.
   b. We have cleaned the classroom.
   c. We have read three stories this semester.
   d. We have been reading stories this semester.

5 Practice

PROCEDURE
1. Refer to General Guidelines for Practice, page x.
2. Do with the whole class.

Answers: When both are possible, the more common is given first. 1. have been looking for/have looked for; have looked for 2. has called; has been calling 3. have been going out; have gone out 4. has been putting on; has put on 5. have written; have been writing 6. has practiced; has been practicing 7. have been reading; have read 8. have rebuilt; have been rebuilding

> **Workbook:** *pages 44-45, exercises C, D*

4 Presentation 🔲

Present perfect vs. present perfect continuous

Sometimes the present perfect and the present perfect continuous have different meanings.

1. When we talk about repeated action in a period of time in the past, only the present perfect shows that something happened on distinct and countable occasions.

   They **have had** two big arguments in the last week.
   (PRESENT PERFECT: The arguments occurred on two distinct occasions in the indefinite past.)

   Gino **has been having** problems with his boss recently.
   (PRESENT PERFECT CONTINUOUS: The problems have been continuing.)

2. The present perfect shows an activity is complete, while the present perfect continuous shows it is incomplete.

   Gino and Cristina **have cleaned** the new apartment.
   (PRESENT PERFECT: Complete)

   They **have been cleaning** the new apartment.
   (PRESENT PERFECT CONTINUOUS: Incomplete)

5 Practice

Complete the sentences with the present perfect or the present perfect continuous of the verb in parentheses. Sometimes both are correct; sometimes only one.

1. I lost my wallet. I _____ it for a week. In fact, I _____ it in every corner of the house. (look for)
2. Your sister _____ twice this morning. Your brother _____ all morning. He's driving me crazy. (call)
3. I like my boyfriend/girlfriend a lot. We _____ for six months. We _____ once this week. (go out)
4. Terry is getting heavy. He _____ weight very gradually. He _____ five pounds this month. (put on)
5. I'm working on a novel. I _____ a chapter this week. It's a lot of work. I _____ it for two years. (write)

6. Sue isn't ready for the concert. She ＿＿ only twice this week. Rafael is ready. He ＿＿ all week. (practice)
7. I adore this book. I ＿＿ it all morning. I ＿＿ it twice before. (read)
8. Mike and Ted ＿＿ three car engines and sold them. They ＿＿ the engine of a family car for two weeks. (rebuild)

6 Presentation

Asking and answering questions using the present perfect continuous

A: Has Liz been living in Winfield recently?
B: No, she hasn't.
A: Where has she been living?
B: In New York with her friend Sue.

7 Interaction

Talk to your classmates and find people who have been doing the following things recently. Ask questions using *where, why, what,* and *how long*. Then continue the conversation using other verb tenses.

1. exercise a lot lately (where, why)
2. look for something recently (what, how long)
3. worry about something lately (what, why, how long)
4. share something lately (what, why, how long)
5. save money recently (why)
6. practice something recently (what, why)
7. study hard lately (what, why)
8. work on something recently (what, why, how long)

6 Presentation

PROCEDURE
1. Refer to General Guidelines for Presentation, page ix.
2. Before beginning this Presentation, you might want to review yes/no and wh-questions in the present perfect tense.

7 Interaction

PROCEDURE
1. Refer to General Guidelines for Interaction, page x.
2. Demonstrate the Interaction with a student. Have two students do number 1. Offer help as needed.

Interaction follows this pattern.

A: Have you been exercising a lot lately?
B: Yes, I have.
A: Where have you been exercising?
B: In my house. I do aerobics.
A: Why have you been exercising/doing aerobics?
B: I like to keep in shape.

3. Have students write 1-8 on their papers, leaving space for three or four names and details below each item.
4. Give students 10 minutes to talk to their classmates and jot down names and information.
5. Regroup the class. Ask students to tell you what they learned about their classmates.

■ EXPANSION ACTIVITY: What's been happening lately?
1. Have students read the newspaper for a week or so and keep a log of events that they notice keep occurring over and over or that have been going on all week. For example: *the police have been stopping drunk drivers this week. The President has been visiting the Soviet Union this week.*
2. Have students talk to other students, asking them *What have you been reading about this week?* When they find someone who has been reading about the same topic, they share their sentences on the news and put one good sentence on the board.
3. Have a class discussion of the currents events that students have written about on the board.

Workbook: *page 46, exercise E*

8 Presentation

PROCEDURE
1. Refer to General Guidelines for Presentation, page ix.
2. Write the model sentences on the board. Mark the main clauses *situation* and the dependent clauses *result*.
3. To expand the Presentation, write the following on the board and ask students to suggest words that can go in the blanks: **a.** so ____ that **b.** *such a ____ that* **c.** *such ____ that* **d.** *such an ____ that*
4. Write the following statements on the board and have students suggest completions:
   a. I'm so busy lately that ____.
   b. Things are so expensive now that ____.
   c. It's such a beautiful day today that ____.
   d. Some people say such awful things about their friends that ____.

9 Practice

PROCEDURE
1. Refer to General Guidelines for Practice, page x.
2. Do with the whole class.

Answers: **1.** so **2.** such **3.** such a **4.** so **5.** such an *Possible Answers:* **6.** so fast that (we can't understand them). **7.** such an expensive car that (most people can't afford one). **8.** such terrible traffic that (it takes a long time to get places). **9.** such a good listener that (everyone wants to talk with her). **10.** so (cold) yesterday that (I didn't want to come to class). **11.** such long tests that (we can't finish them). **12.** so lazy that (they can't keep a job).

■ EXPANSION ACTIVITY: Completing sentences with results

To give students more practice with result clauses using *so* or *such (a/an)* have pairs compete to complete these sentences in interesting ways.

a. The textbook/test was so easy/difficult/interesting/ boring that ____.
b. Yesterday I was so thirsty/tired/hungry that ___.
c. Yesterday was so hot/cold/windy/rainy that ____.
d. The cost of living is so high that ____.
e. Some people are so _____ that ____.

■ EXPANSION ACTIVITY 8A: Explaining results (page 192)

Workbook: *page 46, exercise F*

---

8 Presentation

Talking about situations and their results

> To talk about situations and their results, use:
> **so** + single | adjective | + **that**
> | adverb |
> **such (a/an)** + adjective + noun + **that**

1. In New York City, the rents are **so high that** Liz can't afford to live alone.
2. New York has **such high rents that** Liz can't afford to live alone.
3. Sue has **such a small apartment that** Liz has to find another place to live.

9 Practice

Complete the sentences with *so* or *such (a/an)*. For items 6-12, give a result clause also.

1. I was ____ tired that I fell asleep over my homework.

2. Kathy and Ron are ____ good dancers that they usually win first prize in dance competitions.

3. New York is ____ big city that you could live there all your life and never see half of it.

4. Eduardo studied ____ late last night that he couldn't wake up in the morning.

5. Math is ____ important subject that everyone has to study it.

6. Some English speakers talk ____ fast that . . .

7. A Rolls Royce is ____ expensive car that . . .

8. Big cities often have ____ terrible traffic that . . .

9. Elena is ____ good listener that . . .

10. It was ____ hot/cold/windy yesterday that . . .

11. Some teachers give ____ long tests that . . .

12. Some people are ____ lazy that . . .

10 Presentation 📼

Telling and reacting to news

• Telling news

_____ told me that _____ .

Did you hear that _____ ?

Have you heard that _____ ?

• Reacting to news

Good news: I'm (so) glad to hear that.

That's | terrific! |
        | wonderful! |

How nice.

Surprising news: I | don't | believe it!
      | can't |

Wow!

What | a | _____ !
      | an |

You're kidding!

Where did you hear that?

Are you sure? I thought _____ .

Really? I didn't know that.

Bad news: I'm (so) sorry to hear that.

That's too bad.

A: Did you hear that Ed had another accident?

B: Impossible! Who told you that?

---

11 Interaction

With a partner, write four pieces of imaginary news. Then, share this imaginary news with another pair or with the whole class. Other students will react appropriately to the news. Then continue the conversations.

> A: Did you hear that we won't have a final exam in this course?
> B: You're kidding! Where did you hear that?
> A: A friend heard it from the teacher.
> B: I don't believe it! Not in a million years.

---

10 Presentation

PROCEDURE
1. Refer to General Guidelines for Presentation, page ix.
2. Work with the reactions to news first. Give students a news items and have them respond appropriately.
3. Then work with the three ways to tell news. Have students tell some news; other students will react appropriately.

CULTURAL NOTE
Reacting to news in ways such as these is an important part of the communication process. They show a person's interest and help keep the conversation going.

11 Interaction

PROCEDURE
1. Refer to General Guidelines for Interaction, page x.
2. After students write the news with a partner, put two pairs together to share and react to the news.
3. Recap with the whole class. Ask students for the best/funniest/most interesting news they heard. This will offer an opportunity to reenter reported speech. I heard that _____. _____ told us that _____.

Variation: Make this Interaction into a game in which pairs of students compete for points given by the rest of the class for the best news or reaction. For example, pair 1 gives its news and pair 2 reacts. Then pair 2 gives its news and pair 1 reacts. The class/teacher then decide which pair gets the point for best news and which for best reaction.

12 Interaction

PROCEDURE
Refer to General Guidelines for Interaction, page x.

Workbook: *page 47, exercise G*

13 Reentry

PROCEDURE
1. Refer to General Guidelines for Reentry, page x.
2. Have students discuss possible completions for each sentence and write the best on a single paper for turning in.

Possible answers: **1.** she was still working at the telephone company **2.** she decided to accept the job at Worldwide Airlines **3.** didn't know if she should accept it or not **4.** she accepted the job **5.** she started to work at the airline **6.** they came back from their honeymoon **7.** they spoke with their landlady **8.** he was talking to a friend at work **9.** they liked it immediately **10.** they moved into their new place

■ EXPANSION ACTIVITY: Where's the other half?

(*Note:* This activity requires advance preparation.)

1. Have students work with a partner and write imaginative sentences with the conjunctions *before, after, when, while*, and *since*. Tell them to write sentences that suggest a whole story, such as: *While she was working, someone entered her apartment and stole her TV and some jewelry.*
2. Collect the sentences and choose the best ones, one for every two students in class.
3. Write the first clause of each sentence on one index card and the second clause on another. Give each student a card.
4. Have students move around the room and find the other half of their sentence. Then with their new partner have students plan and write a short story (no more than eight to ten sentences) that includes the sentence.
5. Before students tell or read their stories, have them read the combined sentence aloud that listeners must find in the story.

Workbook: *page 48, exercise H*

12 Interaction

Work with a partner and write a conversation in which one of you has a lot of news to tell the other. Make sure you find out several details about the news. You might want to begin the conversation with one of the following questions.

- How have you been?
- What have you been doing lately?
- What's new with you?
- What's the news from _____ ?
- How's everyone at _____ ?
- What's happening in _____ ?

13 Reentry

Time clauses with *before, after, when, while*, and *since*

Work with a partner. Talk over possible ways to complete the sentences. Write the best sentence you think of on a piece of paper. Compare your sentences with those of other students in your class.

> Liz started looking for a job when _____ .
>
> Liz started looking for a job when she realized that she was bored with her old one.

1. Liz began to think about changing jobs while _____ .
2. She talked with her parents and friends before _____ .
3. When Worldwide Airlines called to offer her a job, she _____ .
4. She called her friend Sue in New York after _____ .
5. Liz has been living with Sue since _____ .
6. Gino and Cristina lived in Gino's old apartment after _____ .
7. When they started having problems with the plumbing, _____ .
8. One day Gino heard about a vacant apartment while _____ .
9. When Gino and Cristina saw the apartment, _____ .
10. They haven't had any problems since _____ .

14 Presentation 📼

Talking about the duration of situations

To talk about the duration of situations, use clauses with **until**.

1. When the main clause uses the future, the **until**-clause uses the *present tense* or **can**.

   Liz will live with Sue **until** she **can** find an apartment.

   ⎣____ main clause ____⎦ ⎣____ **until** + clause ____⎦

   Bob won't be able to drive alone **until** he **passes** the road test.

2. When the main clause uses the past, the **until**-clause uses the *past*.

   Liz looked for a job **until** she **found** what she wanted.
   Liz didn't leave the telephone company **until** she **had** the job with Worldwide Airlines.

15 Practice

Work with a partner. Write an interesting end to each sentence. Share your sentences with another pair or with the whole class.

1. Nobody can be happy until ____ .

2. Our trip was perfect until ____ .

3. We won't have peace in the world until ____ .

4. Most people don't appreciate things until ____ .

5. The world won't be a safe place to live until ____ .

6. We were best friends until ____ .

7. You can't love another person until ____ .

8. It's easy to think you're perfect until ____ .

9. It's best not to make a decision until ____ .

10. I'm going to keep studying and practicing English until ____ .

11. Business was good in the center of town until ____ .

12. The party was going well until ____ .

14 Presentation

PROCEDURE
1. Refer to General Guidelines for Presentation, page ix.
2. To expand the Presentation, have students suggest ways to complete these sentences. Be sure students use a whole sentence in *b*.
   a. ____ until I was ____ years old.
   b. I would like to ____, but I can't until ____.

LANGUAGE NOTE
Until, like *before* and *after*, is both a preposition and a conjunction. If students give examples of the prepositional use (for example, *until Friday*), show them that here they must use a clause that will have a subject and a verb.

15 Practice

PROCEDURE
Refer to General Guidelines for Practice, page x.

Possible Answers: 1. he/she learns to like himself/herself 2. I lost my wallet 3. we learn to accept the fact that people are different 4. they lose them 5. we eliminate child abuse 6. he/she talked about me behind my back/gossiped about me 7. you love yourself 8. you get to work with two different shoes on 9. you have thought carefully about every alternative 10. I learn to use it well 11. the big shopping mall opened at the edge of town. 12. the electricity went off

■ EXPANSION ACTIVITY 8B: Are you still doing that? (page 192)

Workbook: *page 48, exercise I*

16 Listening

PROCEDURE

1. Refer to General Guidelines for Listening, page x.
2. Play the tape or read the script for the Listening. The tape includes the directions on page 116.
3. *If reading the script:* For the First Listening give students 30 seconds to write the answers to statements 1-5. For the Second Listening, give students 45 seconds to write answers to statements 6-10.
4. For script and answers, see page 199.

■ EXPANSION ACTIVITY: Liz and Dave's next date

1. Ask several pairs of students to role play a conversation between Liz and Dave when they meet somewhere in New York to talk over the future of their relationship. Extra students, the best in class, can be assigned the role of director of the skit. Groups should think about the place Liz and Dave are going to meet, for it can play a large role in the seriousness or humor of the skit.
2. Before the role plays are presented, have the class establish a set of awards for the most realistic, the funniest, the most probable/improbable, After the role plays, have students vote for the awards and then talk about the differences and similarities in the scenes. Then have a little awards ceremony.

Variation: Use extra students as a panel of judges to count the votes and make the presentation of the awards.

16 Listening

First Listening

Number your paper from 1-10. Listen to a telephone conversation that Liz Young had recently. Write *T* (True), *F* (False), or *NG* (Not Given) for statements 1-5.

1. Lenore and Liz talked to each other last week.
2. Lenore and Liz are cousins.
3. Liz's boyfriend, Dave, is studying communications.
4. Liz hasn't done anything in New York City except look for an apartment.
5. Lenore wants to visit Liz in New York City.

Second Listening

Listen to the conversation again and find answers to questions 6-10.

6. How did Lenore get Liz's new phone number?
7. Why is Dave upset?
8. What has Liz done in New York?
9. Why can't Lenore visit next weekend?
10. In what month is Lenore calling Liz?

17 Reading

Before You Read

1. Do you have brothers and sisters? What is your position in the family? Are you the oldest? The youngest? In the middle? How do you feel about your position?
2. How do children sometimes feel when a brother or sister gets more attention than they do?
3. If you have any brothers and sisters, do you have a lot in common with them? Do you agree or disagree with them on most issues?

First Reading

Read these questions before you read Jennifer Harrison's essay. Look for the answers as you read.

1. What is Jennifer's position in her family?
2. How did Jennifer feel when her sister Laurie was born? Why?
3. At which ages did Jennifer and Laurie fight?
4. Where is Jennifer now and how do she and Laurie get along?

My Favorite Sister

by Jennifer Harrison

1   I am the oldest. I am the first child, grandchild, cousin, and niece. This puts me in the position of also being the first to go to school, graduate, get a job, and attend college. I was always in the limelight° as a child, and I won't say I didn't love it. But then my sister Laurie was born; she was new and I was "old stuff." I was in the middle of my "terrible twos" that April, and Laurie was very sick right after she was born. Her doctors didn't think she would live through her first week. Mom and Dad were always worrying and trying to take care of her, and I was totally bewildered° because I wasn't the center of attention anymore.

the center of attention

confused, didn't understand

2   I guess I have always been jealous of her because everything she did was "cute." When I did it, the first time, it was an accomplishment.° When Laurie did it, she was "cute." Through grade school and up into our junior high years, there was a constant struggle° for attention. I strove to do bigger and better things than she could do.

something you have done or learned

difficult fight

3   We had many, many fights, most of them verbal, but some of varying° degrees of violence. The one I remember most was the day she was seven, bouncing° on Mom's mattress. I was nine and wise; I ordered her to stop immediately, but she continued her bouncing, then miscalculated the next jump and started falling headfirst toward the floor. I grabbed her arm and pulled her back up onto the bed, but I had jerked her elbow out of its socket,° and I got yelled at for "being rough" and "hurting Laurie." To this day, Laurie recounts° the story of how "Jenn pulled my whole arm out of its socket," which just plain irritates me.

different

jumping

hollow place in a bone where another bone fits

tells

4   As we grew into our teens, the battles took on new meanings. Fighting over bathroom times, who was using whose shampoo, one of us screeching at the other to get off the phone, and sneaking° clothes out of each other's closets were minor wars. Reading each other's letters or diary

taking secretly

---

17 Reading

PROCEDURE
1. Refer to General Guidelines for Reading, page x.
2. "Second Reading" part A can be discussed with a partner, in a small group, or with the class.
3. Have students do "Second Reading" part B individually, so they have feedback on their own ability to infer meaning from context. Then discuss answers as a class.
4. Use some of the discussion questions suggested in *Reacting to the Reading* on page 119.

LANGUAGE NOTES
1. *In the dead of night* (4) means *in the middle of the night*. Students can probably guess its meaning.
2. *Bub*, Laurie's nickname for Jennifer, is slang for *brother, boy,* or *buddy*. Here we see language change occurring. Though once used exclusively to refer to males, *buddy* (and here *Bub*) are being used to refer to females.
3. *Pest* is a person who bothers someone continuously.
4. A *tag-along* is a person who always follows another.

Answers: First Reading: **1.** the oldest **2.** bad, like "old stuff," confused because she wasn't the most important child at the moment, jealous of Laurie who was sick when she was born **3.** Grade school age (when Jennifer was 9 and Laurie was 7) and during their teens **4.** in college and they are best of friends (buddies)

A. 1. When Laurie was born she was sick so she got more attention at that time. Everything Laurie did was cute, but Jennifer says that when she did the same things, they weren't cute but "accomplishments." The parents apparently babied Laurie more than Jennifer. This encouraged Jennifer to compete with Laurie and try to get her parents' attention. Her parents apparently believed Jennifer was rough and hurting Laurie even without checking. They blamed her for all the fights. **2.** No. Laurie was falling off the bed and Jennifer tried to catch her and keep her from hitting the floor. **3.** The parents, because they seemed to favor Laurie. All problems were Jennifer's fault. **4.** Jennifer tried to do bigger and better things than Laurie could do. **5.** Bathroom times, shampoo, phone, taking each other's clothes secretly. Major fights were over reading private correspondence, scaring the other in the middle of the night, leaving the other sister with all the dishes to wash. **6.** Jennifer tried to keep Laurie from hitting the floor when she fell from the bed. Laurie was worried that Jennifer wouldn't miss her when she went to college. Jennifer cried. **7.** Now she likes to spend time with her sister. They go everywhere together. They talk until late at night. **8.** Possibly because the parents couldn't balance the attention they gave to the girls. Possibly because the parents didn't let the children handle their own problems and disagreements. Possibly, because it's normal for siblings to fight. **B. 1.** b **2.** a **3.** c **4.** a **5.** c **6.** b **7.** a **8.** c **9.** a **10.** b **11.** c **12.** b

without permission, sneaking up° and scaring° each other in the dead of night, and leaving one sister with all the dishes to wash — these were major fights. For some reason, we just couldn't get along at all. — *coming up secretly / frightening*

5 We had our last big blowup in early August, a week before I was to leave for college. She was pestering me to get off the telephone so she could call someone, and finally I lost my temper. I yelled, "I can't WAIT until I go to college, 'cause I won't have to listen to you whine° anymore!" She screamed right back, "Well, I can't wait 'til you leave, either! I'm looking forward to it!" After a moment of silence to let this all sink in, Laurie said very softly, "Aren't you going to miss me?" I burst into tears° because I was already beginning to miss her. We hugged each other, which rarely ever happened, and Mom's eyes bugged out° (she had come into the room to split us up). — *talk in a crying voice started to cry* / *started to cry* / *opened very wide*

6 After coming to college I realize that I do miss my sister, and I write to her once a week to keep her up on the latest news. She writes me two or three letters a week and fills me in on° all the happenings at our high school. When I call home (collect), Laurie and I talk for ten to fifteen minutes, or until Dad takes the phone out of her hand. I go home about every other weekend, and we go everywhere together and sit up late, jabbering. She keeps my room swept and cleaned, and when I went home for Thanksgiving there was a huge, crayoned banner taped to my wall that read, "Welcome Home, Bub!" I loved it. It's like I have found a new friend, somebody who's been there all the time except I didn't know it. — *tells me about*

7 It's a little sad that I had to leave home to discover how much I love and miss my sister. I look forward to vacations and summertime, when I'll be with her. After sixteen years of being "The Pest" and "Tag-Along," now I can honestly say my sister is my very best buddy.

Second Reading

A.   Read the story again and answer the questions.

1.   In what ways did Jennifer's parents treat her and Laurie differently?

2.   Did Jennifer pull Laurie's elbow out of its socket on purpose?

3.   Who yelled at Jennifer for "being rough" and "hurting Laurie?" Why?

4.   How did Jennifer try to show she was superior to Laurie?

5.   What were the topics of their teenage fights? Which were the really "major fights?"

6.   What evidence is there that Jennifer and Laurie cared about each other before Jennifer left home?

7.   Why does Jennifer look forward to going home? What is her new relationship with her sister like?

8.   Why do you think Jennifer and Laurie couldn't get along? Do brothers and sisters always fight?

B.   Find the following words in the story and choose the best meaning.

1.   strove (2)   **a.** played   **b.** worked hard   **c.** cried
     (from <u>strive</u>)

2.   grabbed (3)   **a.** took quickly   **b.** threw away   **c.** hit

3.   jerked (3)   **a.** pushed   **b.** cut   **c.** pulled

4.   irritates (3)   **a.** makes upset   **b.** makes happy   **c.** makes sad

5.   battles (4)   **a.** sad times   **b.** happy times   **c.** fights

6.   screeching (4)   **a.** smiling   **b.** screaming   **c.** singing

7.   blowup (5)   **a.** fight   **b.** conversation   **c.** game

8.   pestering (5)   **a.** hitting   **b.** talking to   **c.** bothering

9.   lost my temper (5) **a.** got angry   **b.** cried   **c.** smiled

10. jabbering (6)   **a.** writing   **b.** talking   **c.** thinking

11. banner (6)   **a.** song   **b.** picture   **c.** sign

12. pest (7)   **a.** friend   **b.** person who bothers you   **c.** sister

Reacting to the Reading: Discussion Questions
1. What are the particular problems of the oldest, middle, or youngest child?
2. What do children need most from their parents? Why?
3. What things about a family member have irritated you? What should we do when this happens?
4. Tell about a time you blew up or got very angry at someone. Why did it happen? How did the situation end?
5. What are possible main ideas or themes for this composition? (We learn the value of something when we no longer have it. It's important to grow in our relationships.)

18 Writing

PROCEDURE

1. Refer to General Guidelines for Writing, page xi.
2. Give students time to talk about relationships they have and what makes them good or bad.
3. Have students make notes about the person and relationship they are going to write about.
4. After students write the first draft of their paragraphs, have a class discussion about what makes relationships good and bad.

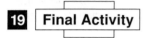

19 Final Activity

PROCEDURE

1. Refer to General Guidelines for Final Activity, page xi.
2. Set the stage for a series of talk show interviews with different famous people. With the class, brainstorm a list of famous guests.
3. Have pairs of students choose one name from the list and write the interview conversation including the opening (*Thank you for being with us tonight/ taking time out of your busy schedule*), a few questions and answers, and a closing. Students can memorize their part or put their lines on 3 x 5 cards.
4. Have pairs role play their dialogs without using the famous person's name. After each interview, someone in the audience names the famous person and tells what clues gave him/her the answer.

Workbook: *page 49, exercise J*

18 Writing

A. Talk with one or two classmates about relationships you have with friends or family members. What makes relationships good or bad?

B. Write a short essay of three or four paragraphs to answer one of these questions. Follow the general model below.

1. Describe a good relationship you have with another person. Why is it good? Give examples of what you do for each other.
2. Describe a problem relationship you have with another person. Why isn't the relationship in good condition now? What could you or the other person do to make it better?

PARAGRAPH 1: **Introduction**
Mention your topic, the person, and the quality of the relationship. Try to include something to get the reader interested in reading more.

PARAGRAPH 2 (3): **Body Paragraph(s)**
Discuss why the relationship is good or bad. Give details.

PARAGRAPH 4: **Conclusion**
Make a final comment on the relationship. You might summarize what you have said or talk about the future of the relationship.

C. Share your ideas about good and bad relationships with your classmates. What makes good relationships? What causes problems in relationships?

19 Final Activity

Work with your classmates and make a list of famous people it would be fun to interview. Put the list on the board. Work with a partner and plan a short interview of one of the people. Use the *Suggested language*. In your interview don't mention the name of the famous person. Can your classmates guess who it is?

Suggested language:

Thank you for _____ .
What have you been doing since _____ ?
Oh, really! Have you been _____ lately?
And what are your plans for the future?
I can't _____ until _____ .

UNIT 9

COMMUNICATION
Talking about possessions ▪ Borrowing, lending, and returning things ▪ Telling what you see or hear ▪ Starting a conversation ▪ Referring to different, but related items ▪ Emphasizing

GRAMMAR
Possessive pronouns ▪ Sense verb + object + verb+-*ing* ▪ *Another, others, the other(s)* ▪ *Pretty* + adjective/adverb

SKILLS
Listening to conversations about celebrations ▪ Reading an article about holidays ▪ Writing about a festival or holiday

Time to Celebrate

The school year is drawing to a close at Winfield High. This year the Logans and the Youngs are right in the middle of the end-of-year celebrations because Bob and Mike are graduating. The celebrations began in April with a dance called the senior prom, a formal occasion with tuxedos and evening gowns. Bob finally got his driver's license in March, and his dad lent him the family car for the dance.

It's now June. Bob and Mike are busy with the plans for the class picnic and a special party for their friends at Mike's house this weekend.

BOB: Everything's ready for the party, isn't it?

MIKE: Yeah. We've got a stereo with a cassette player and a CD so we can play any music the kids bring.

BOB: Terrific! Gloria helped me plan the refreshments. We'll do the shopping Friday. Now I just need to find something neat to wear.

MIKE: Why don't you talk to Sam? Liz told me she saw him wearing a wild purple shirt at the college dance a couple of weeks ago.

BOB: Not a bad idea.

SAM: Hey, Bob. You're looking on *my* side of the closet. What's up?

BOB: I need a really neat shirt for the party this weekend. Can I borrow one of yours?

SAM: Sure, but the shirts I wear to parties are pretty wild.

BOB: Perfect. Exactly what I want.

SAM: How do you like this one?

BOB: It's OK. Let me see another one.

SAM: Another? You mean THE other. I've only got two wild shirts.

BOB: OK. Let me see THE other.

Useful materials: pictures of things people commonly borrow; pictures related to American holidays

Time to Celebrate

PROCEDURE
Refer to General Guidelines for Opener, page ix.

COMPREHENSION QUESTIONS

Now answer these questions.

1. Why are the Logans and Youngs celebrating at the end of this school year? *Bob and Mike are graduating.*
2. What are Bob and Mike planning? *A class picnic and a party at Mike's house.*
3. What is Mike taking care of? *The music.*
4. What are Bob and Gloria going to do Friday? *Shop for the refreshments.*
5. Why does Mike suggest that Bob talk to Sam? *To find something neat to wear to the party.*
6. Why was Bob looking on Sam's side of the closet? *To see what shirts he has.*
7. Why is Sam's shirt perfect for Bob? *It's wild.*
8. How many wild shirts does Sam have? *Two.*
9. Is Gloria going to wear her mother's outfit to the party? *No, she's not, because it's too big.*
10. Why does Gloria want something new for the party? *She doesn't have anything to wear and it's an important occasion.*

DISCUSSION QUESTIONS
1. Why do you think Bob wants a wild shirt for the party?
2. What do you know about the activities that are often part of a U.S. high school graduation? How do you celebrate graduations in your country?

CULTURAL NOTES
1. A typical U.S. high school graduation ceremony is held at the school auditorium or athletic field. It includes speeches from one or two student speakers and an invited guest, and music from the school band or chorus. Students wear graduation caps and gowns and receive their diplomas from the principal.
2. Other common graduation events are a senior dance or prom, class picnic, and sometimes a senior trip.
3. Soft drinks and snacks are the usual refreshments at teenage evening parties. A meal is uncommon.

1 Vocabulary in Context

PROCEDURE
Refer to General Guidelines for Vocabulary in Context, page ix.

Answers: **1.** ending, coming to an end **2.** graduation dance **3.** event, activity **4.** formal clothing for men and women **5.** gave him the car to use **6.** beverages and light food **7.** great, different **8.** crazy, colorful, different **9.** a good idea **10.** What's happening? What are you doing? **11.** think, guess **12.** quite important

> **Workbook: *page 50, exercises A, B***

2 Presentation

PROCEDURE
1. Refer to General Guidelines for Presentation, page ix.
2. Read each pair of sentences in the grammar box and have students repeat, e.g., *This isn't my car. Mine is older.*
3. Ask students to tell you when to use the possessive adjective and when to use the possessive pronoun.
4. To practice *his* and *hers*, use the following model and small objects that we frequently misplace.
   SAM: I need an eraser. Can I borrow yours?
   TOM: Sorry, I don't know where mine is. Talk to Ana. Maybe you can borrow hers.
   ANA: I don't know where mine is either. Talk to Carlos. Maybe you can borrow his.

LANGUAGE NOTE
The possessive adjective always comes before a noun. The pronoun replaces the noun and stands alone.

3 Practice

PROCEDURE
Refer to General Guidelines for Practice, page x.

Optional: Have students write completed sentences on the board. Ask them to circle the pronouns and draw an arrow to the nouns they refer to.

Answers: **1.** Hers, his **2.** His, theirs **3.** mine **4.** ours **5.** mine, yours **6.** His, hers **7.** yours, mine **8.** hers, his **9.** yours, ours **10.** Hers, his, theirs

---

Scene 3

Gloria is trying to decide what to wear to Mike's party.

GLORIA: Mom, you know your black outfit with the sequins? Do you think I could borrow it for Bob and Mike's party this weekend?

MRS. RIVERA: If it fits, honey, but I think it might be too big for you.

GLORIA: I suppose you're right. Oh, Mom. I don't have anything to wear to this party. Could I buy something new? It's a pretty important occasion. Bob's graduating this year, you know . . .

MRS. RIVERA: Well . . . OK. Let's see what we can find.

1 Vocabulary in Context 📼

> Sit in a small group and reread the two conversations and introductions. Locate the words and phrases below. Discuss each one and decide on a definition or different way to say the same thing. Share your work with other groups.
>
> 1. drawing to a close
> 2. senior prom
> 3. a formal occasion
> 4. tuxedos and evening gowns
> 5. His dad lent him the car.
> 6. refreshments
> 7. something neat to wear
> 8. wild purple shirt
> 9. Not a bad idea.
> 10. What's up?
> 11. I suppose you're right.
> 12. pretty important occasion

2 Presentation 📼

Talking about possessions

Subject	Possessive adjective		Possessive pronoun
I you he she we they	This isn't	my your his her our their	car.	Mine Yours His Hers Ours Theirs	is older.

A: I need a wild shirt for the party. Can I borrow **yours**? *your shirt*
B: Sorry, I don't know where **mine** is. *my shirt*

Ex: I see your book. where's mine?

3 Practice

Complete the sentences with the correct possessive pronoun(s).

1. Ted and Joyce both have cassette players. *Hers* is bigger than *his* .
(she) (he)

2. Sam and his parents have cars. *His* is older than *theirs* .
(he) (they)

3. I have a portable radio, but that one isn't *mine* .
(I)

4. We have a volleyball, but that one isn't *ours* .
(we)

5. I know you have a blue pen, but this one is *mine* . I don't know
(I)
where *yours* is.
(you)

6. Bob and Gloria both have tennis racquets. *His* is a little heavier
(he)
than *hers* .
(she)

7. Our cats certainly look alike, but I think *yours* is a little bigger than
(you)
mine .
(I)

8. Ted and Lisa both lost their wallets last month. She has found *hers* ,
(she)
but he hasn't found *his* .
(he)

9. Our suitcases look so similar, I can't tell which is *yours* and which is
(you)
ours .
(we)

10. Mary, Phil, and the Jones all have 1990 Demgos. *Hers* is red, *his*
(she) (he)
is blue, and *theirs* is white.
(they)

■ EXPANSION ACTIVITY: Whose is it?

1. Have students bring a pen, pencil, or other common object to class that they can identify as their own. Put the objects on your desk.
2. Write this model on the board and have students practice in a chain drill.

> A: Ana, is this your pencil?
> B: No, it's not mine. Mine is shorter (Mine is red). Ask Mara. Maybe it's hers.
> (Why don't you ask Pedro? Maybe it's his.)

3. Have two students leave the room. Choose four of the objects and identify whose they are for the rest of the class. Remove all other objects.
4. Call the students back and tell them to find the owners of the four objects. They take turns talking to students and can confer with each other. Classmates give them clues (*Mine isn't on the desk. Mine is green/shorter.*) that might be true.
5. Repeat with other students and other objects.

Optional: Instead of common objects, have students bring something interesting or different to class. After owners are located, have students talk about what they brought.

■ EXPANSION ACTIVITY: Distinguishing possessive adjectives and pronouns

Dictate the following sentences to give students practice in distinguishing possessive adjectives and pronouns.

1. A: That's the Youngs' house, isn't it?
   B: No, their house is brown.
   C: Then that other house is theirs because that house is brown.
2. A: That's Ted's bike, isn't it?
   B: I can't tell because I'm colorblind. His bike is green.
   C: Then that's not his. That bike is silver.
3. A: Those are Joyce's skates, aren't they?
   B: No, her skates are black.
   C: Those might be hers because they're black.
4. A: That's our car, isn't it?
   B: No, our car is a 1990 model.
   C: That might be ours. It's a 1985 model and that's what we have.

> **Workbook:** *pages 51-52, exercises C, D*

4 Presentation

PROCEDURE

1. Refer to General Guidelines for Presentation, page ix.
2. If possible, practice with objects or pictures of them.

CULTURAL NOTE

Americans usually teach their children that if they borrow something, they must return it in the same condition it was borrowed. If not, they will have to replace it.

5 Practice

PROCEDURE

1. Refer to General Guidelines for Practice, page x.
2. Have students demonstrate this Practice for the class before group work. You may need to remind them to change *a* to *some*, *it* to *them*, and *Here is* to *Here are*.

Answers: Answers will follow models A and B in *4* or this plural model.

> A: Do you have some chairs I could borrow?
> B: I sure do. Just a minute. I'll get them.
> *Later:*
> A: Here are your chairs. Thanks for letting us use them.
> B: You're welcome. Any time.

LANGUAGE NOTE

Excuses like these are used when literally true and when one does not want to lend something because it is brand new or because one never lends things in that category. However, it might help students to learn to say *Sorry, but my parents won't let me lend ____*.

> Workbook: *page 52, exercise E*

---

4 Presentation

Borrowing, lending, and returning things

A
> A: Do you have a volleyball I could borrow?
> B: I sure do. Just a minute. I'll get it.
> *A few hours later . . .*
> A: Here's your volleyball. Thanks for letting us use it.
> B: You're welcome. Any time.

B
> A: Do you have a volleyball I could borrow?
> B: Sorry. My brother is using mine. Check with the Logans. Maybe you can borrow theirs.
> A: OK. Thanks anyway.
> *A few hours later . . .*
> A: Here's your volleyball, Mrs. Logan. Thanks for letting us use it.
> C: That's not ours. Ours is black and white. I think that one belongs to Gino.
> A: OK. And don't worry. I'll find yours.

5 Practice

Mike and Bob need to borrow some things for the party at Mike's house. Work with a partner and practice borrowing and returning things, following the models in 4. Sometimes you choose to lend the item; sometimes you give an excuse for not lending it.

1. chairs

2. punch bowl

3. cooler

4. basketball

5. volleyball and net

6. radio

7. barbecue

> **Useful language:**
>
> *Excuses for not lending*
>
> | Mine | is | broken. |
> | Ours | | not working. |
> | | | lost. |
> | | | in the repair shop. |
>
> | My | sister | is using | it. |
> | | brother | | them. |

6 Presentation

Telling what you see or hear

To tell what you see or hear, use:

sense verb + object + verb+-*ing*

Some sense verbs:

see	hear
watch	listen

1. Liz saw Sam at the dance. **+** He was wearing a wild purple shirt. **=**

   Liz **saw Sam** at the dance **wearing** a wild purple shirt.
   Liz **saw Sam wearing** a wild purple shirt at the dance.
2. We **watched the children playing** on the playground.
3. I **see you hiding** behind the couch.
4. We **heard them discussing** the plans for the party.
5. The **teacher listened to the students talking** in small groups.

7 Practice

Combine the following ideas into one sentence.

1. I heard you. You were talking on the phone yesterday.
2. I saw you in the park yesterday. You were walking with someone new.
3. I saw you in the cafeteria yesterday. You were sitting with the new girl.
4. I heard you. You were arguing with your boyfriend yesterday.
5. I saw you. You were reading a letter in the cafeteria.
6. Lisa saw Joyce. Joyce was swimming at the pool.
7. The coach heard the players. The players were arguing about something.
8. Gloria watched Ted. He was playing soccer.
9. The teacher watched the students. They were performing a play.
10. The parents watched their children. The children were dancing at the prom.

6 Presentation

PROCEDURE
Refer to General Guidelines for Presentation, page ix.

LANGUAGE NOTE
Both *verb + -ing* and *base verb* can be used in these sentences. *Verb + -ing* suggests continuing action and communicates that you witnessed part of the activity. The *base* communicates that the person witnessed the complete activity or performance from beginning to end. Note these contrasts:

   a. I saw Sam **filling out** his application for a scholarship. (I saw him working on it.)
      I saw him **fill out** his application for a scholarship. (I saw him start and finish it.)
   b. I heard you **singing** the national anthem.
      I heard you **sing** the national anthem.

7 Practice

PROCEDURE
1. Refer to General Guidelines for Practice, page x.
2. Have students write out the new sentences individually. Check answers with the whole class.

Answers: **1.** I heard you talking on the phone yesterday. **2.** I saw you walking in the park yesterday with someone new./I saw you walking in the park with someone new yesterday. **3.** I saw you sitting in the cafeteria yesterday with the new girl./I saw you sitting in the cafeteria with the new girl yesterday. **4.** I heard you arguing with your boyfriend yesterday. **5.** I saw you reading a letter in the cafeteria. **6.** Lisa saw Joyce swimming at the pool. **7.** The coach heard the players arguing about something. **8.** Gloria watched Ted playing soccer. **9.** The teacher watched the students performing a play. **10.** The parents watched their children dancing at the prom.

8 Practice

PROCEDURE

1. Refer to General Guidelines for Practice, page x.
2. Write the verbs on the board.
3. Give students about one minute to study the picture before they close their books.

Optional: Do as a game or group competition. Have groups write as many sentences as they can about the party. The group with the most correct sentences wins.

Possible answers: I saw a lot of people dancing. I heard some people talking about the food. I watched the drummer playing his drums. I listened to the guitar player playing a solo.

> **Workbook:** *page 53, exercises F, G*

9 Presentation

PROCEDURE

1. Refer to General Guidelines for Presentation, page ix.
2. To expand the Presentation, write a common situation on the board; for example, *You and a classmate are in the hall at school. Your watch shows the next class has already started.* Possible openers: *We're late to class, aren't we?* or *I just saw the hall clock. We're late again.*

10 Practice

PROCEDURE

1. Refer to General Guidelines for Practice, page x.
2. If you prefer, have students write openers with a partner and discuss them in small groups. Be sure students understand that even though all three openers might be possible, one will probably be better than the others for a given situation.

Possible answers: **1.** You aren't going to use your car Friday night, are you? / I saw you cleaning the car yesterday. Are you going to use it this weekend? / You know the dress you bought at Warners? **2.** Your van can hold ten people, can't it? / I see your van in the driveway. I guess it's working now. / You know the math club at school, Dad? ... Well, we're having a picnic Friday. Do you think we could use the van?

8 Practice

Study the picture carefully. Close your books. Imagine you were at that party. Talk about things you *saw, watched, heard,* or *listened to* at the party.

9 Presentation

Starting a conversation

Here are three ways to start a conversation:

1. Use a tag question:

   Everything's ready for the party, isn't it?

2. Comment on something you have observed and then ask a question:

   Hey, Bob. You're looking on my side of the closet. What's up?

3. Mention some object, event, or person you want to talk about:

   Mom, you know your black outfit with the sequins?

10 Practice

Read each of the following situations. Try to write three openings for the conversation, one using a tag question, one beginning with an observation, and one mentioning an object or event. Sometimes one of the ways is not possible. Then talk with a partner about which opening is the best and why.

1. You have a special date. You want to borrow a brother's or sister's car or favorite piece of clothing.
2. Your club is having a picnic. You need to borrow someone's van to take the group to the lake.

3. You're going on a bike ride. Your bike is broken. You would like to borrow a friend's brand new bike.
4. You have lost your English book and there is a big test tomorrow. You really need to borrow a book from a classmate.
5. Your club is having a dance. You would like to use your teacher's stereo, cassette player, or CD player.
6. You are moving to a new apartment. You would like to borrow a friend's truck.

11 Interaction

A. With your class, brainstorm a list of things that you might want to borrow from someone else, not necessarily from a classmate.

B. Now work in a group of three. Write a conversation in which one of you tries to borrow something in the list from one or both of the others in the group. Open the conversation in the most convincing and effective way to get what you want. The others can agree to lend you what you want or give an excuse.

12 Presentation 📼

Referring to different, but related, items

> To refer to different, but related, items use
> **another, others, the other(s).**

In the United States, each state determines its official holidays. Banks, government offices, and many businesses close on official holidays. The United States government gives its employees ten holidays a year, called Federal Public Holidays. Most states celebrate these and sometimes other local holidays.

1. There are two federal holidays in the summer. One is Independence Day. **The other** is Labor Day.
2. There are four federal holidays in the winter. One is Christmas. **Another** is New Year's Day.
3. There are ten federal holidays. One is Veterans' Day. **Others** are Martin Luther King Day and Thanksgiving.
4. There are four federal holidays in the winter. Two are Christmas and New Year's Day. **The others** are Martin Luther King Day and Presidents' Day.

3. You have a new bike, don't you? I don't suppose I could use it, could I? Mine is broken. / I saw you riding your new bike the other day. It's great. I don't suppose I could borrow it. / You know the bike I got for my birthday last year? ... The gears are broken, and I need a bike for the weekend.   4. You heard I lost my English book, didn't you? / I saw you studying for the test in the cafeteria. Are you finished? / You know the English grammar book. ... Well, I lost mine. Do you think I could borrow yours?   5. You know about the French club party, don't you, Mrs. Wilson? / The class has a stereo, doesn't it, Mrs. Wilson? / I saw you cleaning the closet the other day, Mrs. Wilson. Did I see a stereo?   6. You have a truck, don't you? / You heard that I'm moving to a new apartment, didn't you? / I saw you driving a pickup truck the other day. Is that yours? / You know your father's old pickup truck. Does it work?

11 Interaction

PROCEDURE
Refer to General Guidelines for Interaction, page x.

Workbook: *page 54, exercise H*

12 Presentation

PROCEDURE
1. Refer to General Guidelines for Presentation, page ix.
2. Write the names of the U.S. holidays (page 128) on the board in their seasonal groups. Talk with students about each. Be sure they know what is celebrated (see notes on page 128) and how to pronounce the names.
3. As students read the sentences on page 127, point to the names of the holidays on the board.
4. Ask for a paraphrase of the meaning of the pronouns. (See Language Note below.)

LANGUAGE NOTE
Like the articles *a/an* and *the*, these pronouns are general (*another* and *others*) and specific (*the other* and *the others*).
- *Another* means *one of the others* or *any other one*. *Others* means *some/any others*.
- *The other* means *the one remaining*. *The others* means all the remaining, the rest.

CULTURAL NOTE

Martin Luther King Day: a celebration of civil rights in memory of the birthday of the civil rights leader slain in 1968

Valentine's Day: a day for friends and lovers to express their love through cards and gifts; typical symbol on valentine cards is a red heart

Presidents' Day: a single holiday, combining the former birthday celebrations of George Washington and Abraham Lincoln

Memorial Day: originally in memory of veterans, but now more generally understood to be in memory of all one's deceased relatives and friends

Independence Day: commemorates the signing of the Declaration of Independence in 1776

Labor Day: celebrates the contribution of working people to the society

Columbus Day: originally October 12; commemorates the discovery of the western hemisphere by Christopher Columbus in 1492

Halloween: secular celebration on the evening before All Saints' Day; children dress in costumes and ask neighbors for treats of candy or they supposedly will play a trick ("Trick or Treat")

Veterans' Day: commemorates the end of World War I and the contribution of veterans in the protection of the rights stated in the U.S. Constitution

Thanksgiving: a day set aside to express thanks for one's country, family and life according to one's own religious beliefs

■ EXPANSION ACTIVITY 9A: Library project on American holidays (page 192)

13 Practice

PROCEDURE

Refer to General Guidelines for Practice, page x.

Answers: **A. 1.** Another **2.** Others **3.** The others **4.** the other **5.** Others

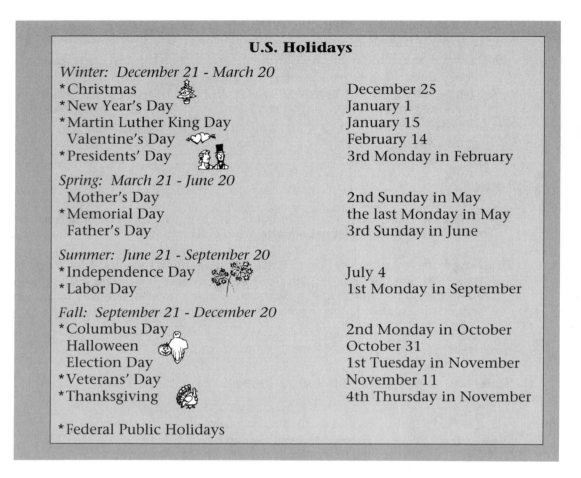

U.S. Holidays

Winter: December 21 - March 20

*Christmas	December 25
*New Year's Day	January 1
*Martin Luther King Day	January 15
Valentine's Day	February 14
*Presidents' Day	3rd Monday in February

Spring: March 21 - June 20

Mother's Day	2nd Sunday in May
*Memorial Day	the last Monday in May
Father's Day	3rd Sunday in June

Summer: June 21 - September 20

*Independence Day	July 4
*Labor Day	1st Monday in September

Fall: September 21 - December 20

*Columbus Day	2nd Monday in October
Halloween	October 31
Election Day	1st Tuesday in November
*Veterans' Day	November 11
*Thanksgiving	4th Thursday in November

*Federal Public Holidays

13 Practice

A. **Complete the sentences about United States federal and minor holidays using** *another, others*, **and** *the other(s).*

1. There are three federal holidays in the fall. One is Columbus Day. _____ is Veterans' Day.

2. There are several minor holidays in the United States. One is Valentine's Day. _____ are Father's Day and Mother's Day.

3. There are four federal holidays in the winter. Two are Martin Luther King Day and Presidents' Day. _____ are Christmas and New Year's.

4. There are two federal holidays in the summer. One is Labor Day and _____ is Independence Day.

5. There are ten federal holidays. One is Veterans' Day. _____ are Memorial Day and Labor Day.

B. Work with a partner and write five more sentences like these about holidays in your home country. Use *another*, *others*, *the other*, and *the others* at least one time. Share your sentences with another pair.

14 Presentation

Emphasizing

> Use **pretty** + *adjective* or *adverb* to show a moderate degree of emphasis.
>
> | **light emphasis** | **moderate emphasis** | **strong emphasis** |
> |---|---|---|
> | a little tired | **pretty** tired | very tired |

A Bob's usually a little tired after school.
Bob's **pretty** tired after he cleans the yard.
He's very tired after playing basketball all afternoon.

B A: The students worked for weeks on the prom.
B: It must be a **pretty** important occasion.

C A: How wild are Sam's shirts?
B: They're **pretty** wild. I think one is purple.

15 Practice

A. Read each statement. Draw a conclusion using *pretty* plus an adjective of your choice. Follow model B in *14*.

1. Lisa won an essay contest.
2. Elinor's been working nights for a week.
3. Joyce has been in bed for a week.
4. Ted got a bad grade on his last math exam.
5. The Youngs are having 20 people for dinner Saturday.

B. Now ask a question with these cues. Another student will answer using *pretty* + adjective or adverb. Follow model C in *14*.

1. expensive / sports cars
2. cold / New York in the winter
3. fast / Bob run
4. often / watch a movie on TV
5. important / holidays to you

■ EXPANSION ACTIVITY: Do you want another?
1. Have students bring one of something to class; for example, one pen, one pencil, one soft drink can, one cookie, etc.
2. Demonstrate the use of the pronouns by giving instructions to students to give you or take *another*, *the other* or *the others*.
3. Have students give instructions to other students.

Optional: With edible items you can set up a role play in which a rather pushy host/hostess is always telling his/her guests to *Have another. Please have the other. Please finish the others.* Students can learn to defend themselves in many ways. *Thank you, but I'm on a diet. Thank you, but I've already had more than I should. Thanks, but I'm just not hungry.*

> Workbook: *page 55, exercise I*

14 Presentation

PROCEDURE
1. Refer to General Guidelines for Presentation, page ix.
2. Teach correct intonation for these phrases:
   a little tired, pretty tired, very tired.

LANGUAGE NOTE
This use of *pretty* as an intensifier is heard frequently when people draw conclusions (model B) and in warnings (model C).

15 Practice

PROCEDURE
Refer to General Guidelines for Practice, page x.

Possible answers: **A. 1.** She must be pretty happy. **2.** She must be pretty tired. **3.** She must be pretty sick. **4.** He must be pretty upset with himself. **5.** They must be pretty busy. **B. 1.** How expensive are sports cars?/They're pretty expensive. (They cost at least $15,000.) **2.** How cold is New York in the winter?/It's pretty cold. (It's about 20°–30°.) **3.** How fast can Bob run?/ He can run pretty fast. (He can run a mile in 7 minutes.) **4.** How often do you watch a movie on TV?/Pretty often. (About 5 times a week.) **5.** How important are holidays to you?/Pretty important.

> Workbook: *page 55, exercise J*

PROCEDURE

1. Refer to General Guidelines for Listening, page x.
2. Play the tape or read the script for the Listening. The tape includes the directions and list of parties with their definitions on page 130.
3. *If reading the script:* For the First Listening, give students 10 seconds to write the name of the celebration. For the Second Listening give students 20 seconds to write answers to 1-4 in each conversation.
4. For script and answers, see page 199.

First Listening

Write A, B, C, D in a list on your paper. Leave four lines between the letters. Listen to Conversations A, B, C, D, and write the name of the celebration the people are talking about or enjoying. Choose from:

- **birthday party**
- **graduation party**
- **retirement party**
- **wedding anniversary:** yearly remembrance of the date of a wedding
- **bridal shower:** a party for a bride-to-be before the wedding at which gifts are given
- **baby shower:** a party for a woman before the birth of her baby at which gifts are given
- **family reunion:** a party to bring all family members together, especially those who don't see each other often

Second Listening

Write the numbers 1-4 below each celebration. Listen again, and write *T* (True), *F* (False), or *NG* (Not Given) for each statement.

Conversation A

1. Men are always included in this kind of party.
2. The party is a surprise for Maribelle.
3. Tom will help surprise Maribelle.
4. The party will be at Tom's mother's house.

Conversation B

1. Betsy and Billy are brother and sister.
2. Billy is two days older than Betsy.
3. The children will eat at the park.
4. There is a pretty good possibility of rain.

Conversation C

1. A mother calls her son to ask for details about a party.
2. There was a live orchestra at the party.
3. Ann is Bill's wife.
4. Ann and Bill had the party for their parents' 30th anniversary.

Conversation D

1. Sara Randall is getting married.
2. Sara has been teaching history for 30 years.
3. The plate is a gift from the school principal.
4. Sara is sad on this day.

17 Reading

Before You Read

1. What do you know about the American holiday called Thanksgiving?
2. Do you know on which holidays Americans give gifts?
3. On which holidays do people give gifts in your country?

First Reading

Skim the article below and look for answers to these questions. After reading, discuss the answers in small groups.

1. Is the article a news article? What type of article is it?
2. What is the writer's main idea?

WINFIELD DAILY NEWS   **OCTOBER 19, 1991**

Nobody asked my opinion, but . . .

By Richard Balestreri

1   Well, the holidays are just around the corner. The Christmas decorations are up at the mall, and advertisers everywhere are bombarding us with their latest jingles and telling us we'd better get working on our lists. There are only 65 shopping days before Christmas. In fact your catalog orders for Christmas should have been placed last week.

2   How different things are from when I was young! When I was a kid, I waited anxiously for the day after Thanksgiving when the stores would take on their festive Christmas look. And from there to Christmas was a manageable and exciting 32 days. We had a calendar on the wall and marked off each one with a big X, waiting excitedly for the morning when, among other things, we found a big, beautiful apple in the toe of our mother's old nylon stocking.

3   Now advertisers are encouraging my grandkids to begin counting in October, and frankly young kids can't count to 65. And they certainly can't be excited about something for 65 days. They can, however, begin to drive Mom and Dad crazy telling them about all the gifts they want that they have seen on TV. And kids have over two whole months to succeed.

4   The commercialization of holidays isn't limited to Christmas. Businesses try to convince us that gifts are necessary on Valentine's Day, Mother's Day, Father's Day, birthdays, wedding anniversaries, retirement — almost any occasion. And on TV at least, there is always the suggestion that the more we spend, the more meaningful our gifts will be.

5   But buried under all this holiday hype, there is one thing that we can still be grateful for, one holiday I give thanks for, and that is Thanksgiving. No one has yet managed to turn it into a gift-giving occasion. The only thing we give on Thanksgiving is thanks. Let it always be so.

■ EXPANSION ACTIVITY 9B: Reading about Thanksgiving (page 192)

17 Reading

PROCEDURE

1. Refer to General Guidelines for Reading, page x.
2. When presenting the "First Reading" instructions and questions, be sure students know what to read when skimming (title, date, the first and last paragraph, and the first sentences of other paragraphs). With this short article, the first sentences of paragraphs 1-4 and all of paragraph 5 should give them the main idea.
3. Give students about 30 seconds to skim the article. Be sure they don't have time to read it.
4. Discuss the answers to the questions in the "First Reading" with the whole class and follow instructions for the "Second Reading."

Possible answers: First Reading: **1.** No, it isn't. It's an editorial. It gives a person's opinion. **2.** American holidays are too commercialized. Only Thanksgiving is not. Therefore, he gives thanks for Thanksgiving.

Possible answers: Second Reading: **1.** October 19. 65 days before Christmas and the stores are already decorated for Christmas. The date is important because without this combination of facts, the writer has nothing to complain about. **2.** He criticizes the commercialization of holidays. He praises Thanksgiving because it is an important holiday on which Americans do not give gifts. **3. a.** near, but 65 days is not exactly near to Christmas (used ironically) **b.** shooting at, but here used figuratively to mean we hear a lot of ads **c.** most recent easily remembered songs, poems, or words of advertising **d.** a shorter period of time that small children can relate to or handle and therefore enjoy **e.** bother them, make Mom and Dad lose their calm/cool and get angry **f.** two months from October to December to drive Mom and Dad crazy **g.** holiday exaggeration, exaggerated advertising; *hype* is slang for exaggerated advertising, talk, or activity; it comes from a Greek prefix *hyper-* meaning *over* or *above* **h.** be thankful for, be happy about **i.** succeeded in making it

Reacting to the Reading: Discussion Questions

1. Are holidays in your country getting too commercialized?
2. Which holiday do you like best and why?

18 Writing

PROCEDURE

1. Refer to General Guidelines for Writing, page xi.
2. After students talk about a national or family celebration with a partner, have them make notes of things they want to include in their compositions.

PROCEDURE

Note: This Final Activity shows a way to handle student talks, especially in large classes. First, all students present their talks in small groups. You circulate and listen. Then give students guidelines on selecting who will talk to the class. The first time you might ask for a volunteer, another time the most interesting talk from a person who has not presented, etc. Over a period of weeks or a semester, everyone can report once.

1. Refer to General Guidelines for Final Activity, page xi.
2. Do this activity after students turn in their compositions so they talk about the celebrations, rather than read their compositions.
3. Give students time to make some notes on 3 x 5 cards before collecting the papers.

■ EXPANSION ACTIVITY: Panel report on a holiday

1. Form groups of students who come from the same country or, if all students are from the same country, on some other basis.
2. Each group chooses a holiday or celebration from their/your country and plans a short report about it.
3. Members should divide the oral report more or less evenly. One student can give the introduction; others talk about the history and meaning, ways of celebrating, etc.; another gives the conclusion.
4. Give students time to plan and practice their presentation in class if possible. Encourage them to include pictures and objects connected with the celebration.

Workbook: *page 56, exercise K*

Second Reading

Read the article and answer the following questions.

1. When was the article written? Why is the date important?
2. What does the writer criticize? What does he praise?
3. What do the following words or expressions used in the article mean? In some cases you will have to think about the usual meaning of the words as well as an exaggerated meaning.
   a. just around the corner (1)
   b. bombarding (1)
   c. latest jingles (1)
   d. a manageable and exciting 32 days (2)
   e. they can begin to drive Mom and Dad crazy (3)
   f. They have two whole months to succeed. (3)
   g. holiday hype (5)
   h. be grateful for (5)
   i. managed to turn into (5)

18 Writing

A. **Talk with a partner about national or family celebrations that you particularly like. Tell him or her what you do on one of these special days.**

B. **Write three or four paragraphs about a celebration or festival in your country or family. Follow this general outline.**

PARAGRAPH 1: **Introduction**
Introduce the reader to the celebration, its name, purpose, and date.

PARAGRAPH 2 (3, 4): **Body**
Describe one or more of the events and the role people play in them.

PARAGRAPH 3: **Conclusion**
Give your opinion or reaction to this celebration.

C. **Ask your partner to read your paper and give you suggestions on ways to improve it. Make a final copy of your composition.**

19 Final Activity

Meet with a small group of your classmates. Listen to each student talk about the celebration he or she wrote about in *18*. Ask each student at least one question about the celebration. Then, choose one of your group members to talk and make the same presentation to the whole class. After all of the presentations, talk about similarities and differences in the celebrations.

UNIT 10

COMMUNICATION
Emphasizing ▪ Verifying information ▪ Responding to other people's comments ▪ Talking about what makes a good employee

GRAMMAR
Still with the present perfect ▪ Tag questions with *did* and *didn't* ▪ Short responses with *think, hope, guess*

SKILLS
Listening to job interviews ▪ Filling out a job application form ▪ Reading about successful job interviews

Waiting for a Call

Tom, Adela, Bob, and Lisa Logan have moved to Texas; Sam decided not to move with them at this time. Soon after the Logans arrived in Dallas, Adela and Bob started looking for jobs. Bob found a part-time job at a sandwich shop right away, but it hasn't been that easy for Adela. She is still looking. Just last week, she heard about an opening for a computer programmer at the Dallas Electric Company, and she applied for the job. She filled out her application carefully and turned it in, along with her résumé. Now she is waiting to be called for an interview. Living in a new city, looking for a house, and applying for a job have made Adela pretty nervous.

TOM: How's it going, darling? Are you ready for the interview?

ADELA: I think so, but they still haven't called. I'm afraid with no paid experience in programming, they won't be interested in me.

TOM: But you *do* have job experience. You worked at Wells for two years before we were married, and you did some programming with your instructors. What's more, you've managed our home better than I ever could.

ADELA: Managed our home? What do you mean?

TOM: Why . . . you're the greatest money manager I know! Look at what you were able to do with my salary. And you're really good at getting people to work for you — just ask me and the kids about that!

ADELA: Ha! . . . But I see what you mean. I guess I'm not looking at my talents from the right point of view.

Useful materials: newspaper employment ads; map and pictures of places in Texas

Waiting for a Call

PROCEDURE
Refer to General Guidelines for Opener, page ix.

COMPREHENSION QUESTIONS
Now answer these questions.
1. Which of the Logans didn't move to Texas? *Sam.*
2. Is Bob looking for a job? *No, he isn't. He found a job at a sandwich shop.*
3. Has Adela found a job? *No, but she has applied for one.*
4. What is Adela waiting for? *A call for an interview.*
5. Has Adela had a paid job as a computer programmer? *No, she hasn't.*
6. What kind of work, paid and not paid, has Adela done? *She has worked at Wells Travel Agency. She has worked with the PTA and with her instructors, and she has managed the family home.*
7. What talents does Tom think Adela has? *Tom thinks Adela is a good manager of money and people.*
8. Has Adela worked with the PTA at school? *Yes, she has.*
9. What should Adela talk about in the interview? *All the things she has done.*
10. Does Adela have all A's from the Technical Institute? *Maybe. She has good grades.*

DISCUSSION QUESTIONS
1. Why is Adela nervous and a little worried about the interview?
2. What does Tom say to give Adela confidence?

CULTURAL NOTE
Women returning to the work force after or while raising a family should consider the work they do in the home as an important part of their qualifications. Successful homemakers have developed good managerial skills that can transfer to business. They have learned to work well with other people, among them children who are not the easiest people to work with. They have managed the schedules of several other people and still done their own work in the home. Often they have managed the finances of the family.

■ EXPANSION ACTIVITY 10: Texas montage (page 192)

1 Vocabulary in Context

PROCEDURE

Refer to General Guidelines for Vocabulary in Context, page ix.

Answers: **1.** opening **2.** application, apply for **3.** interview **4.** experience **5.** résumé **6.** References **7.** transcript

> **Workbook: *pages 57-58, exercises A, B***

2 Reentry

PROCEDURE

1. Refer to General Guidelines for Reentry, page x.
2. Have students work independently or with a partner.
3. Check answers with the class.

Answers: **1.** get **2.** returning, bring it back **3.** completed, wrote in all the information **4.** completed, wrote in; forget, omit **5.** returned by mail, read it again, checked **6.** (hand) carry, deliver in person.

Optional: Have students ask and answer wh-questions for each item. In this way they will review separating these transitive phrasal verbs for pronoun objects. For example: *A: When did Adela pick up the application? B: She picked it up last week.*

> **Workbook: *pages 58-59, exercises C, D***

TOM: Now you're making sense. You put your volunteer work with the PTA on your application and résumé, didn't you?

ADELA: Sure. I really worked hard for the school.

TOM: Honey, you're one of the hardest-working people I know. And you're so well-organized. In the interview you just have to talk about all the things you've done. I'm sure you can sell yourself.

ADELA: I hope so. But none of that will mean much if they don't think I can program well.

TOM: Take it easy. You've got great references from your instructors at the technical institute. Your grades are good. They're going to be very impressed with your transcript. Just be patient. If they received a lot of applications, it will take them time to look them over and decide who to call for an interview.

ADELA: I guess you're right.

1 Vocabulary in Context 🔊

> **Complete the definitions with vocabulary from Tom and Adela's conversation or from the introduction.**
>
> 1. A vacancy for a job is called a/an _____ .
> 2. The form you fill out to get a job is a/an _____ . When you turn it in, you _____ the job.
> 3. A/An _____ is a conversation you have with a representative of a company to find out if you are the person they are looking for and if the company is right for you.
> 4. If you have worked before, you have job _____ .
> 5. In your _____ , you summarize essential information about your education, work experience, and skills.
> 6. _____ are people who know you and who are willing to write letters of recommendation for you.
> 7. A/An _____ is an official school document showing the courses you have taken and the grades you received.

2 Reentry

Separable phrasal verbs

Think of a good paraphrase for the underlined phrasal verbs that are often used when talking about job applications.

1. Adela went to the Dallas Electric Company to <u>pick up</u> an application.
2. She was careful to ask the secretary about the deadline for <u>turning</u> it <u>in</u>.

3. She took the application home and <u>filled</u> it <u>out</u> carefully.

4. She <u>filled in</u> all the information. She didn't <u>leave</u> anything <u>out</u>.

5. Before she <u>sent</u> the application <u>back</u>, she <u>looked</u> it <u>over</u> carefully to be sure she hadn't forgotten anything.

6. At the last minute she decided to <u>take</u> it <u>back</u> to the company herself rather than mail it.

▓3▓ Presentation 🔲

Emphasizing with *still* and the present perfect

> **Still** + *the present perfect* has the same meaning as **yet**, but it is more emphatic. It suggests a long time, and often a degree of frustration.

> TOM: Has the Electric Company called yet?
> ADELA: No. They **still haven't called.**

▓4▓ Practice

Five people in an English class have said that they are going to apply for a special scholarship to help pay their college tuition and expenses. Look at the chart and ask and answer questions about what these people have and haven't done.

Name	Pick up	Fill out	Turn in
Jose	6/1	6/3	
Ana	6/1		
Yara			
Li Ping	6/3	6/3	
Pierre	6/2		

> A: Has Jose picked up his application yet?
> B: Yes. He picked it up June 1st.
> A: Has he filled it out?
> B: Yes, he has, but he still hasn't turned it in.

▓3▓ Presentation

PROCEDURE

1. Refer to General Guidelines for Presentation, page ix.
2. To expand the Presentation, ask other questions that students answer using *still* and the present perfect; for example: *Have you found your ____ yet? Has the teacher returned your papers yet? Have you seen (the best movie in town) yet?*

LANGUAGE NOTE

Still and *yet* can both be emphasized with the following difference in meaning:

*I **still** haven't done it.* (And I don't know if or when I will.)

*I haven't done it **yet**.* (But I am going to do it.)

▓4▓ Practice

PROCEDURE

1. Refer to General Guidelines for Practice, page x.
2. Ask a few yes/no questions to be sure students can find information in the chart. (*Has Jose picked up the application?*)

Answers: Answers will follow the model.

■ EXPANSION ACTIVITY: She still hasn't decided

1. Have students bring pictures showing people doing various things; for example, cleaning the house, fishing, studying, playing football.
2. Put the pictures on the wall and have students write five statements using the present perfect continuous to tell what the person has been *planning to do, thinking about doing,* or *worrying about*. The statements should contain a clue to help others identify the picture. For example, *He has been worrying about getting hurt.* (football player)
3. A student reads one of his/her statements. Another student identifies the picture and says something about what still hasn't happened. *He still hasn't gotten hurt.* or *He still hasn't decided to leave the football team.*
4. The student who correctly identifies the picture and makes a correct statement with *still* has the next turn to read a sentence.

Workbook: *page 60, exercise E*

5 Presentation

PROCEDURE
1. Refer to General Guidelines for Presentation, page ix.
2. Refer to Language Notes for Presentation 9, on page 29, for general comments on tag questions.

6 Practice

PROCEDURE

Refer to General Guidelines for Practice, page x.

Optional: Personalize this Practice by having students write statements with tag questions to check information about their classmates. For example, *You started studying English this year, didn't you?*

Answers: Responses to the tag questions will vary. #1 and 2 are given as examples. **1.** A: The move went well, didn't it? B: Not really. Their furniture arrived three weeks late. **2.** A: Sam didn't move to Texas, did he? B: No, he didn't. He liked his job, and he wanted to keep on studying at the Community College. **3.** didn't he? **4.** didn't she? **5.** didn't she? **6.** didn't she? **7.** did she? **8.** didn't they? **9.** did she? **10.** didn't they?

> **Workbook: *pages 61-62, exercises F, G***

5 Presentation

Verifying information

> To verify information in a past tense statement, use tag questions with **did** and **didn't**.

A: The Logans moved to Texas, **didn't** they?
B: Yes, they did.
A: Lisa didn't want to move, **did** she?
B: No, she didn't.

6 Practice

With a partner, check the accuracy of the following statements by adding a tag question. In some cases you must use your imagination in the response.

1. The move went well.

2. Sam didn't move to Texas.

3. Bob found a job easily.

4. Adela started looking at the same time as Bob.

5. Adela applied for a job at the Dallas Electric Company last month.

6. Adela put her work with the PTA on her application.

7. She didn't forget anything on her application.

8. Adela and Tom both worked at Wells Travel Agency.

9. Adela didn't go to college after high school.

10. Adela and Tom both wanted to move to Texas.

Short responses with *think, hope, guess*

A Responding with what you believe

> A: Did you have a good interview, Sue?
> B: I **think** so. I answered all the questions.
> A: Did you forget anything important?
> B: I don't **think** so. I prepared well.

B Responding with what you hope

> A: Do you think they will call you for a second interview?
> B: I **hope** so, but it's been a week and they still haven't called!
> A: Do you think they lost your application?
> B: I **hope** not!

C Responding with reluctance

> A: Do you think you're going to get the job?
> B: I **guess** not. I haven't heard anything, and it's been over a month.
> A: Would you take the job if they did offer it to you?
> B: I **guess** so, because I need a job, but I really wasn't very impressed with the company.

PROCEDURE
1. Refer to General Guidelines for Presentation, page ix.
2. To expand the Presentation, ask questions such as: *Are you going to have a nice weekend? Are you going to find the book you lost? Are you going to break a leg in the next soccer game?*

LANGUAGE NOTE
We also express reluctance with *I'm afraid not* or *I'm afraid so*. Since students often misunderstand these expressions as communicating real fear, they can be taught to use them to express reluctance by associating them with the expressions with *guess*.

8 Practice

PROCEDURE
1. Refer to General Guidelines for Practice, page x.
2. Put half the pairs on one side of the room, half on the other. Questions from one side are answered initially by students on the other side. Continue with class discussion of those questions that interest students.

■ EXPANSION ACTIVITY: Adela's future (Reentry of future obligations and possibilities)

Have students talk or write about Adela's and the Logans' future if she gets the job at the Dallas Electric Company and if she does not. Give students the following sentences to complete, using *will (won't)/ might (might not)* and *have to* or *be able to.*

1. If Adela gets the job at the Dallas Electric Company, ____.
2. If she doesn't get the job, ____.

Workbook: *page 62, exercise H*

9 Vocabulary in Context

PROCEDURE
1. Refer to General Guidelines for Vocabulary in Context, page ix.
2. Elicit the new words by giving the definitions only.

Optional: Review relative clauses by asking students to complete definitions such as: *An honest person is a person who ____.* or *A person who perseveres will ____.*

8 Practice

Work with a partner. Write four questions that ask for your classmates' opinions about topics of interest in the world, your country, city, or school. Then ask your classmates for their opinions. Begin your answers with one of the expressions with *think, hope,* and *guess* in 7. Continue talking about those topics that interest you. Here are some possible questions:

> Is there life on other planets?
>
> Are gas prices ever going to go down?
>
> Do brothers and sisters always fight?

9 Vocabulary in Context

Talking about what makes a good employee

When interviewers talk with job applicants, they are looking for people who will be good employees. What kinds of people make good employees?

1. **Honest** people tell the truth. They don't lie.
2. **Enthusiastic** people are excited about what they are doing.
3. **Hardworking** or **industrious** people know how to work hard and get good results.
4. **Imaginative, creative** people use their minds to find new ways to do things.
5. **Well-organized** people can find things when they want them or need them. They keep things organized systematically. They are usually good at planning.
6. **Responsible, dependable** people do what they say they will do.
7. **Cooperative** people work well with other people. They listen to others; they share information and work together.
8. Good employees **take the initiative**. Nobody has to tell them to do something. When they see something that needs to be done, they do it.
9. People who can make changes quite easily are **adaptable**. They are always ready to learn a new way to do something.
10. Employers always want people who will **persevere**, who will **keep going** even when the situation gets very difficult. **Persevering** people usually get results because they **finish what they start**.

10 Practice

Bob Logan got one of the two jobs at the sandwich shop. Four other people applied for the other opening. First read the ad that Bob and the others saw in the newspaper. Then complete the recommendations for each applicant with the correct words from 9. Finally, talk with a classmate about which applicant you think should get the job and why. Share your opinion with the class.

SANDWICH SHOP
Need two part-time employees afternoons, evening, weekends. No experience necessary. For interview appointment: **Call Ms. De Castro** **671-9848**

May Ling

INTERVIEW NOTES: high school junior, has done babysitting, free after 3:00 PM, neat appearance and application, quiet but a good communicator

Recommendation from Ms. Julie Wagner, teacher
May Ling is a great addition to class. She is intelligent, hardworking, and _____; she makes changes easily. She is _____ and works well on a team because she knows how to share work with others. She's quite _____, too. She comes up with lots of interesting ideas, and she is a good artist.

Ron Tishler

INTERVIEW NOTES: high school junior, no experience, but president of his class, free after 3:00 PM, very talkative and outgoing, seems sure of himself

Recommendation from Mr. Anthony Silva, principal
Ron is very _____. If he says he will do something, he will do it. He's also very _____. He keeps the details of all class projects up-to-date and in good order. Without a doubt he is one of our best young leaders.

Eduardo Toledo

INTERVIEW NOTES: college freshman, two years in the army, free after 5:00 PM, very self-confident

Recommendation from Sgt. John Nelson, 102nd Infantry Division
Pvt. Toledo was a great addition to the unit. He accepted any job we gave him, and he got it done. Nothing stopped him; he _____ even under the worst conditions. He's also a very happy and _____ person. He is interested in and excited about everything. He knows how to work hard and have fun.

10 Practice

PROCEDURE
1. Refer to General Guidelines for Practice, page x.
2. Read the instructions and have students read the ad. Ask simple questions to check their understanding of this background information.
3. Have students work independently on the completion exercise and compare their answers with a classmate. Remind them it is sometimes necessary to read beyond the blank to know how to complete a sentence.
4. Check answers to the completion exercise with the whole class.
5. Have students read the interview notes and discuss which applicant should get the job.
6. Record the choice of each pair of students on the board to see how much agreement there is. Discuss any differences of opinion, having pairs give their reasons for choosing one applicant over another.

Answers: **May Ling:** adaptable; cooperative; creative, imaginative; **Ron Tishler:** dependable, responsible; well-organized; **Eduardo Toledo:** kept going, persevered; enthusiastic; **Helen Langstrom:** hardworking, industrious; takes the initiative; honest

■ EXPANSION ACTIVITY: I'm hardworking
If students are going to interview for jobs, they will benefit from practice in demonstrating their personality traits by telling about something they have done. They can begin by saying *I'm hardworking* or *I take the initiative,* but then they must tell about an experience in which they worked hard or took the initiative. Most students need this practice in talking about themselves and selling their good qualities.

Workbook: *page 63, exercise I*

11 Listing

PROCEDURE

1. Refer to General Guidelines for Listening, page x.
2. Play the tape or read the script for the Listening. The tape includes the directions on page 140.
3. *If reading the script:* For the First Listening, give students 10 seconds after each comment to decide which question was asked. For the Second Listening, give students 20 seconds after each comment to write at least one characteristic.

Script

Comment 1
I haven't had a paying job, but I've always helped my father fix things around the house. He's a good teacher. I've learned to do just about everything. I can paint, take care of the yard, repair the car, and fix the plumbing. One time I noticed that the kitchen sink was leaking, and I fixed it before my father came home from work.

Comment 2
Yes, my family just moved to this town. It has been a little difficult. We were living in Houston when my dad got this chance to come to Winfield. I wasn't too happy at first because Winfield is so small; but I've made some new friends and I really love it now.

Comment 3
I'm taking the secretarial program at Westlake High and I'll be graduating in June. I've always wanted to be a secretary. I like the idea of working with other people, meeting the public, and I really like to keep things organized. I'm happiest when everything is in its place, and I can find it easily. Also my teachers have told me that I am good at following instructions, and a secretary certainly has to be able to do that.

Comment 4
No, I haven't, but I love to play basketball with my friends. I once thought maybe I could play on the varsity team at school, but I guess I'm just not tall or fast enough. I keep practicing, and I try out for the team every year, but I guess I have to understand that professional basketball is not in my future.

Helen Langstrom

INTERVIEW NOTES: high school senior, worked six months in a fast food restaurant, free after 3:00 PM, serious, quiet

Recommendation from Mr. Fred Lau, manager of Freddie's Diner
Helen is very ____ . You can give her any job and she will work overtime if necessary to finish it. She also ____ ; if she sees something needs doing, she does it. Nobody is more ____ than Helen. She tells you what she really thinks.

11 Listening

First Listening

Number your paper from 1-4. Leave three lines between numbers. You will hear comments made by students in job interviews. First decide which question the interviewer asked.

1. **a.** What do you like to do in your free time?
   b. Tell me about some of the jobs you have had.
   c. Do you help your father around the house?
2. **a.** Are you new in town?
   b. Have you always lived here?
   c. Which do you like better, your old hometown or your new one?
3. **a.** Do you like to build things?
   b. What do you do best?
   c. Tell me a little bit about yourself.
4. **a.** What's your favorite subject in school?
   b. Do you like to participate in sports?
   c. Have you ever played on a team?

Second Listening

Listen again and write down at least one characteristic from *Vocabulary in Context* 9 that each person demonstrates. There may be more than one good answer. Be ready to explain your choice(s).

12 Writing

A. **Pretend you are applying for a job at Sandwich Ranch. Discuss the various sections of the application with a partner.**

B. **Fill out the application.**

C. **Read your partner's application. Ask questions if something is not clear.**

EMPLOYMENT APPLICATION FOR GENERAL RESTAURANT WORK

───────── **PERSONAL INFORMATION** *(please print clearly)* ─────────

NAME _____ TEL. # (____) _____
      Last   First   Middle   Area Code

ADDRESS: _____ CITY _____ STATE ____ ZIP _____
SOCIAL SECURITY NO. _____

Ever Work for Sandwich Ranch Before? ❑ Yes ❑ No If yes, when/where _____

In Case of Emergency Notify:
NAME _____ TEL. # (____) _____
      Last   First   Relation   Area Code

ADDRESS _____ CITY _____ STATE ____ ZIP _____

───────── **AVAILABILITY** ─────────

What type of position are you seeking? ❑ Part-Time ❑ Full-Time

	M	T	W	T	F	S	S
HOURS From							
AVAILABLE To							

───────── **SCHOOL MOST RECENTLY ATTENDED** ─────────

NAME _____ ADDRESS _____
Counselor _____ Last Grade Completed _____ Grade Average _____
GRADUATED? ❑ Yes ❑ No NOW ENROLLED? ❑ Yes ❑ No
Sports or Activities _____

───────── **MOST RECENT EMPLOYMENT** ─────────

Company _____ Address _____ Tel: # _____
Position _____ Supervisor _____ Dates Worked: From ___ To: ____
Wage _____ Reason for Leaving _____

Company _____ Address _____ Tel: # _____
Position _____ Supervisor _____ Dates Worked: From ___ To: ____
Wage _____ Reason for Leaving _____

───────── **PHYSICAL** ─────────

Any Health or Physical limitations that could affect your employment? ❑ Yes ❑ No
If yes, please explain: _____

I CERTIFY THAT THIS INFORMATION IS ACCURATE AND COMPLETE. GIVING INCOMPLETE OR FALSE INFORMATION IN AN APPLICATION FOR EMPLOYMENT IS A SERIOUS MATTER AND IS GROUNDS FOR DISMISSAL. I HEREBY ACKNOWLEDGE NOTIFICATION THAT SANDWICH RANCH MAY REQUEST INFORMATION REGARDING MY CHARACTER, GENERAL REPUTATION OR MODE OF LIVING.
DATE _____ SIGNATURE _____

───────── **FOR OFFICE USE ONLY** ─────────

Interviewer or Reference Comments _____

Answers: First and Second Listening: **Comment 1**: b. **Possible characteristics**: honest, hardworking, responsible, takes the initiative **Comment 2**: a. **Possible characteristics**: honest, adaptable **Comment 3**: c. **Possible characteristics**: cooperative, well-organized, enthusiastic **Comment 4**: c. **Possible characteristics**: honest, hardworking, persevering

12 Writing

PROCEDURE
1. Refer to General Guidelines for Writing, page xi.
2. Have two students read the application together and talk about things they do not understand.
3. Have students fill out the application independently.
4. Have students exchange papers with a partner and check each other's applications. They can make changes.

Optional: Use these words from the application to give additional practice in guessing the meaning of words from context and paraphrasing: *availability/available* (can start work), *seek* (look for), *enrolled* (presently in school), *wage* (salary), *accurate* (correct), *dismissal* (firing, you have to leave the job), *acknowledge notification* (agree that somebody told/notified me), *regarding* (about), *character* (what kind of person I am morally), *reputation* (what people think of the way I act), *mode of living* (lifestyle, the way I live).

13 Reading

PROCEDURE
1. Refer to General Guidelines for Reading, page x.
2. After students read the interview silently, have them discuss answers to the "First Reading" questions in small groups and give you a single written copy of the group's answers.
3. Have students discuss and write answers to the "Second Reading" questions with a partner.

Answers: *First Reading:* **1.** Suggestion #1. Plan well; #2. Be yourself; #3. Relax and have a conversation with the interviewer; #4. Don't give simple yes-no answers. Always give examples; Last suggestion: See things from the interviewer's point of view. **2.** In some cases, no. But in other cases, yes. Therefore, "Be your self. It's really important for the interviewer to like you and want to give you a chance."

---

13 Reading

Before You Read

1. What do you think a Director of Personnel would know a lot about?
2. Suppose you want to have a very good job interview. What should you do or not do?

First Reading

Read the questions below before reading "Succeeding in a Job Interview." Think about the questions as you read. After reading the interview, answer the questions in complete sentences. Discuss the answers in small groups.

1. What are Mr. Lee's basic suggestions?
2. Do you have a chance for a job if you don't have experience?

Succeeding in a Job Interview: Four Essentials

We are grateful to Mr. Raymond Lee, Director of Personnel at the Dallas Electric Company, for giving us permission to print the following transcription of a recent conversation we had with him.

Intercom 2000: As Director of Personnel at the Dallas Electric Company, you have interviewed a lot of people for a lot of different jobs. Could you give us some suggestions for succeeding in a job interview?

Mr. Lee: I certainly could. First, plan well. One type of planning is to list all paid or volunteer work you have done, where you did it, who your boss was, exactly what you did, and what you learned there — that is, how the experience helped you grow professionally. You also need to think about what kind of person you are, what you like to do and why. If you haven't thought about things like that ahead of time, you're asking for trouble.

Intercom 2000: And what if you have no work experience at all?

Mr. Lee: Well, in some cases you won't have a chance without experience. That's just a fact of life. But in other cases, remember my second suggestion — be yourself. It's really important for the interviewer to like you and want to give you a chance. Show enthusiasm for hard work, talk about how you have handled daily problems well, show that you want to succeed in what you do.

Intercom 2000: You mean qualifications aren't everything?

Mr. Lee: In most cases, there is more than one applicant who has the basic qualifications. The people who make the final decision usually hire people they would like to work with.

Intercom 2000: I see.

Mr. Lee: My third and fourth suggestions are related. Number 3 — relax and have a conversation with the interviewer. Number 4 — no simple yes-no answers. Always give examples. Talk about yourself and what you've done enthusiastically and in detail. Interviewers don't want to hear only general comments like "I like to work hard." Talk about some hard work you did, for example, how you fixed your family car or took care of younger brothers and sisters so your parents could work. The only way interviewers can tell what you are going to do in the future is from what you have done in the past.

Intercom 2000: Before you go, Mr. Lee, do you have any other suggestions you would like to make?

Mr. Lee: Yes, I do. This may sound like common sense, but try to see things from my point of view. I'm looking for someone who will do good work for my company and represent my company well in public. Be sure you know what kind of business my company or organization does. And be sure you dress for business, not for a sporting event. In a brief interview like this, I think that's the best advice I can give.

Second Reading

Now work with a partner and talk over answers to these questions.

1. In planning for a job interview, what should you write out and what should you think a lot about?

2. Why is it important for an interviewer to like you?

3. What's wrong with answering "I like to work hard"?

4. What does Mr. Lee mean when he says, "Try to see things from my point of view"?

5. Make a list of the things interviewers are looking for.

PROCEDURE

1. Refer to General Guidelines for Final Activity, page xi.
2. Have partners work together and prepare a 3 x 5 card for each question. It should include the question at the top and notes to remind the speaker of the answer. Then have partners decide how to divide the oral report and each speaks from the appropriate notes.
3. If students use ads from local newspapers, have them make a large copy of the ad to put on the wall.
4. Try to have each pair report about a different ad. *Optional:* In large classes using only the ads in the text, have students report first in small groups where all pairs have prepared different ads. Regroup the class and select one pair to report on each ad to the class.

Workbook: *page 64, exercises J, K*

Work with a partner. Choose one of the employment ads on this page or find one in your local newspaper. Talk with your partner about answers to the following questions. Together give a short oral report about the job.

1. What do you know about the employer?
2. What kind of job is available?
3. What qualifications does the applicant have to have?
4. Where can you get more information if you are interested in this job?
5. What would your life be like if you accepted this job?
6. Who would you recommend this job to?

Travel Agent

★ Full-time
★ Minimum two years experience
★ Excellent health plan and travel benefits
673-8675 / 673-8676

The friendliest hotel in area is looking for a HOUSEKEEPING SUPERVISOR

If you meet the following requirements:
✂ Bilingual: English-Spanish
✂ Friendly and enthusiastic
✂ Well-organized
WE WOULD LIKE TO MEET YOU!!
Please submit résumé to:
PERSONNEL DIRECTOR
P.O. Box 3809
Winfield, New York 11500

COMPUTER OPERATOR

Requirements:
Data entry, word processing, and spreadsheet software
12:00 PM-8:00 PM weekdays
Please send résumé to:
P.O. Box 1367
Winfield, New York 11500

Dental Assistant

Experience required.

Send résumé and references.
P.O. Box 446
Winfield, New York 11500

Growing consulting company is seeking:

Secretary
Requirements:
◆ Associate or Bachelor's Degree
◆ Self-motivated
◆ Willing to assume additional responsibilities
◆ Able to work for more than one individual
◆ Experience not necessary

Purchasing Agent
Requirements:
◆ Bachelor's Degree
◆ Minimum three years experience
◆ Self-motivated
◆ Willing to work long hours
◆ Salary and fringe benefits commensurate with experience

Please Send Résumé:
PERSONNEL DEPARTMENT
P.O. Box 550
Winfield, New York 11500

UNIT 11

COMMUNICATION
Talking about past habits or customs ▪ Talking about changes ▪ Selling your abilities in an interview

GRAMMAR
Used to + verb ▪ Present perfect questions with *ever* ▪ Gerunds after prepositions

SKILLS
Writing about a change in one's life ▪ Listening to a job interview ▪ Reading a letter to a newspaper advice columnist

Adela's Interview

Several days ago, the Dallas Electric Company called Adela for an interview. Adela has just greeted the Personnel Director, Mr. Lee, and his assistant, Ms. Ruiz.

MR. LEE: Why don't you start by telling me a little bit about yourself, Mrs. Logan.

ADELA: Well, I just finished a two-year program in computer programming at the Technical Institute in Winfield, New York, where I lived until about a month ago. Now I'm interested in putting my skills to work.

MR. LEE: From your résumé I see that you have not had a full-time job as a programmer. Could you tell us something about the programming experience you *have* had?

ADELA: First of all, my courses at the Institute were very good and offered a lot of practical programming experience. In addition, I worked for a year with one of my instructors. I helped customize certain software programs for businesses in Winfield. One was for a pharmacy and another was for an insurance company.

Useful materials: résumé models; pictures showing people or situations before and after

Adela's Interview

PROCEDURE

Refer to General Guidelines for Opener, page ix.

COMPREHENSION QUESTIONS

Now listen to these sentences. Say *Yes, that's right, No, that's wrong,* or *I don't know. Maybe.*

1. Adela begins by telling Mr. Lee about her education. *Yes, that's right.*
2. She tells Mr. Lee that she has moved to Dallas recently. *Yes, that's right.*
3. Mr. Lee asks Adela to tell him about all the jobs she has had. *No, that's wrong.* (He asks about her experience in programming.)
4. Adela explains her work with her instructor in detail. *Yes, that's right.*
5. Dallas Electric Company is looking for a person who can work well with other people. *Yes, that's right.*
6. Adela didn't like the work with the PTA. *No, that's wrong.* (The work was satisfying.)
7. Adela wants paid work now because her family needs money. *I don't know. Maybe.*
8. Adela taught herself to use the school computers. *I don't know. Maybe.* (Maybe students taught her.)
9. Adela decided to study programming because she was always good at math in high school. *Yes, that's right.*

DISCUSSION QUESTIONS

1. What do you think Mr. Lee, Ms. Ruiz, and Adela said to each other before the start of the conversation?
2. What should a person do and not do if he or she wants to make a good impression in a job interview? Point out ways in which Adela makes a good impression.

LANGUAGE NOTE

In addition to greeting Adela and inviting her to sit down, Mr. Lee or Ms. Ruiz might open the conversation with some small talk. Typical small talk at an interview might be about the weather, the candidate's trip to the interview, or the company facilities.

■ EXPANSION ACTIVITY: Writing a résumé

If your students are going to need a personal résumé in the not-too-distant future, provide them with a model from a business textbook and help them prepare their own. Begin by having the class write a résumé for Adela Logan, based on the information in Units 10 and 11. Invent important information not found in the units, such as address and telephone number. Then have students write their own résumé.

1 Vocabulary in Context

PROCEDURE
Refer to General Guidelines for Vocabulary in Context, page ix.

Answers: **A. 1.** full-time **2.** courses **3.** supervisory; supervised **4.** volunteer **5.** challenge **6.** keep **7.** Personnel **B. 1.** said hello to **2.** adapt a computer program to the needs of a special business/user **3.** help, guide, encourage (The idea is people will work together well because she is a good supervisor.) **4.** made **5.** motivate people to talk openly to each other **6.** learn what people's abilities are and give them that kind of work

Workbook: *page 65, exercises A, B*

MS. RUIZ: I'm sure that was good experience. We're also interested in finding someone who has supervisory experience. Have you ever supervised other people?

ADELA: Yes, I have, in my volunteer work with the PTA in Winfield. I was president for two years, and I learned a lot about getting along with people and getting them to work well together. The important thing, I believe, is to encourage open communication and to find the right job for each person. Not everybody can do everything well. A supervisor has to find out what people's talents are and put those talents to work.

MR. LEE: I certainly agree with you. It sounds like your work with the PTA was very valuable. . . . Now, why did you decide to go back to school?

ADELA: The PTA work was very satisfying . . . in fact it was a real challenge and I used to be happy doing that kind of volunteer work . . . but it also opened my eyes to some other possibilities. Students helped us keep our records on a computer. They were so excited about their work that they got me excited, too. I was always good at math in high school, so studying programming seemed like the right thing to do.

1 Vocabulary in Context 🔲

A. **Complete the following definitions with words from Adela's interview with Mr. Lee and Ms. Ruiz and from the introduction.**

1. If you work an eight-hour day in the United States, you work ____ .

2. Classes at a university or college are often called ____ .

3. If you have worked as a boss or manager, you have ____ experience. You have ____ other employees.

4. Non-paid work is called ____ work.

5. If a job is not easy for you, it offers you a/an ____ .

6. When you save information on paper or in a computer, you ____ records.

7. The ____ Office handles matters related to the employees of a company.

B. Now talk about what these sentences mean. Say them in a different way. Be sure to paraphrase the underlined words.

1. Adela has just <u>greeted</u> the Personnel Director.

2. I helped <u>customize</u> certain software programs for businesses.

3. Adela can <u>get</u> people to work well together.

4. The students <u>got</u> Adela excited about computers.

5. The important thing is to <u>encourage open communication</u>.

6. A supervisor has to <u>find out</u> what people's <u>talents</u> are and <u>put those talents to work</u>.

2 Presentation

Talking about past habits or customs

> Use **used to** + *base form of the verb* to talk about something that was true for a period of time in the past, but is not true anymore.

Affirmative:	**used to**
Negative:	**didn't use to**
Interrogative:	**Did** . . . **use to** . . . ?

A Adela **used to** be satisfied doing volunteer work. (She isn't satisfied anymore.)

B Adela **didn't use to** want a full-time job.

C
INTERVIEWER:	Mrs. Logan, **did** you **use to** work for a travel agency?
ADELA:	Yes, I did. I worked at Wells Travel Agency for two years.

2 Presentation

PROCEDURE
1. Refer to General Guidelines for Presentation, page ix.
2. Before beginning this Presentation, review talking about present habits using adverbs of frequency: *I usually study in the library. I always eat breakfast. I never go to bed before 10:00 PM.*
3. To expand the Presentation, have students write a sentence beginning *I used to _____.* (For example; *live in a different city, go to a different school, study a different language.*)
4. Have students practice in a chain. One student reads his or her statement. The next one asks a question with *used to*; for example, *Where did you use to live/ go to school/work?*

LANGUAGE NOTES
1. *Used to* is a past tense modal auxiliary expression and is used before a base verb. Questions and negative statements use *did* and *didn't + use to.*
2. *Anymore* (one word) is an adverb meaning *now, at this time. Any more* (two words) refers to any more of something; for example, *Thanks for offering me more cake, but I don't want any more.*

3 Practice

PROCEDURE

PROCEDURE

1. Refer to General Guidelines for Practice, page x.
2. Talk about the pictures and do part A with the class.
3. Pair students for Part B. Circulate and offer help as needed. End with a class discussion.

Answers: **A. 1.** used to/rich **2.** didn't use to/relax more often **3.** didn't use to/he spends a lot of money on clothes **4.** used to/she is a businesswoman **5.** used to/she sits at a desk **6.** didn't use to/she reads reports every day **7.** didn't use to/they have three **8.** used to/their car is old and scratched **9.** used to/ they stay home with the kids **10.** didn't use to /the kids leave toys everywhere. *Some possible answers:* **B.** Harry used to wear jeans all the time. Now he wears expensive suits. Sumie didn't use to work in an office. Now she has a beautiful office with a nice desk. Salvador and Betty used to watch mystery movies. Now they watch cartoons.

■ EXPANSION ACTIVITY: He used to be on top

1. Have students write two paragraphs to finish this story about J. G. Moneybundle. In one paragraph, they write about the way things used to be and about the things he won't be able to do anymore. In the other paragraph, they write what they think J. G. is going to do next.
2. Have students read their endings or put them on the wall for others to read.

J. G. Moneybundle used to be on top of the world. He used to make billions of dollars a year. He was the battery king, the maker of the longest-lasting battery on Earth. It could power your flashlight for five years. But J. G. Moneybundle didn't know that someone would invent the permanent battery, one that wouldn't wear out. This new invention brought the Moneybundle Corporation to its knees, and in a matter of months J. G. didn't have a penny to his name. Now in the street in tattered clothing, he remembers how his life used to be before Millie and the children left him. . . .

3 Practice

A. Complete the sentences about the people in the pictures using *used to* and *didn't use to*. Then make a comment about what is true now.

Harry then   **Harry now**

1. Harry _____ be a poor, hardworking farmer. Now he is _____ .
2. He _____ have a lot of free time. Now he can _____ .
3. He _____ wear expensive clothes. Now _____ .

Sumie then   **Sumie now**

4. Sumie _____ be a waitress. Now _____ .
5. She _____ work on her feet. Now _____ .
6. Reading _____ be part of her job. Now _____ .

Salvador and Betty then   **Salvador and Betty now**

7. Salvador and Betty _____ have any kids. Now _____ .
8. They _____ have a brand new car. Now _____ .
9. They _____ go out a lot. Now _____ .
10. They _____ have a lot of toys around the house. Now _____ .

B. Now work with a partner and write four more sentences about each set of pictures — two sentences about how things *used to* be and two about how they are *now*. Talk with your partner and decide what you think caused the change. Share your ideas with the class.

4 Interaction

Write down three things that you used to do but you don't do anymore. For example: *I used to smoke, I used to play the guitar,* and *I used to drive too fast.* (Don't write your name on your paper.) Give your paper to your teacher who will distribute the lists around the class. Ask your classmates questions and find the person whose paper you have. Then talk with the person and find out:

- when he or she started doing each thing
- how long he or she did each thing
- when and why he or she stopped doing each thing

After finding out the answers, report the information to the class.

5 Presentation

Present perfect questions with *ever*

> Use **ever** in present perfect questions when you mean at any time in the past.

Ms. Ruiz:	**Have** you **ever supervised** other people?
Adela:	Yes, I have. A lot of people worked for me when I was president of the PTA.
Mr. Lee:	**Have** you **ever had** trouble getting along with people?
Adela:	No, never. I like working with other people. I've always learned a lot from other people.

6 Practice

Work with a partner. Ask and answer questions using the cues. Make an additional comment. Verbs and verb tenses in the response will vary.

> Adela / do volunteer work (PTA)
> A: Has Adela ever done volunteer work?
> B: Yes, she has. She did volunteer work for the PTA.

1. Adela / have a full-time job (yes / travel agency)
2. Gloria / live in Puerto Rico (no / born in New York)
3. Gloria's mother / live in Puerto Rico (yes / born there)

4 Interaction

PROCEDURE
1. Refer to General Guidelines for Interaction, page x.
2. Demonstrate the Interaction to be sure students practice the correct question (*Did you use to ____?*).

Optional: Collect students' three sentences at the end of one class. Use in the next or a later class.

■ EXPANSION ACTIVITY: Expanded Interaction report

Have students write a paragraph about one thing that has changed in the life of the person they talked to in Interaction 4. They should begin by telling who they talked to and what he or she used to do. Then they continue with information about how long the person did that thing and when and why he or she stopped. They can add other information they learned about the change from the conversation, possibly including the person's attitude toward the change. (Is he/she happy with the change or not? Why or why not?)

■ EXPANSION ACTIVITY 11A: What did you use to think? (page 193)
■ EXPANSION ACTIVITY 11B: Changes (page 193)

> Workbook: *page 66, exercises C, D*

5 Presentation

PROCEDURE
Refer to General Guidelines for Presentation, page ix.

6 Practice

PROCEDURE
1. Refer to General Guidelines for Practice, page x.
2. Do as a whole class or pair practice.

Answers: **1.** Has Adela ever had a full-time job? / Yes, she has. She worked in a travel agency. **2.** Has Gloria ever lived in Puerto Rico? / No, she hasn't. She was born in New York. **3.** Has Gloria's mother ever lived in Puerto Rico? Yes, she has. She was born there.

Answers (continued):   **4.** Have the Youngs ever lived in New York City? No, they haven't. They have always lived in Winfield.   **5.** Has Mike ever gone to Mexico? Yes, he has. He spent one summer in Mexico City. **6.** Has Bob ever been to Mexico? No, he hasn't. He has not been out of the U.S.   **7.** Have the Logans ever bought a new car? No, they haven't. They have bought used cars.   **8.** Have you ever written a poem or story? **9.** Have you ever made a mistake while cooking? **10.** Have you ever bought something you didn't like?

7 Interaction

PROCEDURE
1. Refer to General Guidelines for Interaction, page x.
2. Have students take turns being the questioner. A secretary can keep count for each survey.
3. Have groups report their totals, question by question, and keep a record on the board. Talk about the most interesting experiences.

Optional: Substitute one or more of the following experiences for those in the book: *changed jobs; called someone in another country; stayed up all night; missed an important plane, train, or bus; performed in a play; gotten a famous person's autograph.*

■ EXPANSION ACTIVITY: Things I've never done, but would like to do

1. Without prior class discussion, have students write a paragraph about things they have never done, but would like to do.
2. Have students read their paragraphs or talk about their dreams.
3. Talk with the class about dreams they have in common and how their dreams differ and why.

Workbook: *page 67, exercises E, F*

8 Writing

PROCEDURE
Refer to General Guidelines for Writing, page xi.

9 Listening

PROCEDURE
1. Refer to General Guidelines for Listening, page x.
2. Play the tape or read the script for the Listening. The tape includes the directions on page 151.
3. *If reading the script;* For the First Listening, give students 15 seconds to answer questions 1-3. For the

4. the Youngs / live in New York City (no / always lived in Winfield)
5. Mike / go to Mexico (yes / spend one summer in Mexico City)
6. Bob / be to Mexico (no / not be out of the U.S.)
7. the Logans / buy a new car (no / used cars)
8. you / write a poem or story
9. you / make a mistake while cooking
10. you / buy something you didn't like

7 Interaction

Form a group of four or five. Find out how many people in your group have ever done the following. Ask additional questions about their experiences.

1. moved from one city to another (when, why)
2. visited another country (which, when, why)
3. been in a car accident (when, with whom, what)
4. seen a ghost or UFO (where, when, what)
5. done volunteer work (what kind, where, when, why)
6. worked part-time or full-time (where, when, how long)

> **Useful vocabulary:**
>
> **ghost** =
>
> **UFO** (Unidentified Flying Object) =

Report your findings to the class. Share any interesting stories you heard or information you learned.

8 Writing

A.   Talk with a classmate about a change in your life or in the life of a person you know well. It might be a change in residence, schools, jobs, or hobbies.

B.   Write three paragraphs about this change. Use this outline as a guide.

PARAGRAPH 1: **Introduction**
What was the change? When and where did it happen?

PARAGRAPH 2: **Body**
Describe things before and after the change. Make comparisons if possible.

PARAGRAPH 3: **Conclusion**
Evaluate the change. Did the change make your life better or worse? Would you do things again the same way or would you do something differently?

C.   Read your partner's paper and ask questions if something isn't clear.

9 Listening 📼

Number your paper from 1-3. Quickly reread the interview Adela had with Mr. Lee and Ms. Ruiz on pages 145-146.

First Listening

Now listen to the rest of the interview. Then choose the correct answers to questions 1-3.

1. What is Mr. Lee's first question?
   a. Where did you work before?
   b. Why would you like to work for us?
   c. Would you rather work by yourself or with others?

2. What worries Mr. Lee?
   a. Adela might not be a good employee.
   b. Adela might not like the company.
   c. Adela might not stay in Texas.

3. What does Adela ask about?
   a. taking classes
   b. vacations
   c. salary

Second Listening

Listen again and discuss answers to these questions with your classmates. If there is no information given, say so.

1. What does Mr. Lee say to give Adela a hint or idea that he thinks she is a good applicant?

2. Where did Adela get the information about the Dallas Electric Company?

3. Why does Adela think she will like working at Dallas Electric?

4. When will Adela know if she gets the job or not?

5. What words does Mr. Lee use to close the conversation? How does Adela respond?

Second Listening, discuss answers to questions 1-5 with the class.

Script

MR. LEE: Very interesting, Mrs. Logan. It sounds like you have many of the qualities we're looking for. Now why do you think you would like to work for us?

ADELA: I've read the information your secretary gave me on Dallas Electric very carefully. One of the things I like about your company is that you seem to emphasize teamwork, but at the same time you encourage people to take the initiative.

MR. LEE: I think that's a fair picture of our company.

ADELA: I'm glad to hear that because as I mentioned before, I believe I'm good at working with and learning from other people, but I am somewhat more experienced than the usual graduate. When I see something that needs doing, no one has to tell me to do it.

MR. LEE: I understand. I have just one other question, Mrs. Logan. You mentioned a moment ago that you've been living in Dallas for only a month. Do you plan to stay here for a while?

ADELA: Oh, yes. My husband is a new partner of the Lone Star Travel Agency, so we've made a permanent move.

MR. LEE: That's good to hear. Do you have any questions for me?

ADELA: Just one. Does Dallas Electric have continuing education programs?

MS. RUIZ: Yes, we do. That's my special area in dealing with personnel. If everything works out well, you'll be able to take more course work at one of the many colleges or universities in town.

ADELA: I'm very glad to hear that.

MR. LEE: If you have no more questions, I'd like to thank you for coming. You can expect to hear from us in the next week or two.

ADELA: Thank you. I'll look forward to hearing from you.

Answers: First Listening: **1.** b **2.** c **3.** a
Answers: Second Listening: **1.** He says it sounds like she has many of the qualities they're looking for. **2.** From the secretary. **3.** The company seems to emphasize teamwork but also encourages people to take the initiative. **4.** In the next week or two. **5.** Mr. Lee says, "I'd like to thank you for coming." Adela says, "I'll look forward to hearing from you."

■ EXPANSION ACTIVITY 11C: A terrible interview (page 193)

10 Reentry

PROCEDURE
1. Refer to General Guidelines for Reentry, page x.
2. Have students do the exercise individually. Check answers with the class.

Answers: **1.** having **2.** working **3.** taking care of
4. managing **5.** doing **6.** studying **7.** looking for
8. living

> Workbook: *page 68, exercises G, H*

11 Presentation

PROCEDURE
Refer to General Guidelines for Presentation, page ix.

12 Practice

PROCEDURE
1. Refer to General Guidelines for Practice, page x.
2. Have students do the Practice individually. Check with the class.

Answers: **1.** telling **2.** studying/majoring in
3. finding/having/working at **4.** getting **5.** learning
6. fixing/rebuilding/repairing/designing **7.** going
8. being **9.** giving **10.** hearing

> Workbook: *pages 68-69, exercises I, J*

10 Reentry

Gerunds as objects of verbs

Complete the sentences with the *-ing* form of one of these verbs: *do, have, live, look for, manage, study, take care of, work.*

Adela Logan went to work at Wells Travel Agency after she graduated from high school. She met Tom there, and when they started (1) _____ children, she stopped (2) _____ at Wells. While her children were young, she enjoyed (3) _____ them and (4) _____ their home. She also enjoyed (5) _____ volunteer work at Winfield High School.

When her children were almost grown, Adela started (6) _____ computer programming at the Winfield Technical Institute. Just about the time she graduated, Tom got a good offer in Texas, so they moved there. After they arrived in Dallas, Adela began (7) _____ a job. No move is easy, and there have been problems in Dallas, but she still enjoys (8) _____ there.

11 Presentation 🔲

Common interview language; gerunds after prepositions

1. Why don't you start **by telling** me a little bit about yourself?
2. We're interested **in finding** someone with supervisory experience.
3. I learned a lot **about getting** along with people.
4. I believe I'm good **at working** with other people.
5. I'd like to thank you **for coming**.
6. I'll look forward **to hearing** from you.

12 Practice

Complete the comments that might be heard in job interviews with the *-ing* form of appropriate verbs.

1. I would like to start by _____ you something about a project I'm working on.
2. Before I entered accounting, I was thinking about _____ math.
3. I'm interested in _____ a challenging job.
4. I believe I'm good at _____ along with people.

5. I definitely want to keep on ____ more about computers.
6. I've learned a lot about ____ cars in the program.
7. Instead of ____ to college, I decided to study machine repair.
8. The job at the fast food restaurant taught me a lot about ____ polite to all kinds of people.
9. I'd like to thank you for ____ me the opportunity to talk with you.
10. I'm looking forward to ____ from you.

13 Reentry

Using superlatives to sell your abilities in an interview

Complete the sentences with information about yourself. Then share your ideas with a partner.

1. One of the things I am proudest of is ____ .
2. One of the things that makes me happiest is ____ .
3. One of the things I'm best at is ____ .

14 Reading

Before You Read

1. What do you read in a newspaper advice column?
2. Have women worked outside the home as much in the past as they do now?
3. Think of a woman who has a family and works outside the home. What problems might she write about in a letter to an advice columnist?

First Reading

Read the questions below before reading the "Dear Jennifer" column. Think about the questions as you read. After reading, write answers to the questions. Discuss your answers in small groups.

1. Why is the lady "Almost Dead in Derby"?
2. Is she satisfied with her job? Why or why not?
3. Is she satisfied with her husband's and children's contributions? Why or why not?
4. What advice does she expect?

13 Reentry

PROCEDURE
1. Refer to General Guidelines for Reentry, page x.
2. Do the exercise with the class or in small groups.
3. It might help your students if you complete each sentence about yourself as an example.

CULTURAL NOTE
Most people find it difficult to talk about their good qualities, but it is more difficult for people from some cultures than from others. For that reason, think about your students' personalities before deciding whether to do this Reentry in small groups or with the class. Although most students might prefer to talk with friends, job interviews require us to say good things about ourselves to a complete stranger. Therefore, students will benefit from sharing these modest "brags" with the whole class.

Workbook: *page 69, exercise K*

14 Reading

PROCEDURE
1. Refer to General Guidelines for Reading, page x.
2. Follow the instructions in the students' text.
3. Use some of the discussion questions suggested in *Reacting to the Reading* on page 154.

Possible answers: First Reading: **1.** She is working very hard as a wife, mother, and supervisor. **2.** She doesn't express dissatisfaction, but says she wishes she didn't have to work. She works for necessities. **3.** With her husband's contribution, yes. Her husband works just as hard as she. With her children's contribution, no. They don't volunteer to help on the weekends. **4.** She will be happy to get any advice about how to handle the situation.

Possible answers: Second Reading: **1.** A matter of opinion. She apparently encourages her children to study during the week. Maybe she is too pushy. If they drive her crazy, maybe she gets angry at them. She says she doesn't have enough time to enjoy them; maybe she doesn't see them much. **2.** Too much work. (She could get the children to do more work for her.) Not enough fun. (She could make time for fun with the family.) Being overweight. (She could go on a diet and exercise program.) Her husband works night shift now. (Maybe he can change that.) She's letting her kids run her. (She should take charge of them.)

Reacting to the Reading: Discussion Questions

1. What do children need to receive from their parents to be happy?
2. How are the chores divided in your family? Do you think the division of housework is fair?

■ EXPANSION ACTIVITY: An answer from Jennifer

After students have written their responses, have them compare their ideas with Jennifer's.

Dear Almost Dead,

You have a problem. You supervise people in the factory, but you don't seem to be willing to supervise your kids' work at home. Why do you expect them to volunteer? You and your husband have to hand out the work because children need to learn that they have jobs that are their contribution to the family. It's my guess that the stress in your life is made worse because you feel someone is taking advantage of you. But nobody takes advantage of us unless we let them. Take charge of the kids, and I'm pretty sure you'll take charge of your eating habits too.

If I were you, I would call a family conference. Prepare a list of all the jobs that need doing and give the kids their choice of two, three, or whatever it takes. Flip a coin to see who chooses first. But you should do something soon, or you'll be dead in Derby.

Jennifer

DEAR JENNIFER

Dear Jennifer,

I'm almost too tired to write this letter. Why? Because I work three jobs. I'm a wife, a mother, and a supervisor at a clothing factory. No, I don't work at the factory for luxuries. I work because it takes more than one salary to keep food on the table, clothes on our backs, and a roof over our heads. After eight hours of handling other people's problems, I come home to work — the cooking, the cleaning, and money-saving jobs like sewing.

Frankly, I wish I didn't have to work. I don't have enough time to enjoy my kids. Before I know it, they will be grown and on their own. I wish I could put more time into the house, too. It could look a lot better than it does. I also wish I had some time for myself. I have a weight problem, and it doesn't take a doctor to tell me what's wrong. I didn't use to be overweight, but now every time I'm under stress, I eat.

Where's my family in all this? Well, my husband is working as hard as I am. He does most of the shopping, he fixes things around the house, and he drives the kids to church activities, ball games, etc. Until recently, he used to pick them up from their activities too, but now he can't because he has to work the 3-11 PM shift. Now they have to wait an hour or more for me.

The kids, a boy 14 and a girl 12, don't have time to help during the week. They're always busy with homework or school and church activities. They study a lot on weeknights. They're good students, but not brilliant; so if they're going to be successful in the future, I don't want to cut into their study time with chores. It's their attitude on weekends that's driving me crazy. They have some activities, of course, but they also have time to help and they don't volunteer to do anything. Can't they see how hard their father and I work? Why won't they just pitch in? Do I have to get down on my knees and beg them to help? Jennifer, I will appreciate any advice you can give me.

ALMOST DEAD IN DERBY

Second Reading

A. Read the letter again and discuss these questions in a small group.

1. Do you think that the writer has a positive or negative relationship with her children? Find evidence in her letter to support your opinion.
2. Where does the stress in her life come from? Could she change anything to reduce the stress?

B. As a group, write a response to "Almost Dead in Derby" and share it with your class.

WANTED

Lion tamer for immediate employment. **Experience a must!**

Call: R. J. Landowsky 903-337-5487

CIRCUS!

A. Work with a partner to create a job interview role play. First, list several occupations for which you might interview and choose one. (Perhaps you are interested in the job in the ad shown on this page!) List the qualifications for the job. Check off those that the applicant has.

B. Decide what questions the interviewer will ask. Talk about how the applicant will respond. Use some questions you have practiced in Units 10 and 11.

C. Practice the conversation twice, exchanging roles. Role play the interview for the class.

■ EXPANSION ACTIVITY: Writing letters to an advice column

1. Have students work alone or with a classmate and write a letter to an advice column about a problem, real or imaginary. Although the problems can be about any situation, if students write about problems related to changes in people's lives (for example, a person has changed jobs, moved to a new city or school or wants to make a change in his or her relationships with other people), students will use many of the structures emphasized in this unit.

2. Collect these letters. Have students form small groups. Give each group several letters to read and discuss.

Optional: Have pairs of students write a single letter. Have pairs exchange letters and write an answer to the letter they get.

15 **Final Activity**

PROCEDURE

Note: The ad for the lion tamer is meant to suggest that students should have fun with this interview role play. Real job interviews are boring because they are serious and predictable. Only if your students are going to interview for jobs, will they be motivated to practice real answers to the questions.

Refer to General Guidelines for Final Activity, page xi.

Workbook: *page 70, exercises L, M*

Useful materials: pictures that suggest what has just taken place (as for Unit 5); pictures of people you and students admire

New Directions

PROCEDURE
Refer to General Guidelines for Opener, page ix.

COMPREHENSION QUESTIONS

Now answer these questions.

1. Why are Sam and Sekila at Gino and Cristina's new apartment? *To help Gino refinish the kitchen cabinets.*
2. What are they doing now? *They are taking a break for lunch.*
3. What's the news from Adela? *She got the job with the Dallas Electric Company.*
4. What did Lisa do recently? *She joined a local swimming team.*
5. How do you think Lisa felt in her first weeks in Texas? *She missed Winfield and her friends.*
6. What is Bob talking about now that he has a job? *Getting a used car.*
7. What does Gino want to do? *Start his own restaurant with Cristina.*
8. What worries Cristina? *Getting the money. Competition from the Roma.*
9. Is Sam worried about competition from the Roma? *No, he isn't. He thinks it's Gino who makes the Roma special.*
10. Is Sekila against the idea of the restaurant? *No, she isn't. She says they should check everything before they decide.*

DISCUSSION QUESTIONS
1. Why didn't Lisa want to move to Texas?
2. Who is more optimistic about starting a business, Gino or Cristina? What evidence can you find in the conversation to support your opinion?
3. Would you start your own business if you were Gino or Cristina? Why or why not?

UNIT 12

COMMUNICATION
Verifying information ▪ Emphasizing that something is close in time or place ▪ Talking about a change

GRAMMAR
Tag questions with auxiliary verbs ▪ Compound modifiers ▪ *Right* as an intensifier ▪ *Get/Be used to* + noun/verb + -ing

SKILLS
Listening to one side of a conversation ▪ Reading a short biography and tribute to a famous person ▪ Writing about a person you admire

New Directions

It's early August. Sam and Sekila are at Gino and Cristina's new apartment. They've been helping Gino refinish the kitchen cabinets. They've been working all morning, and they've just taken a break for lunch.

GINO: What do you hear from your folks, Sam?

SAM: Everything's going really well for them. Mom has a job with the Dallas Electric Company. Dad sounds just terrific. Things are even looking up for Lisa. She didn't want to go to Dallas, but I guess she's getting used to it. She joined a local swimming team, so she'll be making some friends pretty soon.

SEKILA: What about Bob? Has he applied to a college yet?

SAM: Not yet. But he found a part-time job right away. He's working at a sandwich shop. He's already talking about getting a used car. I've got a two-week vacation in December. I just might go down to Texas for Christmas.

GINO: Well, honey, Adela and Tom are doing something new. Maybe we should think about a change, too.

CRISTINA: You've got something in mind, don't you?

GINO: As a matter of fact, I do. I'm sick and tired of working for someone else, especially someone like Williams. His values aren't the same as mine. I think that you and I should start our own restaurant.

CRISTINA: Well . . . I don't know. That's a pretty big step, Gino. Where would we get the money? Would we be able to make a go of it? Two Italian restaurants in Winfield just might be one too many.

SAM: That may be true, but think of how much Gino does for Williams, Cris. Williams isn't Italian. It's Gino who makes the Roma special.

CRISTINA: I guess so, but it's still a very big step. Starting a new business is risky.

GINO: That's true. We'll have to work very hard, but I think we can do it!

CRISTINA: Mmmm . . . what do you think, Sekila?

SEKILA: It won't be easy, but before you say no, you should check it out, shouldn't you?

CRISTINA: You've got a point.

GINO: Yeah. In fact, I'm going to call the bank right after lunch.

CRISTINA: Gino, hold on! Please give me some time to get used to this idea.

1 Vocabulary in Context

Sit in a small group and read through the conversation and its introduction again to locate the words and expressions listed below. Discuss each one and decide on a definition or different way to say the same thing. Share your work with other groups.

1. taken a break
2. hear from your folks
3. looking up
4. sick and tired of
5. His values aren't the same as mine.
6. a pretty big step
7. risky
8. make a go of it
9. check it out
10. You've got a point.

1 Vocabulary in Context

PROCEDURE
1. Refer to General Guidelines for Vocabulary in Context, page ix.
2. Have students work with a partner if you prefer.

Possible answers: 1. stopped working for a while 2. What's the news from your parents/family? 3. improving/getting better/looking better 4. have had enough of/disgusted with/unhappy about 5. The things he thinks are important, I don't./We have different ideas about what is important. 6. a rather big decision/change 7. not sure/there's a possibility of failing 8. make the business successful/succeed 9. investigate/find out about it 10. Your idea is worth thinking about./I should think about that idea.

Workbook: *page 71, exercises A, B*

2 Presentation

PROCEDURE
1. Refer to General Guidelines for Presentation, page ix.
2. Before beginning this Presentation, review tag questions with *be*, *do*, *does*, and *did*, if necessary. Use statements based on the Opener such as:
   1. Tom is a partner at Lone Star Travel.
   2. Adela got the job.
   3. Lisa didn't want to move to Texas.
   4. Bob works at a sandwich shop.
   5. Lisa doesn't have many friends in Dallas yet.
   6. It wasn't easy for Adela to find a job.
3. To expand the Presentation, write statements like these on the board. Have students check the information with you.
   1. We're going to have a test Friday.
   2. It will cover chapters 11 and 12.
   3. We can use our dictionaries on the Reading.
   4. We have finished chapter 11.

3 Practice

PROCEDURE
1. Refer to General Guidelines for Practice, page x.
2. Do the Practice in pairs or as a whole group.

Answers: Responses to these questions will vary.
1. have they? **2.** hasn't he? **3.** has he? **4.** has she? **5.** hasn't she? **6.** can they? **7.** should she? **8.** won't they **9.** will they? **10.** won't she? **11.** can he? **12.** shouldn't we?

Workbook: *page 72, exercise C*

2 Presentation 📻

Verifying information; tag questions with auxiliary verbs

1. Gino and Cristina have been married less than a year, **haven't they**?
2. Gino hasn't been happy at the Roma lately, **has he**?
3. You should check it out, **shouldn't you**?
4. Gino and Cristina will make a go of it, **won't they**?
5. They can get a loan from a bank, **can't they**?

3 Practice

With a partner, check the accuracy of the following statements by adding tag questions. You can use your imagination in answering.

1. The Logans haven't found a house yet.
2. Bob has started working.
3. He hasn't gotten paid yet.
4. Lisa hasn't made many friends yet.
5. Adela has found a job.
6. The Logans can't find a house.
7. Adela shouldn't worry about that.
8. They'll find one before long.
9. The Logans won't go back to Winfield.
10. Lisa will make friends soon.
11. Bob can't buy a used car yet.
12. We should keep studying English.

4 Reentry

> Use **just** after **has/have** in the present perfect to show that something has happened very recently.

A. Say the same idea using the present perfect.

> Gino and the others **just took** a break for lunch.
>
> They **have just taken** a break for lunch.

just took =
has/have just
taken

1. Adela just found a job.

2. They just called from the Dallas Electric Company.

3. Tom just became a partner at Lone Star Travel.

4. Bob just got a job at a sandwich shop.

5. Lisa just joined a new swimming team.

B. Tell your class or a partner about something that you have just started, finished, or stopped doing recently.

> I've just started taking a course in auto mechanics.
>
> I've just finished fixing my car.

5 Presentation

Using numbers to create compound modifiers

> Sometimes a number is used before a noun to form an adjective. The words are connected by a hyphen to show that they work together to form one meaning.

1. Sam has a vacation in December. It will be two weeks long.
   Sam has a **two-week** vacation in December.

2. Adela had a **twenty-minute** interview.

3. Tom and Adela have a **twelve-year-old** daughter.

4 Reentry

PROCEDURE
1. Refer to General Guidelines for Reentry, page x.
2. Have students do part A individually. Check answers with the class. Do part B with the class.

Answers: **A.** **1.** has just found **2.** have just called **3.** has just become **4.** has just gotten **5.** has just joined

LANGUAGE NOTE

Just + simple past and *just* + present perfect have the same meaning. The former is more common in speech and the latter is more common in writing, especially when a writer is bringing a reader up-to-date on the events of the past.

5 Presentation

PROCEDURE
1. Refer to General Guidelines for Presentation, page ix.
2. Ask students what they observe about the nouns in these compound adjectives. (They do not take the plural *s*.)
3. To expand the Presentation, list some nouns on the board such as *test* and *book*. Ask for a variety of examples for each noun.

6 Practice

PROCEDURE
1. Refer to General Guidelines for Practice, page x.
2. Have students write out the new sentences. Check answers with the class. Check pronunciation of the compound modifiers.

Answers: **1.** four-door car **2.** eight-week-old puppy **3.** fifteen-year-old son **4.** ten-dollar bill **5.** three-page letter **6.** four-hour movie **7.** fifteen-second commercial **8.** three-bedroom house **9.** three-minute call **10.** four-hour meeting.

■ EXPANSION ACTIVITY: Using compound modifiers
1. Write the first twenty concrete nouns that your students give you on the board.
2. Divide the class into teams of three members. Each team appoints a secretary.
3. Choose one of the nouns and give students thirty seconds to write as many compound modifiers using numbers as they can that make sense with that noun.
4. The team with the most correct compound modifiers wins the point for that noun. Continue with the nouns in the list. The team with the most points is the winner.

■ EXPANSION ACTIVITY: Compound modifier scavenger hunt
1. Have students bring pictures of things to class that can be described with compound modifiers (a ten-story building, a $200-dollar radio).
2. Have students describe a picture they brought, using at least one compound modifier.
3. Select ten pictures, put them on the board and number them.
4. Have students write a sentence about each picture with a compound modifier spelled correctly.

> Workbook: *page 72, exercise D*

7 Presentation

PROCEDURE
Refer to General Guidelines for Presentation, page ix.

---

6 Practice

Say the same idea using a compound modifier.

1. Bob wants to buy a car with four doors.
2. Liz just got a puppy that is eight weeks old.
3. The Youngs have a son who is fifteen years old.
4. I lost a bill that was worth ten dollars.
5. I wrote a letter to my sister that was three pages long.
6. I'll never go to a movie that lasts four hours again.
7. That was a commercial that lasted only fifteen seconds.
8. The Logans are looking for a house with three bedrooms.
9. I asked the operator for the cost of a call that lasts three minutes.
10. We had a meeting that lasted four hours.

7 Presentation

Emphasizing that something is very close in time or place

> To emphasize that something is very close in time or place, use **right** + *adverb* or *adverb phrase*.

1. Bob found a part-time job **right away**. (immediately)
2. Gino wants to call the bank **right after lunch**. (immediately)
3. I can't help you **right now**. (at this very minute)
4. Mary will be **right here**. (in just a minute)
5. I'll be **right with you**. (in just a minute)
6. Your notebook is **right there** on the table. (very close)
7. The school is **right across** from the police station. (very close)

8 Interaction

Work with a partner. Write a four-line conversation for one of the following situations. Use an expression from *7* and some of the *Useful expressions*. If appropriate, use *just* with the present perfect or a tag question. Role play your conversation for the class.

> **Useful expressions:**
> a one-o'clock appointment
> a ten-dollar watch
> my two-year-old brother
> a three-day conference
>
> have just found/lost it
> has just come in/gone out
>
> You haven't _____ , have you?
> I should _____ , shouldn't I?
> You can wait a moment, can't you?

a. A person comes to an office to see someone on business.

b. A person is looking for someone in a crowded place.

c. A person has lost something and is looking for it.

8 **Interaction**

PROCEDURE
Refer to General Guidelines for Interaction, page x.

Workbook: *page 73, exercise E*

9 **Presentation**

PROCEDURE
1. Refer to General Guidelines for Presentation, page ix.
2. To expand the Presentation, write the expressions *get used to* and *be used to* on the board. Have students complete sentences like these: *Pepe just bought some new shoes. He* ____. (is getting used to his new shoes) *Elena has been wearing her new shoes for a week. She* ____. (is used to her shoes)

9 **Presentation**

Talking about a change

To talk about adapting to something new, use:

| get | used to + noun/pronoun/ |
| be | verb + **-ing** |

Used to means something different when used alone or when following **be** or **get**. Compare the two meanings below.

get used to = to be in the process of adapting
be used to = already adapted

The Logans **used to live** in Winfield. Then they moved to Dallas.

They **are getting used to living** in a very big city. Bob **is used to it**; Lisa still **isn't used to it**.

10 Practice

10 Practice

PROCEDURE

1. Refer to General Guidelines for Practice, page x.
2. Do Part A with the whole class.

Answers: **A. 1.** am getting used to; was used to
2. get used to **3.** get used to **4.** isn't used to
B. Answers will vary.

11 Interaction

PROCEDURE

1. Refer to General Guidelines for Interaction, page x.
2. After discussing these situations with the class, have students suggest other situations that force people to change, and discuss the difficulties in each.

■ EXPANSION ACTIVITY: Putting yourself in someone else's shoes

1. Have students bring in pictures of famous people they know quite a bit about.
2. Put the pictures on the wall. Have students write about five of the people using this sentence: *If I were this person, I would have to get used to ____.*
3. One student reads his or her sentence about one of the pictures. The student who correctly identifies the person the sentence was written about, reads the next sentence.

Workbook: *page 73, exercise F*

---

10 Practice

A. Complete the sentences with *get used to* or *be used to*, in the affirmative or negative. Use the correct form of *get* and *be*.

1. I used to work days, and now I work nights. I ____ working nights, but it is hard. I ____ sleeping during the night.
2. Gino and Cristina were single for many years. Now that they are married, they are trying to ____ each other's habits.
3. Bob Logan used to go to a small high school. If he goes to the University of Texas, he will have to ____ a very large school.
4. Gloria used to have her guitar lesson Saturday morning. Her teacher changed it to Wednesday after school. She ____ the new time, and she forgot her lesson last week.

B. Talk with a partner about things that people have to adapt to in the following situations. If you have done any of these things in your life, talk about whether you are used to the change or not.

a. when someone goes to live in a new country
b. when someone moves to a new city or neighborhood
c. when someone changes schools
d. when someone travels in a foreign country
e. when someone starts studying English or something else for the first time
f. when someone becomes a parent for the first time

11 Interaction

Discuss the following situations in a small group.

A. Mark and Shirley Mann were childless for eight years after they got married. Just last summer they had twins, a boy and a girl. The twins are now thirteen months old.

B. Bob and Helen Marcus had six children. Their youngest child is now in college, and the older ones are all married and working.

1. What did these peoples' lives use to be like? What did their daily routines use to be like?
2. What are they used to or getting used to doing now? What do they usually do now?

12 Reentry

Questions with *How long*: past, present, and future

> A The Logans used to live in Winfield.
> A: How long did the Logans live there?
> B: For many years.
> B The Logans are now living in Dallas.
> A: How long have they been living in Dallas?
> B: | For a month. |
> | Since late June. |
> C A: How long will they stay in Dallas?
> B: Who knows. Maybe until something better comes along.

Ask and answer questions beginning with *How long* about each of the following situations. You can use your imagination in answering.

1. Liz used to work for the Winfield Telephone Company. Now she works for Worldwide Airlines. She used to live with Sue. Now she is living with Nilda Rosado.
2. Gino and Cristina used to live in Gino's small apartment. Now they live in a new two-bedroom apartment.
3. Tom used to work for Wells Travel Agency in Winfield. Now he's a partner at Lone Star Travel in Dallas.
4. Adela used to study at the Winfield Technical Institute. Now she's working for the Dallas Electric Company.

13 Reentry

Verb tenses

Complete the paragraph with the correct tense of the verb in parentheses. Use: *simple past, past continuous, present perfect, simple present, present continuous,* or *the future*.

The Logans arrived in Dallas about two months ago. They (1) _____ (be) very busy ever since. Tom (2) _____ (work) at Lone Star Travel for almost a month. He (3) _____ (like) it a lot. Bob (4) _____ (find) a job at a sandwich shop during his second week in Dallas, and he already (5) _____ (know) how to make the most complicated sandwich in 45 seconds.
    Adela (6) _____ (have) a difficult time finding a job, but fortunately one day while she (7) _____ (read) the newspaper, she (8) _____ (see) an ad

12 Reentry

PROCEDURE
1. Refer to General Guidelines for Reentry, page x.
2. Do the exercise in pairs, small groups, or with the class.

Possible answers: **1.** How long did Liz work at the Winfield Telephone Company? How long has she been working at Worldwide Airlines? How long will she work at Worldwide? Answers for 2-4 follow the same pattern. Responses will vary.

13 Reentry

PROCEDURE
1. Refer to General Guidelines for Reentry, page x.
2. Have students complete the exercise individually. Check answers with the class.

Answers: 1. have been 2. has been working/has worked 3. likes 4. found 5. knows 6. has had/has been having 7. was reading 8. saw

Answers (continued): **9.** got **10.** is **11.** was **12.** didn't want **13.** joined (has just joined) **14.** is beginning/has begun **15.** starts **16.** will make

> **Workbook:** *pages 74-75, exercise G*

14 Listening

PROCEDURE
1. Refer to General Guidelines for Listening, page x.
2. Play the tape or read the script for the Listening. The tape includes the directions on page 164.
3. Play the tape a second or third time if necessary for students to do the First or Second Listening exercises.
4. *If reading the script:* Pause two seconds at each #. For the First Listening give students 45 seconds to do the First Listening exercise. For the Second Listening give students 40 seconds to answer statements 1-8.
5. For script and answers, see page 200.

■ EXPANSION ACTIVITY 12: What to look for in a college or vocational or technical school (page 193)

15 Reentry

PROCEDURE
1. Refer to General Guidelines for Reentry, page x.
2. Have individual students write at least one sentence to answer each question.
3. Discuss answers with the class.

Possible answers: **1.** They will have to borrow some money. **2.** If they want the restaurant to be successful, they should keep the prices as reasonable as possible. They should use good ingredients. **3.** They might have problems finding a good location. **4.** They won't be able to take a lot of vacations. They will have to be there all the time in the beginning. **5.** Someday they will be able to find a good manager so they can take a vacation.

> **Workbook:** *page 75, exercise H*

for a job with the Dallas Electric Company. She (9) _____ (get) that job a week ago, and she (10) _____ (be) busier than she ever (11) _____ (be) before. _____

Lisa wasn't too happy about the move originally because she (12) _____ (not want) to leave her friends in Winfield. But she just (13) _____ (join) a new swimming team and she (14) _____ (begin) to make new friends. When school (15) _____ (start) in the fall, she (16) _____ (make) even more.

14 Listening 🔲

Copy the names listed below on your paper. The Logans called Sam the other day. Listen to Sam's side of the conversation.

First Listening

Number the people in the order Sam talks to them — 1, 2, 3, and 4. Then write the letter of one or more topics Sam and the other person talk about.

	Order	Topics
Tom	_____	_____
Adela	_____	_____
Bob	_____	_____
Lisa	_____	_____

a. the weather
b. a new house
c. new friends
d. a vacation
e. a car
f. a job
g. college
h. food

Second Listening

Now number your paper from 1-8. Listen again and write *T* (True), *F* (False), or *NG* (Not Given) for each statement.

1. It has been more than 100° in Dallas recently.
2. Adela is a little worried about Sam.
3. Everything is perfect at Adela's job.
4. Sam is working overtime at the garage.
5. The Logans have found a house in Dallas.
6. Something's wrong with the family car.
7. Tom seems to be worried about Sam, too.
8. Bob is looking at small colleges.

15 Reentry

Using modals to speculate and predict

Gino and Cristina are thinking about starting their own Italian restaurant. Discuss answers to these questions in a small group. Then share your ideas with the whole class.

1. What will Gino and Cristina have to do before they can open their own restaurant?

2. What should/shouldn't they do if they want the restaurant to be successful?

3. What problems do you think they might have with a new restaurant?

4. What won't they be able to do when the restaurant is new?

5. What will they be able to do some day if they work hard now?

16 Reentry

Comparing and contrasting infinitives and gerunds

Complete the sentences with an infinitive (*to* + verb) or a gerund (verb + *-ing*). Sometimes both are correct.

1. Gino is thinking of _____ (start) his own restaurant.

2. He is sick and tired of _____ (work) for someone else.

3. In particular, he dislikes _____ (work) for Mr. Williams.

4. He wants _____ (be) his own boss.

5. Cristina says _____ (start) a business is risky.

6. She knows it's risky _____ (start) a business because you usually have to borrow money.

7. Cristina would like _____ (be) sure that the business is going to be successful.

8. Gino and Cristina aren't afraid of _____ (work) hard so they'll probably be successful.

16 Reentry

PROCEDURE
1. Refer to General Guidelines for Reentry, page x.
2. Review the rules given below if necessary.
   a. Gerunds follow prepositions other than the infinitive marker *to*.
   b. Certain verbs take only the gerund; for example *dislike* and *enjoy*.
   c. Some verbs always take the infinitive form; for example, *want* and *need*. *Would like* meaning *want* is followed by the infinitive, but can be followed by the gerund, in which case it means *enjoy*. (*I would like living there.*)
   d. Gerunds are the most common form for subjects. Infinitives can be subjects but are formal.
   e. Infinitives are used after adjectives.
   f. Some verbs can be followed by either an infinitive or a gerund; for example *like, start, stop. I stopped doing that* (I don't do that anymore) and *I stopped to do that* (for the purpose of doing it) mean different things.

Answers: **1.** starting **2.** working **3.** working **4.** to be **5.** starting **6.** to start **7.** to be **8.** working

■ EXPANSION ACTIVITY: Real or imaginary (Reentry of real and imaginary conditional sentences)

Give the students the following sentences to complete with **will** or **would** + verb.

1. If Gino and Cristina were rich, ____.
2. If they decide to start the business, ____.
3. If the business is successful, ____.
4. If they had a rich uncle, ____.
5. If Sam had a vacation right now, ____.
6. If Lisa makes a few new friends, ____
7. If Bob had his own car right now, ____.
8. If Tom and Adela have to get a new car, ____.
9. If Lisa were still in Winfield, she ____.
10. If Adela doesn't like working at the Electric Company, ____.

Workbook: *page 75, exercise I*

PROCEDURE

1. Refer to General Guidelines for Reading, page x.
2. Have students read the biography of Davis silently and take notes on what they think are the five most important facts about his life. Discuss possible answers with students.
3. Use some of the discussion questions suggested in *Reacting to the Reading*, page 167.

Possible answers to the most important facts about Sammy Davis Jr.'s life: **1.** He was born in Harlem in New York. **2.** His parents were performers. **3.** He learned to sing and dance when he was very young. **4.** He toured with Will Mastin. **5.** He had to join the army. **6.** He met prejudice in the army. **7.** He learned to read in the army. **8.** He was in a car accident and lost an eye. **9.** He performed on Broadway, on television, and in the movies.

Possible answers: First Reading: **1.** An entertainer (he liked to make people happy), a pioneer, a groundbreaker, proud, fearless. He knew how to live. He was flamboyant, self-educated, intelligent, imperfect (he made mistakes), sensitive, and unselfish, and he had a good heart **2.** Yes I can. **3.** People accepted Davis as an equal. He broke racial barriers in the entertainment world. He made it easier for black entertainers (and blacks in general) to get ahead. He opened the road to success for other blacks.

Possible Answers: Second Reading: **A. 1.** proud, fearless, one of the greatest entertainers, flamboyant, self-educated, brilliant, sensitive, unselfish **2.** They were friends and equals. Before, black and white entertainers didn't eat together even though they performed on the same stage. **3.** Jackson knows that Davis opened the way for him. He says, "If you weren't there, I wouldn't be here." **B. 1.** in traveling shows, entertaining in different cities **2.** changed things **3.** nickname of group of friends including Davis, Sinatra, and Martin **4.** really too bad, a pity **5.** difficult times on the way to the top **6.** making mistakes **7.** people criticized him, he took criticism **8.** felt bad about all the criticism

Before You Read

1. Have you ever heard of Sammy Davis Jr.? Why was he famous?

2. What do you know about racial problems in the early 20th century in the United States?

3. What is a pioneer? What do you think a groundbreaker is?

4. Quincy Jones, a record producer and musician, wrote the tribute to Sammy Davis Jr. on pages 167-168 What kind of comments would you expect to find in a tribute?

Before you read the "Tribute to Sammy Davis Jr.", read this short biography of his life. When you have finished reading it, write down what you think are five important facts about this entertainer's life.

A Short Biography of Sammy Davis Jr.

Sammy Davis Jr. was born December 8, 1925, in Harlem, New York City. His father and mother, Sammy Davis Sr. and Elvera Sanchez Davis, were both performers in the vaudeville° troupe of Will Mastin, young Sammy's uncle. Sammy learned to sing and dance at an early age and performed with his father throughout his childhood. Sammy later learned to do many other things. He could do impressions of famous people, play the trumpet, drums, piano, and vibes.°

variety theater of the early 20th century

an instrument like a xylophone

Davis toured with Will Mastin in the late thirties and early forties before he was drafted into the army at the age of 18. He experienced a lot of prejudice in the army because he was black, and he got into a lot of fights with whites in the barracks. But there were benefits from the army experience, too. He learned to read from one of his sergeants and he eventually transferred to Special Services and began to entertain other servicemen.

In 1954 he had a car accident in which he lost his left eye. Despite the accident, he was increasingly in demand. He performed for the rest of his life — on Broadway, in television, and in movies. As a singer he had many hits, among them "Candy Man," "Birth of the Blues," and "Mr. Bojangles." Davis died on May 16, 1990.

First Reading

As you read the "Tribute" below, look for information to answer these questions. When you have finished reading, discuss your answers in small groups.

1. What kind of person was Sammy Davis Jr.?
2. What was his attitude toward life?
3. What did Sammy Davis Jr. do to help other black people?

Tribute

1 Sammy Davis Jr. was born on the road, and he lived his life on the road. He was a total entertainer, true vaudevillian,° and he made a lot of people happy.

performer in vaudeville

2 The thing that has to be said about Sammy is that he was a groundbreaker in every way. He was one proud, fearless man. His first autobiography was called *Yes I Can*, and that really was his attitude toward life. Back in the old days, black entertainers had to sit in the kitchen to eat their dinners — even when they were playing the big room.° Sammy helped turn things around in terms of racial barriers.° His being a member of the Rat Pack with people like Frank Sinatra and Dean Martin created a perception that friends were friends, that it didn't matter what someone's color was. Sammy could do anything that anyone else in that group could. And that was the first time you ever saw anything like that going on. Before that you would just have Rochester° hanging out with Jack Benny, or Bojangles° with Shirley Temple — situations in which the black person was always in some subservient role.° Sammy, on the other hand, was an equal.

the most important show room in a hotel
obstacle, something to stop you

black actor on a radio show / black actor in movies

lower position, like a servant

3 I don't think a lot of young black entertainers truly appreciate all that Sammy Davis Jr. did for them, and that's a real shame. It's so much easier for them to get ahead° these days, and a lot of them assume that their success is totally the result of their own ability. But the truth of the matter is that there's a whole lot of blood on the road to their success. I know for sure

progress, be successful

Reacting to the Reading: Discussion Questions

1. If Sammy Davis Jr. were alive today, what would you like to ask him?
2. What other groundbreakers do you know about?
3. Do we need pioneers in any other situations today? Where?
4. Define success.

that Michael Jackson knows this. Michael understands exactly how much credit someone like Sammy really deserves. He paid a great tribute to Sammy. He said, "If you weren't there, I wouldn't be here." And believe me, there are a lot of people who got places because Sammy Davis got there first. . . .

4   I think Sammy will be remembered as one of the greatest entertainers America's ever seen. He was a man who knew how to live. He was flamboyant in every way. He was self-educated and very brilliant. He made tremendous pioneering efforts, and he made some tremendous mistakes. He did a lot of bumbling along the way, . . . but Sammy always led with his heart, and you really can't blame someone for that. Sammy took a lot of flak, and he suffered every blow, because he was a very sensitive° man. He *man of feelings* wanted desperately to be loved, and he gave a lot of love. In fact, he was the most unselfish giver I ever saw in my life. If he had pneumonia, he would still perform. He always gave 100 percent. He gave every drop° he had. *drop of blood or sweat*

5   Toward the end, he had so much going his way. He loved his wife, Altovise, so much, and in addition to his other kids, he'd adopted° a young son, Manny. *became the legal parent of* And as a singer, he sounded better at the end than he had *ever* sounded. He stopped smoking and started getting some sleep for a change, which probably shocked his body. Bill Cosby called me and said, "Let's try and find some songs for Sammy." And I'd been looking, getting a little collection together, but like everything else, you always wait until it's too late.

6   Sammy lived 150 years in his lifetime, because he did everything. I don't care if it was Broadway, television, records, movies — whatever you name, he could do it. Sammy Davis Jr. did it all the way no one had done it before.

— Quincy Jones

Second Reading

A. Read the tribute again and answer these questions.

  1. List the adjectives Jones uses to describe Sammy Davis Jr. What does each say about him?
  2. What was Sammy Davis Jr.'s relationship to Frank Sinatra and Dean Martin? How was it different from the earlier relationships of black and white entertainers?
  3. What is Michael Jackson's tribute to Sammy Davis Jr.?

B. Look for these words or expressions in the reading and guess their meaning from the context.

  1. on the road (1)
  2. turned things around (2)
  3. the Rat Pack (2)
  4. a real shame (3)
  5. blood on the road to their success (3)
  6. bumbling (4)
  7. took a lot of flak (4)
  8. suffered every blow (4)

18 Writing

A. Think about a person, living or dead, whom you admire. Tell your partner about this person.

B. Write three paragraphs about this person explaining why you admire him or her. Follow this guide.

Paragraph 1: **Introduction**
Give background information on the person: name, age, occupation, relationship to you, etc.

Paragraph 2: **Body**
Tell some of the qualities he or she has/had and give detailed examples of things he or she does/did.

Paragraph 3: **Conclusion**
Write about why you admire the person.

C. Give your paper to your partner and talk about what you have written. Do you admire the same or different qualities in the people you wrote about?

18 Writing

PROCEDURE
1. Refer to General Guidelines for Writing, page xi.
2. Have students make notes before beginning to write.
3. Discuss the questions in part C with the class if you prefer.

■ EXPANSION ACTIVITY: People we admire

Have students decorate a bulletin board with pictures, names, maps of native countries, quotations, and paragraphs written by them of famous and lesser known people they admire.

PROCEDURE

1. Refer to General Guidelines for Final Activity, page xi.
2. Read the instructions in part A and give students an identity card made according to the instructions on page 174.
3. Read the instructions for part B and circulate and offer help as students work in their groups.
4. Before the final part of the activity, tell students to listen carefully because they will have to write a comment about one of the groups later.
5. Bring the "families" to the front of the room one at a time. Have the family members introduce themselves to the class. Then the class can begin the questioning.
6. After all families have been interviewed, have students write two or three sentences telling you which family they think was the most interesting and did the best job. You might want to give some sort of award.

Workbook: *page 76, exercises J, K*

Find Your Family

A. Your teacher will give each of you a card that tells you where your "family" used to live and the place to which you have just moved. Move around the classroom and find the other members of your "family," using these questions:

> Did you use to _____ ?
> Are you getting used to _____ ?

B. When you find your family, sit together and create a family story about your move. First give each member a name, age, and occupation. Then answer these questions:

1. Why did you have to move?
2. How did you react to the move?
3. What did you use to do that you can't do anymore?
4. What are you getting used to? What are you already used to?
5. Are you happy with the move? What are your plans for the future?

C. In the final part of this activity, the class will interview each family about their move. Use these questions and any other appropriate ones.

> **Suggested questions:**
>
> Where did you use to live?
> How did you like _____ ?
> How long did you _____ ?
> Where do you live now?
> How do you like _____ ?
> How long have you been _____ ?
> Would you _____ if you could?
> Would you like to _____ ?
> What will you do if _____ ?

Appendix

UNIT 1

16 Interaction

CLUES FOR STUDENT A
1. Ellen's Unisex Hair Salon is #2.
2. #16 and #17 are both clothing stores.
3. The new Nelson's Pharmacy is next to Bell's Supermarket.
4. The Kitchen Shop is the smallest store on the south wing.
5. The ice cream parlor is next to the Main Entrance and across from the bookstore.
6. Value Slacks is at the end of the west wing, next to the door.

CLUES FOR STUDENT B
1. Music Lovers, Inc. is #12.
2. Allen's men's store is closer to Warner's than Mary Jo's women's store.
3. Small World, the children's clothing store, is next to the hair salon.
4. Harlan's Shoes is in the north wing and smaller than its neighbors.
5. The Sports Shop is the big store across from the ice cream parlor.
6. Jenson's Jewelry is across from the camera shop and the ice cream parlor.

CLUES FOR STUDENT C
1. #24 is Fast Photo, a camera store.
2. #8 and #9 are both fast food restaurants.
3. The toy store is on the west side of the north wing.
4. Hal's Electronics Store is next door to the biggest store in the mall.
5. The bookstore is one of the two large stores near the fountain.
6. The people at Smart Shoes hear music next door.

CLUES FOR STUDENT D
1. The office supply store is #6.
2. Taco Place is next to the hardware store, and Burger Place is next to the bookstore.
3. Rosemary's Boutique is between the toy store and the office supply store.
4. Lamps and Lighting is next door to the smallest store on the south wing.
5. The bank is next to an unknown (?) store.
6. The hardware store is at the end of the west wing next to the door.

UNIT 4

11 Interaction

CLUES FOR STUDENT A
1. The stove is between the sink and the counter with a curved end.
2. There's a table with six chairs in the center of the dining room.
3. There's a round rug in the middle of the living room floor.
4. There's a long, low bookcase on the wall across from the living room couch with a television in the middle of it.

CLUES FOR STUDENT B
1. The sink is under the kitchen window.
2. There's a microwave oven on the counter between the kitchen and the dining room.
3. The living room couch is under the front window.
4. There's a recliner in front of the right living room window.

CLUES FOR STUDENT C
1. The dishwasher is in the middle of the counter on the right side of the kitchen.
2. There's a square table with a plant on it in the corner of the dining room between the windows.
3. There's a long coffee table on the edge of the rug in front of the couch.
4. There's a desk in the study under the window, and bookcases at both ends.

CLUES FOR STUDENT D
1. The refrigerator is in the middle of the back wall of the kitchen.
2. There are three high stools in the dining room in front of the curved counter.
3. There are end tables with lamps on them at both ends of the sofa.
4. There's a bed in the middle of the back wall of the study to make it a guest room. There's a table with a lamp on it between the bed and the wall next to the stairs.

19 Reading

What happens to recycled trash?

Recycling has always been the public-spirited thing to do — it saves resources and cuts down on pollution. But now it's becoming essential as cities and states struggle to cope with the burden and expense of garbage disposal.

The Environmental Protection Agency estimates that only 10 percent of America's municipal solid waste is now recycled. This includes 30 percent of our newspapers, 40-45 percent of cardboard, 10-15 percent of office paper, 50 percent of aluminum cans, 10 percent of glass bottles, and 2 percent of plastic products. But more could be recycled. "For instance," says Cynthia Pollack Shea of the Worldwatch Institute in Washington, "recycling all copies of just one Sunday edition to *The New York Times* could leave 75,000 trees standing!"

What happens to discards once they're taken to the recycling center? The chart below shows some of the new products that can be made from your recycled garbage.

—*L.J.B.*

Plastic	Paper	Glass	Aluminum
• Fiber filling in jackets and pillows • Flowerpots • Paintbrush bristles • Plastic "lumber" for fences and boat docks • Plastic-strapping for shipping boxes	• Game boards • Record jackets • Egg cartons • 50% of grocery-store food boxes • Book covers • Gift boxes • Jigsaw puzzles • Paper matches • Game/show tickets	• Bottles (90% are made into new bottles) • "Glasphalt" used in street paving • Used in bricks • Used in tile • Used in reflective paint for road signs	• Cans (almost 100% are made into new aluminum cans) • Other aluminum items, such as lawn chairs and window frames, are made into similar products or castings for car parts

UNIT 12

19 Final Activity

Making "Family Cards" for "Find Your Family"

1. Prepare a card for each member of each family with the information suggested below.
2. If all students don't fit in four families, add #5 and #6 together. (If you add *only* 5 or *only* 6, it will be easier for that one group to form than for the others.)
3. Relationships in the families are suggestions only, but the number in each family should be about the same.

FAMILY #1:
father, mother, kids (as needed)
You are the/a _____ .
You used to live in a big city.
  (about 500,000)
You used to have a small apartment.
You are getting used to a small town.
  (about 15,000)
You are getting used to a big house.

FAMILY #2:
father, kids (as needed)
You are the/a _____ .
You used to live in a big city.
  (about 500,000)
You used to have a small apartment.
You are getting used to a farm in the country.
You are getting used to a very small house.

FAMILY #3:
mother, two or three kids, a grandparent
You are the/a _____ .
You used to live on a farm in the country.
You used to have a big house.
You are getting used to a big city.
  (about 500,000)
You are getting used to a small apartment.

FAMILY #4:
mother, father, kids, grandparents
  (as needed)
You are the/a _____ .
You used to live on a farm in the country.
You used to have a big house.
You are getting used to a small town.
You are getting used to a small apartment.

FAMILY #5:
father, mother, kids (as needed),
  grandparent
You are the/a _____ .
You used to live in a small city.
  (about 50,000)
You used to have a small apartment.
You are getting used to a farm in the country.
You are getting used to a big house.

FAMILY #6:
mother, kids (as needed)
You are the/a _____ .
You used to live in a small city.
  (about 50,000)
You used to have a small apartment.
You are getting used to a very small town.
  (about 10,000)
You are getting used to a big house with a big yard.

VOCABULARY: Book 4

This vocabulary list contains the productive words as well as most receptive words in Book 4. A list of vocabulary words from Book 3 is found on page 181. Productive words are those that students should know how to use. The unit number refers to when the word is first introduced productively. Receptive words are those that students need only understand. The unit number for these words is in parentheses. (*n*) = noun; (*v*) = verb; (*adj*) = adjective; (*adv*) = adverb; (*pron*) = pronoun

A

a bit of   (4)
a couple of   5
above   4
absolutely   (7)
academic   (7)
accelerator   2
accept   (2), 7
accommodation   (5)
accomplishment   (8)
according to   (4)
accuracy   (10)
accurate   (10)
acknowledge   (10)
across   (5)
action   (1)
active   (2)
ad   1
adapt   (12)
adaptable   10
addition   (10)
adequate   (4)
adjective   (2)
admire   (12)
adopt   (12)
adult   (2)
advanced   (3)
advantage   6
advertisement   (1)
advertising   (3)
affect   (1)
afford   (1), 3
afraid   (10)
against   (2)
agree   1
agreement   (1)
ahead   (10)
air-conditioning   (2)
alcohol   (2)
alike   (5)
almost   (11)
alone   (2), 6
already   (1), 7
alternative   (6)
amazing   1
among   (2)
amusement rides   1
anniversary   (5)
announcer   (1)
another   9
any chance   5
any time   9

anymore   (1), 11
anyone   (8)
apology   7
appear   4
appearance   (10)
appliance   4
applicant   10
application   10
apply   (7)
apply for   10
appreciate   5
appreciation   (5)
appropriate   (1)
approximately   (4)
archaeologist   (4)
architecture   1
area   6
area code   (10)
argument   (4)
armchair   4
army   (10)
article   (2)
artistic   1
as a matter of fact   (12)
as many...as   6
as much...as   6
assignment   5
assistant   (11)
assume   (10)
at all   (2)
at least   6
athletic events   (6)
athletic field   (3)
atmosphere   (4)
attend   (10)
attitude   (11)
attraction   (6)
auto   (1)
autobiography   (12)
automobile   (2)
availability   (10)
available   (5)
average   (10)

B

baby shower   (9)
back seat   2
back up   (2)
background   (12)
bake   (4)
banner   (8)
barbecue   (9)

bargain   3
barrier   (12)
barter   (3)
based on   (7)
basic   (10)
battery   (4)
battle   (8)
be grateful for   (9)
be used to...   12
beauty   2
been   4
behind   4
believe   2
belong   9
below   (1), 4
bench   (3)
benefit   (6)
besides   (7)
best   1
bet   2
better   1
between   4
bicyclist   (5)
bigger   1
biggest   1
bill   (3)
biodegradable   (4)
biography   (12)
blame   (12)
blank   (1)
blanket   (5)
blender   4
blowup   (8)
body   (7)
bookcase   4
boring   1
borrow   2
boss   (3), 8
bother   (3)
bottom   (7)
bought   5
bounce   (8)
brainstorm   (9)
brake   2
brand new   (2)
bridal shower   (9)
broken   5
built   1
bumbling   (12)
burst   (4)
bury   (4)
business   (5), 11
business owner   (1)

C

c'mon   (2)
cabinet   (3)
cafeteria   (9)
calculator   (3)
call back   (3)
camera shop   (1)
camped   5
camping   (6)
capital   (2)
care   2
carefully   (2)
careless   (2)
carelessly   (2)
carnival   1
carry out   (2)
cash   2
cassette player   (9)
casual   (1)
catalog   (9)
catch up on   8
caught   (6)
cause   (11)
ceiling   (4)
center   (1)
century   (6)
ceremony   (7)
certain   (1), 11
certainly   (9)
certify   (10)
chain   (1)
chair   (9)
challenge   11
challenging   (11)
chance   (1)
change (*n*)   10
change my mind   6
chapter   (2)
character   (1)
characteristic   (10)
chart   (1)
cheap   (2)
check out   (1)
check it out   12
childhood   (12)
choice   (2)
choose   (1), 3
chore   (5)
circle   7
claim   (1)
classical music   (6)
clause   (2)

clearly   (10)
clinic   (7)
clogged   5
cloth   (2)
clothing   3
cloudy   (1)
clutch   2
coast   (5)
coffee table   4
collect   (5)
collection   (12)
college   (10)
column   (2)
combine   (9)
come a long way   5
come back   (3)
come up with   (10)
comfortable   (1)
commensurate   (10)
comment   (6), 9
commercial (*adj*)   (2)
commercial (*n*)   (12)
common   (1)
common sense   (10)
communicate   (7)
communication   (2)
communicator   (10)
commute   7
compact car   (2)
company   (1), 10
compare   (1)
comparison   (2)
complete (*v*)   (1)
complete (*adj*)   (2)
completely   (2)
complex   (7)
complicated   (12)
composition   (9)
compound   (12)
conclusion   (4)
condition   (2), 4
conference   (6)
confirmation   (2)
confusing   (1)
connect   (6)
conserve   (6)
consider   (4)
constant   (8)
consult   (5)
consulting   (10)
consumer   (1)
container   (4)
contest   (9)
context   (4)
contract   (2)
contribution   (11)
convenient   1
convince   (2)
cooler   (9)
cooperative   10
copy   (1)
correct   2

correctly   (2)
couch   4
could   2, 7
couldn't be better   4
council   (5)
counselor   (6)
count on   (1)
counter   4
course   (8), 11
cover   (2)
create   (1)
creative   10
credit   (1)
critic   (7)
criticize   (9)
cross (*v*)   (6)
crossing (*n*)   (7)
crowd   1
crowded   (1), 6
cue   (3)
culture   (2)
cushion   (6)
custom   11
customer   (1)
customize   11
cut off   (6)
cute   4

D

daily   (2)
dance (*n*)   (2)
dangerous   2
darker   (3)
darling   (10)
darn   3
data entry   (10)
date   (9)
day camp   (7)
deadline   (10)
dealer   2
decide   7
decision   (1), 7
decision-making   (7)
decorate   (1), 7
decrease   (3)
defend   (6)
definitely   (11)
definition   (4)
degree   10
demand   (12)
demonstrate   (3)
dental assistant   (10)
department store   (1)
depend on   (1)
dependable   10
depreciate   2
deserve   (12)
designate   (5)
desirable   2
desperately   (12)
despite   (12)

destination   (6)
detail   (1)
determine   9
development   (6)
diamond   7
differently   (4)
difficult   3
dig   (4)
director   (10)
dirtier   (2)
disadvantage   6
disagreement   (2)
discard   (3)
discount   (1)
discover   (5)
discuss   (1), 9
dislike (*n*)   6
dislike (*v*)   (12)
dismissal   (10)
distance   (6)
distinct   8
distribute   (11)
document   10
don't miss it   1
done   4
doubt   (1)
draft   (7)
drafted   (12)
drainage   (4)
draw to a close   9
drawer   4
drilling   (4)
drive...crazy   (8)
driven   5
driver's license   (2)
drop   (3)
drought   (4)
drum   (12)
drunk   (2)
due to   (2)
dump   (4)
duration   (8)

E

easily   10
easy   11
eaten   4
economical   1
economize   3
effective   (9)
elbow   (8)
elderly   (7)
electric   (4)
electrical   (4), 5
electronics   (1)
elegant   1
embarrassed   (5)
emergency   (2)
emphasis   9
emphasize   (5)
employee   (3), 10

employer   10
employment   (10)
empty   4
encourage   (2)
end table   4
engine   2
enough   (1), 2
enroll   (10)
ensure   (5)
enter   (11)
entertainer   (12)
entertainment   1
enthusiasm   (10)
enthusiastic   10
enthusiastically   (10)
equal   6
equally   (7)
equip   (5)
equipment   1
especially   (2)
essay   (7)
essential   10
estimate   (4)
evaluate   7
evening gown   9
eventually   6
ever   (1), 11
evidence   (4)
exactly   (5)
exaggerate   1
exaggeration   (1)
except   (8)
excessive   6
exchange   (3)
excited   10
exciting   (9)
exist   (6)
expect   2
expected (*adj*)   (3)
expense   (7)
experience   10
express   (2)
expression   (1)

F

fabric   3
facility   (5)
facing   (2)
fact   2
fail   2
fairly close   (7)
fall asleep   (8)
falling (*adj*)   (2)
false   (10)
familiar   6
family reunion   (9)
famous   (2)
fan   (1)
far   5
farm   (5)
farther   1

least (5)
leave out (10)
led (12)
left 5
left over 7
lend (5), lent 9
less (2)
lesson (2)
let me know 6
license 2
license plate 2
lie 10
lift 5
like (n) 6
limitation (6)
line (1)
list (7)
live (adj) (9)
loan (n) 12
local (10)
locate 4
lonely 6
look at 3
look for 3
look forward to 6, 11
look over (10)
looking up 12
lose one's temper (8)
lost 4
lot 2
lots of 7
lottery (2)
lower (1)
lucky (3)
luxurious 1

M

machine (4)
magazine (5)
magic (2)
magnet (6)
magnetism (6)
main 7
major (4)
make a go of it 12
make ends meet 3
make sense (1)
manage (10)
manageable (9)
management (4)
manager (10), 11
mark (2)
match (7)
material (4)
matter (10), 11
mattress (8)
maximum (3)
may 1
mayor (2)
meaning (1)
medical care (6)

medium-sized 2
membership (5)
memory 3
mention (1), 9
merchant (1)
merry-go-round 1
message (2)
met 4
might 1
might be able to... 7
mind (n) 10
mine 9
minimum (10)
minor (9)
mirror 2
miss 8
mode (10)
moderate 9
motionless (6)
motor 2
motorcycle 2
move 10
musician (12)
myself 3

N

nation (4)
nearby (1)
neat 9
necessarily (9)
necessary (10)
necessity (7)
negotiations (1)
neighbor (1), 3
neighborhood (1)
net (9)
next door (1)
nicer 1
nicest 1
noisy (2)
noncountable (6)
none of my business 7
not a bad idea 9
not enough 6
note 3
notebook (2)
notification (10)
notify (10)
novel (8)
now where are we? 7

O

object (4), 9
observation 2
observe 9
obstacle (12)
obvious (1)
occasion (3), 9
occasionally 2
occupation (11)

occur 8
ocean (4)
octagon 7
octagonal 7
off and on 5
offer (2), 10
office supply store (1)
official (2), 9
oil 2
old-fashioned (1)
older 1
oldest 1
on board (5)
on his way 5
on purpose (8)
on the other hand (12)
on the road 5
on top of 4
one-way street (7)
open space (6)
opening (4), 10
operation (4)
operator (10)
opinion (2)
opportunity 7
oral (10)
orchestra (9)
order (v) (10)
order (n) (12)
organization (2)
organized (4)
originally (12)
others 9
ours 9
ourselves 3
out loud (3)
outfit 9
outgoing (10)
outline (9)
outside 6
oven 4
over (1), 4
over a 8
overdue (3)
overnight (5)
overseas (5)
overtime 8
owe (3)
own (1)
owner 2

P

page (12)
painter (4)
paraphrase (4)
parent (2)
parentheses (2)
park 2
part-time (10)
partnership (8)
pass (5)

passenger (2)
passing (n) (7)
patient (adj) (10)
patronize (1)
pattern 3
peace (3)
pentagon 7
pentagonal 7
perception (12)
perfect (8)
perfectly (3)
perform (12)
performer (12)
perhaps (7)
period 6
permission (8)
permit 2
persevere 10
personnel (10), 11
pest (8)
pester (8)
pet (5)
pharmacy (1)
physical (10)
piano (12)
pickup truck (2)
picnic (1)
pillow (5)
pioneer (12)
pipe (4)
place (v) (9)
planet (10)
planning (n) 10
plant (4)
plaza (1)
plot (1)
plumbing (4)
poem (7)
poet (7)
poetry (7)
point 6
point of view (10)
polite (2)
politely 1
pollution (6)
population (2)
portable (9)
position (10)
possession (5)
possibility 1
possibly (2)
postcard (5)
posture (3)
power (4)
power brakes (2)
power steering (2)
powerful (2)
practical (11)
praise (9)
precious (6)
predict (12)
preference 1

prejudice (12)
present (4)
preserve (4)
president (11)
press 2
pressure (6)
pretend (10)
prettier 1
prettiest 1
pretty... 9
pretty big step 12
pretty soon (12)
previous 2
principal (4)
print (10
prize (8)
probably (6)
problem-solving (6)
process 12
produce (4)
producer (12)
professionally (10)
prohibit (5)
project (2)
propel (6)
proper (4)
property (5)
prose (7)
proverb (1)
provide (5)
pull out (2)
punch bowl (9)
puppy (12)
purchase (3)
purpose (2)
push (1)
put...to work 11
put away (3)
put back 3
put on (3)

Q

qualification (10)
quality 1
quick (2)
quiet (2)
quit (7)
quite (2), 10

R

rack 3
racquet (9)
radio (9)
rail (6)
raise (1)
ran out 5
range (5)
ranking (3)
react (8)
reaction (9)

ready (2), 9
real (11)
reality (2)
realize (3)
rebuild (8)
recent (10)
recently 4
reckless (2)
recliner 4
recognizable 6
recommend (1)
recommendation (1), 10
record (n) 11
rectangle 7
rectangular 7
recyclable (4)
recycle (4)
reduce (11)
refer to 7
reference 10
refinish 4
refreshments 9
refrigerator 4
refuse 1
regarding (10)
regulation (5)
relate (2)
related (adj) 11
relationship 8
relative 6
relax (10)
reliable (1)
relieved 8
reluctance 10
reluctantly 1
remembrance (9)
remind (7)
remove (3)
rent 4
rental 4
repair (3)
repair shop (9)
repeat (8)
report (2)
represent (6)
representative 10
reputation (10)
request (10)
require 4
requirement (10)
research (6)
residence (11)
resident (5)
residential 6
resolve (5)
respect (2)
respond (6)
responsibility (2)
responsible 10
rest (1)
restrict (5)
result (8)

results 10
résumé 10
return (3), 9
reverse (6)
ridiculous (3)
right... 12
right across 12
right after (8), 12
right away (10), 12
right here 12
right now 12
right there 12
right with you 12
rising (adj) (2)
risky 12
road test 2
robbery (6)
robot (3)
role (4)
room 4
roommate 7
rough (6)
round 7
route 1
rude (2)
rug 4
rule (5)
run into 3
rural (1)

S

safe 2
safely (2)
safest 1
salary 7
sandwich shop (10)
satisfied (7), 11
satisfying (11)
save (1)
savings (1)
saying (1)
scare (8)
scene (2)
scholarship (10)
scratch (4)
scream (8)
screech (8)
seat belt 2
secretly (5)
security deposit 4
security guard (1)
seek (10)
seem (1)
seen 4
self-confident (10)
self-motivated (10)
send back (10)
send out (5)
senior (10)
senior prom 9
sensitive (12)

sent 5
separable (3)
separate (4)
sequin (9)
serious (2)
seriously (3)
servant (12)
service (1)
setting (1)
sew 3
sharp (3)
sheet (5)
shift 2
shock (12)
shopping center (1)
shouldn't you? 12
sick and tired of 12
side 5
sigh (7)
sign 4
signature (10)
silently (7)
similar (1)
simplicity (5)
simply (7)
since (5), 6
sink 4
situation (1), 2
skill (3), 10
skim (9)
slang (1)
slept 5
slow (1)
small appliance 4
smooth (2)
sneak (8)
so...that 8
so far 4
social security (10)
sofa 4
software program 11
soil (4)
solitaire (6)
solution (2)
solve (2)
something comes along (12)
something is wrong 5
sophomore (5)
sorry 7
sounds good to me 1
space (4)
space creature (2)
special (9)
speculate (12)
speed (6)
spent 5
spoken 4
sponsored 1
sporting goods store (1)
sports car (2)
square 7

stand for   (2)
standard shift car   2
stanza   (7)
station wagon   (2)
stay   (4)
stayed   5
steady   (7)
steering   5
steering wheel   2
still...   10
stolen   (7)
stood   (7)
stove   4
stress   (6)
stripe   9
strive/strove   (8)
strong   (2), 9
stuck   5
studying (n)   6
style   (1), 3
subject   (10)
submit   (10)
subservient   (12)
substitute   (2)
suburb   6
succeed   (9)
success   (12)
successful   (2)
such (a/an)...that   8
suggest   10
suggestion   (1)
summarize   (7), 10
summary   (4)
sunlight   (6)
superior   (8)
superlative   1
supervise   (5), 11
supervisor   (10), 8
supervisory   11
supply   (4)
suppose   (6), 9
surprising (adj)   8
synonym   (3)
system   (4), 5
systematically   10

T

table   4
take a break   12
take a lot of flak   (12)
take back   (3)
take it easy   (10)
take notes   (2)
take over   (6)
take place   (1)
take the initiative   10
take time   (10)
take turns   (4)
take up space   (6)
taken   4

tale   (1)
talent   11
talkative   (10)
tallest   1
tape   (8)
technical   (10)
technology   (6)
teenage   (2)
temper   (8)
temporary   (5)
tempt   (7)
tenant   4
test   (1)
the other(s)   9
the rest   8
theirs   9
themselves   3
therefore   (2)
think   10
think about   (8)
throughout   (12)
tire   (4)
toaster   4
together   1
tons   (4)
too   2
too many   6
too much   6
tool   (3)
topic   (2)
totally   (8)
touch   (4)
tough   (1)
tour   (12)
tow truck   (5)
toward   (12)
towel   (5)
track   (6)
trade   (3)
traffic jam   (6)
tragedy   (2)
transcript   10
transferred   (12)
transportation   (6)
traveling (n)   6
treat   (5)
tree   (6)
tremendous   4
triangle   7
triangular   7
tribute   (12)
trouble   (8), 11
trumpet   (12)
trunk   2
truth   10
try on   3
tuition   (10)
turn...in   10
turn down   (3)
turn into   (9)
turn things around   (12)

turn to   (1)
turn up   (3)
tuxedo   9
twin   (12)
type   8
typical   (4)

U

UFO   (11)
uglier   1
ugliest   1
ugly   2
unclear   (3)
uncrowded   (1)
under   (1), 4
underline   (10)
undesirable   2
undone   (7)
unexpected   (1), 2
unfinished   (1)
unfortunately   (6)
unfurnished   4
uni-sex hair salon   (1)
unidentified   (1)
uninteresting   (1)
unit   (10)
university   11
unreliable   (1)
unromantic   (1)
unselfish   (12)
until   (7), 8
up-to-date   (10)
update   (6)
upholstery   (2)
urban   (1)
used   2
used to...   11
useful   (1)
using   2

V

vacancy   10
vacant   4
valid   (5)
valuable   (11)
value   (1), 2
variety   (1)
various   1
vehicle   (2)
verify   (10)
violence   (8)
visa   (6)
visited   5
voice   (8)
volume   (3)
volunteer   (10), 11
vote   (7)

W

wage   (10)
wallet   (2)
war   (4)
warn   (7)
warning   (1)
was   3
was/were just   5
waste   (1)
watch out   7
way   10
we can't help...   7
wear   3
weekday   (1)
welcome   (4)
well-organized   10
went off   5
went up   1
were   2
what...for   7
what's up?   9
whether   (4)
whichever   (5)
whole   (1)
wild   9
willing   10
wind   (1)
windshield   2
wing   (6)
wise   2
without   (3)
witness   (2)
won't they?   12
woods   (5)
word processing   (10)
worry   (3)
worse   1
worst   1
worth   (3)
would   2
would rather   1
written   (2), 5
wrong   (2), 5

Y

yet   (3), 7
you can say that again   6
you're kidding   8
you've got a point   12
young   (2)
yours   9
yourself   3
yourselves   3

Z

zip   (10)

VOCABULARY: Book 3

A

a few   13
a little   13
a lot of   13
ability   (9)
about to   13
above   (1)
absent   (9)
absolute   (5)
abundant   (8)
accept   (8)
acceptable   (1)
according to   (7)
achieving   (8)
acquire   2
acquisition   (2)
acre   (14)
across   (4)
act   (8)
action   (1)
actively   (14)
activity   (2), 7
ad   (2)
add   (1)
additional   (8)
admission   (1)
adore   11
adverb   (5)
advice   (1)
aerobics   (7)
affect   (8)
affectionate   (13)
after   2
afterwards   (14)
against   (14)
age   1
agree   (1)
air   2
airfare   5
airline tickets   (10)
alive   (14)
all   (of)   7
allowed   (8)
almost   (1)
alone   (8)
aloud   (5)
already   (14)
although   (3)
altitude   (12)
always   5
ambulance   4
amount   (5)

ancient   11
angry   (5), 6
animal   5
anniversary   (1)
announce   1
announcement   1
annual   (1)
anonymous   (5)
antique   (2)
anxiously   (10)
any   8
anybody   (4), 9
anymore   (6)
anyone   (13)
anything   5
appear   (2)
appearance   (2)
appetite   (7)
application   (8)
appreciated   (4)
approve   (13)
area   (2)
arena   2
argument   (4)
around   1
arrival   1
arrive   1
as   (1)
as a/an ...   11
ashamed   (5)
aside   (13)
ask   12
asparagus   (8)
assistant   (6)
associate   (14)
astrologer   3
astrology   3
astronomer   (3)
astronomy   (3)
atmosphere   (11)
attack (*v*)   (5)
attend   (4), 14
author   (2)
authority   (5)
available   (2)
avoid   (14)
awareness   (14)
away   (1), 2

B

baby   (1)
back (*adv*)   (7), 9

background   (10)
bacon   (7)
bagel   (7)
baked   (8)
ballet   (11)
balloon   (2)
basis   2
bath   (2)
bathing suit   (11)
battle   (3)
bay   (11)
be born   1
be prepared   3
beading   (10)
became   2
because   6
become   3
begin/began   8, 12
beginning   (5)
behavior   (5)
behind   (5)
belief   5
believe   (3)
bell   (11)
below   (1)
benefit   (7)
best   (2)
best man   10
beverage   (8)
beware   (14)
billion   (3)
birth   1
blender   10
blew   14
blow   14
blow out   10
body   (5)
bon voyage   (12)
bonus   (8)
boring   (6)
boss   (5)
bottom   (1)
bought   10
bouquet   (10)
bowl   8
bowling   (7)
break down   10
breathing   2
bridal attendants   (10)
bride   1, 10
bridesmaid   10
bring   (1), 3
broccoli   (8)

brochure   (12)
broiled   (8)
bronchial   (2)
brought   (1)
brush   6
brutal   (14)
building   2
built   (11)
bulky   (7)
bullet train   11
bureau   (12)
burn   4
business   (3)

C

café   (11)
cafeteria   (7)
calculator   (6)
calendar   (3)
calorie   (7)
camera   (11)
campaign   (2)
candle   (10), 14
cards   1
carefully   (8)
careless   (6)
carpeted   (2)
carrot   (8)
carry   (5), 12
cartoon   (3)
cash   (5)
casserole dishes   10
cassette player   (5)
catch/caught   5
cause   (4)
cavities   6
ceiling   (13)
celebrate   1
celebration   1
celery   (8)
center   (3)
century   (2)
ceremony   (2)
certainly   (7)
champion   (1)
championship   (1)
change   (3)
character   (2)
charge (*v*)   (5)
charming   (12)
chart   (1)
chase   (11)

cheap (8)
cheaper 14
check 3
checkup 6
cheer up (9)
chef (1), 5
chest (9)
chief 5
childish (5)
choice (5)
choose (1)
chores 1
civil (1)
classified ad (5)
clean 6
clear 11
clear up 2
climb (4)
close to 2
cloud 4
clown (2)
club (8), 11
clue (5)
collect (2)
colorful (10)
column (1)
come back 6
come in 6
comfortable (8)
comics (5)
coming (adj) (4)
comment (5)
commit (5)
committee (4)
community (4)
company (1)
compare (3)
comparison (8)
compete 1
competition 1
complain 6
complete (1)
condition (7)
conference 12
connect (12)
conservation (14)
consider (4)
consist of (4)
consult (7)
consume (7)
consumer (14)
contact (4)
contain (2)
contest (13)
context (5)
continent (14)
contrast (3)
contribution (1)
control 4
convenience 2
conversation (1), 5
convicted (5)

convince (6)
correct (1)
correction (5)
correspondent (10)
cost 9, (past) 14
could 9
couldn't 9
counseling (8)
counselor (8)
county (5)
couple 10
cover (6)
crackers (13)
craft (11)
crash (n, v) (4)
crazy (5), 11
cream 8
create (14)
crime 5
criminal (5)
critical (14)
crowded (14)
cruel (5)
cry (4)
crystal glasses 10
cue (4)
culture (13)
cup 8
currently (10)
customer (3)
cut (4), 14

D

daily (8)
damage (5)
damp 11
danger (14)
dangerous (5)
dark (5)
deal with (8)
death (5)
decade (14)
decide 1
decline (1)
decrease (7)
dedicated (4)
deepen (5)
defend (14)
defending (adj) (1)
delicacy (12)
delicate (10)
delightful (11)
delivery (2)
den (2)
dental (6)
dentist 6
depart (10)
depend on (6)
depressed 9
describe (1), 14
description (7), 14

desk clerk (4)
dessert (1)
destroy (14)
detective (5)
detergent 9
develop (3)
devote (5)
dial (4)
diamond (3)
diary (8)
did 4
die (4)
diet (3), 7
difference (3)
different (1)
difficult (1)
director 2
dirty (5)
disagree (1), 4
discomfort (7)
discovered (9)
discovery (3)
disease (9)
disgrace (5)
dish (1)
dislike (14)
dispense (1)
disprove (3)
distance (11)
divorce 1
do 4
donated 2
donation (2)
door (4)
downtown 2
drank 9
draw/drew 11
dream (13)
drink 9
driver (4)

E

each 1
earlier (7)
earth (3)
edge (14)
editor (5)
educated (8)
effect (7)
effective (8)
either (1), 13
election (4)
electric (10)
electricity 2
elegant (10)
elephant (2), 12
elevator (11)
eligible (4)
eliminate (12)
elves (2)
embarrassment (1)

emergency (4)
employ (6)
empty (5)
endangered (14)
ending (3)
endless (11)
energy (7)
engagement 1
enjoy (2), 3
enormous (3)
enough (7)
ensure (8)
enter (4)
entertainment (11)
entitle (1)
entrée (8)
entry (13)
equal (2)
era (2)
escape 5
especially (7)
essential (2)
establish (8)
even 8
ever (8)
every 7
every other 7
everyone 14
exactly (4)
examination 9
examine (6), 9
except (5)
exception (8)
excessive (5)
exchange (2)
excitement (10), 11
excuse 7
exercise 2
exhibit 2
exit (12)
expand (1)
expensive (2), 5
explain (2)
express (13)
extensive (2)
extinction (14)
extra 2
extremely (2)

F

fact (7)
fair (7)
fairly (11)
fall (down) 11
family room (2)
famous (2)
far away 2
fare (10), 12
farthest (12)
fascinated (3)
fat 7

father-in-law 1
fattening 7
favorite (8)
fee (2)
feel 8
fell down 11
felt (1), 8
female (10)
few (1)
fiber (8)
fill 6
fill in (7)
fill out (8), 10
fill up 10
final (1)
finally 3
finals 4
financial (1)
find out (1), 3
fire department (4)
firm (adj) (5)
firmly (1)
fish (8)
fit (adj) (7)
fitness (7)
flat (11)
floor 4
flower (7), 10
fold (3)
follow 7
following (adj) (2)
for 7
for sale (2), 14
forecast (3)
forget 9
forgot (3), 9
fork 8
formal 10
formerly (10)
formula (5)
fortunately (14)
fortune teller (3)
found 3
found out 3
founding (n) (14)
fountain 11
frame 7
free (1)
freeze (5)
frequency (5)
frequent (12)
frequently (7)
fried (8)
friendly (3)
front (4)
full (4)
fun (3), 5
fund (14)
furious (5)
future (2), 3

G

gain weight 7
galaxy (3)
garden (2)
gas (6)
gasoline (10)
gave (1), 9
generous (2)
gently (7)
germ (9)
get engaged 1
get married 1
get up (1)
gift (1)
give 12
glad (1)
glass 8
goal (1)
golf (7)
gone (14)
good-looking (10)
gorgeous (10)
gorilla (14)
government (14)
gown 10
grade (5)
graduate (3)
grapefruit (8)
gravity (3)
grocery (7)
groom 1
guest 1
guide (4)
guidelines (1)
gums 6

H

habit (8)
habitat (14)
half past 2
hall (2)
ham 8
hamburger (7)
handle (4)
handsome (10)
happen (3)
happiness 14
hard-boiled (8)
hardened (5)
harvest (3)
headline (4)
health (7)
healthy (6), 7
heard (1)
heart of (2)
heavy 7
height 7
hemisphere (11)
herbal (8)
heritage (14)

hide/hid 11
high 9
highway (4)
hint (12)
hit 11
hold (10)
hole (11)
holiday (10)
honeymoon 1
honor 2
hope 12
horoscope 3
host (v) (2)
household items 10
housing (2)
how long ... 2
how tall 7
however (14)
hug 14
huge (2)
human beings (3)
hurry up (10)
hurt 6

I

icy (13)
ideal (8)
identify (5)
identity (11)
illegal (14)
illness (4), 9
imaginary (1)
imagination (6)
imagine (2)
immediate (2)
important 5
impossible 5
impractical (7)
impression (12)
improve (7)
in 7
in addition to (2)
in fact (7)
in front of (4)
in order (1)
in-laws (12)
inch (7)
include (1), 2
incomparable (2)
increase (7)
incredibly (1)
independent (12)
indicate (11)
inexpensive 2
infant (5)
infection (2)
informal (1)
information (1)
ingredients (12)
initially (8)
injury 4

inseparable (6)
inside 9
instrument (8)
intense (7)
intention (12)
interested 2
international (2)
interrupted 4
introduce 14
introduction 14
invention (3)
invitation (1), 10
invite (1), 2
island 11
item (7)
itinerary (10)
ivory (14)

J

jaguar (14)
jail 5
jazz (4)
join (8)
jump 4

K

keep (5), 9
key (5)
kick off (2)
kill (5)
kind (2)
king (3)
knee (7)
knife 5, 8/knives 5
know (3)
knowledge (3)

L

lace (10)
lack (1)
ladder 4
land (2)
land (v) 13
last (v) 2
late (1), 8
lately 9
law (3)
lazy 7
lead (n) (5)
leader (1)
leaf/leaves 5
learn to 2
lecture 14
led (1)
legislation (14)
lemonade (12)
length 2
leopard (14)
less ... than 14

less (7)
level (7)
license (10)
life 1
lift (7)
light (3), 14
likely 3
limbo (11)
lime (12)
limited (13)
lined (12)
linens (13)
liquids 9
list (2)
listed (adj) (7)
listing (2)
lit 14
liter (9)
living (n) (5)
loaf/loaves 5
lobby (4)
local (1)
located (13)
location 2
logical (3)
look at 6
look for 6
look up (7)
lose weight 7
lost 3, 8
loud 7
loudly 4
loveliest (13)
lovely (14)
low 5
lower (9)
luck (3)
lucky (3)
luggage 12
luxury 11

M

maid of honor 10
main (1)
maintained (2)
maintenance (8)
major (7)
management office (2)
manners (1)
many 13
map (11)
march (10)
mark (n) (5)
market 14
marriage 1
marry (3)
math (6)
meal 6
mean (v) 2
meaning (n) (1)
measure (8)

meatball (8)
medal 2
medical (5)
medicine 9
medium 7
meeting 4
member (4), 10
membership (4)
menu (8)
met 3
meter (12)
middle-aged (5)
might (6)
mind (5)
mine (1)
minor (7)
miss (4), 8
mistake 3
mix (5)
moderate (7)
modern (2), 14
modification (8)
moment (1), 4
money (1)
monitor (8)
more 1
more ... than 14
most 1
mother-in-law 1
motorcycle (2)
movement (3)
movie star (5)
much 13
mugger (5)
murder (5)
muscle (7)
musical (2)
My goodness! 9
mysterious (3)
mystery (5)
myth (7)

N

napkin 8
narrow (13)
native (10)
natural (8)
natural surroundings 14
naturally (8)
necessarily (7)
necessary (4)
need 12
negative (13)
neighbor (4)
neighborhood 7
neither 14
nephew (14)
never 5
new 1
niece (10)

nightlife 11
nobody 14
noise 1
none of 7
normally (7)
note (1)
nothing 5
noun (3)
nowadays 1
nowhere (12)
numbered (3)
nutrition (8)

O

object (3)
observation (3)
observe (3)
obtain 10
occasion (10)
ocean (11)
of 2
off (7)
offer (2)
office 6
officer 5
official (5)
often 5
on a diet 7
on fire 4
on sale 14
on the premises 2
on time (7)
one-man (1)
one-on-one (2)
operate (1)
opinion (4)
opportunity 2
oral (1)
outdoor 14
outreach (14)
outside (2)
over (5)
over the years 2
overdevelopment (14)
overseas (12)
own (1)

P

pack (12)
page (1)
paid 3
pain (7)
pale (10)
pancake (7)
park (v) 3
part 2
part-time (3)
participate 1
past 2
patient 6

pay 1
peace (4)
pearl 12
pen pal (5)
per (2)
perfect (1)
perform (1), 2
performance (1)
period (7)
permanent (8)
personal (1)
perspire (7)
pet (2)
pharmacist 9
phase (8)
phone call (3), 10
photograph (n) (4)
photographer 4
physical (7)
pick out 10
pick up 10
picture 4
pie (12)
piece (3), 8
pills 9
pilot (5)
place (v) (12)
plan (1), 12
planet (3)
plans 12
plant (v) (3)
plate 8
play (n) (2)
pleased (1)
pleasure (2)
plus (2)
pocket 13
point of view (1)
point out (4)
police officer 4
polite (6)
politely (1)
popular (13)
pork (14)
position 3
positive (8)
possession (14)
possibility (9)
potluck (1)
predict 3
premature (7)
preparation (8)
prepare 4
prescribe 9
prescription 9
president (1)
pretend (1)
pretty (adj) 8
prevent (6)
previous (8)
primate (14)
prince (5)

principal   (12)
principle   (8)
print   (5)
prison   (5)
prisoner   (5)
private   2
probably   (1), 3
processed   (8)
professional   (8)
programming   1
progress   (8)
promise   (4), 12
promotion   (3)
pronoun   (3)
protect   (5), 14
protected (*adj*)   14
protection   12
prove   (11)
provide   (8)
public   (1), 2
pull   6
purchase   (14)
put   14
put in   (4)
put out   10
puzzled   (1)

Q

qualification   (4)
quantity   (8)
quart   8
quarter past   2
quickest   (7)
quiet   (9)
quite   (3)

R

raincoat   (14)
raise   (7)
ran   (4)
rang   11
range (*v*)   (12)
rapidly   (7)
rare   (14)
rarely   5
rather   (8)
reach   (4)
read (past)   3
read   12
ready   (2)
real   (1), 11
really   (1), 3
reason   1
reasonable   2
receive   1
recent   (9)
reception   1, 10
recommend   (13)
record   (6)
recreate   (1)

reduce   (7)
refer to   (3)
refined   (8)
reform   (5)
refrigerator   3
refuse   (1)
regular   2
regularly   7
relative (*n*)   (5)
relatively   (7)
release   (5)
remain   (8)
remember   (1), 6
remote   (14)
remove   (9)
rent   (2)
replaced   (8)
reporter   (1), 4
request   (14)
require   (7)
rescue   4
reservation   (10)
reserve (*n*)   (14)
reside   (10)
resident   (11)
resources   (4)
respected   (6)
response   2
responsible   (8)
rest   (2)
restful   (7)
result   (1)
resume   (12)
retire   1
retired   1
retirement   1
return   (1)
reverse   (3)
review (*n*)   (3)
revise   (5)
revolve   (3)
rewrite   (4)
rhino   12
rich   (1)
rights   (1)
ring   11
risk   (7)
robbed   5
robber   (4), 5
robbery   (4)
role   (3)
roof   5
rose   (10)
round-trip   (10), 12
route   (11)
rude   (1)
rudeness   (1)
ruins   11
rule   (8)
ruler   (3)
runway   (4)

S

safe   (5)
safety   (5)
said   (1)
sail   (12)
sale   (2), 14
salesperson   14
salt and pepper shakers   8
same   (1)
sandy   11
sang   (10), 14
sat down   11
saucer   8
save   (1)
scale   (8)
scan   (2)
scarf/scarves   5
scene   (4)
scenery   (11)
schedule   (8)
scholarship   (1)
scientific   (3)
score   1
scrambled   (3)
scratch   (5)
sculptor   (12)
sculpture   2
sea   11
search   (3)
section   (3)
sedentary   (7)
seem   (7)
selection   (4)
sell   (8), 12
senator   4
send   1
senior   (1)
separable   (10)
separate (*adj*)   (3)
separate (*v*)   (6)
series   (2)
serious   4
serve   (8)
serving dishes   10
session   (8)
set up   (8)
setting   (2)
several   1
shape   7
sharp   (12)
sheets   10
ship   (12)
shop (*v*)   (3)
short of   (1)
shot   (5)
show (*n*)   (1), (*v*) (3), 12
shower   (4)
side   (10)
side order   (8)

sights   (10), 12
sightseeing   12
sign   3
silently   (10)
silverware   8
similarity   (3)
simple   (1), 4
since   (1)
sing   14
sister-in-law   (12)
sit (down)   6
situation   (1)
skim milk   (8)
skin   (8)
sky   3
sleep/slept   8
slice   8
slow down   (7)
smart   (3)
smile   (1), 11
smoke   4
snow   (5)
so   1
so-called   (5)
society   (5)
soft-boiled   (8)
sold   3, 14
solution   (1)
solve   (5)
some   8
some of   7
somebody   4
someday   (3)
someone   (3)
something   5
sometimes   5
song   (2)
sore   (7)
sound   (9)
soup spoon   8
sour   (12)
spare time   (4)
speaker   (6)
species   (14)
specific   (2), 4
spectacular   2
spend   (6), 14
spent   (8), 14
spoon   8
squad   (4)
square   (2)
stadium   (1)
staff   2
stage   (8)
stamp   (2)
star   3
starch   (8)
stare   (13)
start   (1), 4
start over   (7)
state   (1)
statue   (11)

stay   (3)
steak   8
steal   5
steps   4
stole   5
stood   (4)
storm   (5)
straight   (1)
stranger   (3)
strength   (7)
stress   (8)
stroll   (13)
strong   (4)
stuck   5
studio   2
study (*n*)   (7)
stuff   (2)
substance   (9)
success   (8)
such   (1)
suggest   (5)
suggestion   (3)
summary   (2)
sun   (3)
sunset   11
support   (4)
surprise   3
surprised   14
surround   (5)
surviving   (14)
sympathetic   (13)
symptom   (9)
syrup   (7)

T

table   (3)
tablecloth   10
tablespoon   8
take care of   6
take it easy   (9)
take off   10
take turns   (1)
talented   (1)
tape   (13)
target   (14)
tasteless   (1)
taught   (8), 14
tax   (4), 12
teach   14
tear   11
teaspoon   8
techniques   (8)
teeth   6
telescope   (3)
television set   (5)
tell   1
tell time   (2)

teller   (11)
temperature   9
temple   11
test   (3)
than   (9)
than any other   11
there was   4
there were   4
thermometer   9
thief/thieves   5
thin   (6), 9
thing   1
thought   3
throw   4
throw away   (5), 10
ticket   12
tiger   (14)
tiny   (12)
tip   (5)
title   (1)
to   2
toast   8
toaster   10
together   (3)
told   9
took   (1), 5
toothache   6
toothbrush   (9)
top   5
topic   (11)
tore   11
tossed salad   (8)
tour   (11), 14
tournament   (1)
towels   10
town   (1), 2
toy   (2), 11
track   (11)
traffic   4
train (*v*)   (6)
training   (4)
translate   (13), 14
translation   14
transportation   (11)
treasure   2
trip   3
trophy   (1)
tropical   11
trouble   (5)
true   (2), 3
truly   (1)
try   1
tuna   (8)
turkey   (8)
turn (*n*)   (6)
turn off   10
turn on   (4), 10
tuxedo   10

twin   (2)
typical   (10)

U

ugly   (8)
ulcer   (9)
ultimate   (8)
ultramodern   2
unanswered   (5)
unbeatable   2
under control   (4)
unfair   (5)
unhappy   1
unique   (14)
unit   (2)
universe   (3)
unknown   (4)
unlock   (4)
unnecessary   (7)
until   (8)
unusual   2
upon   (3)
upper   (4)
used to   2
useful   (5)
usual   14
usually   5
utilities   2

V

vacant   (5)
value   (2)
van   4
variety   (8)
vase   10
veil   10
victory   (1)
view   (2)
vigorous   (7)
violent   (5), 7
visible   (5)
visit   (2), 12
visitor   (12)
vital   (8)
volunteer   (4)
vote   (13)

W

waiting room   (7)
walk-in closets   (2)
wall   4
way   (1)
wed   1
wedding   1
wedding party   10

weekly   (8)
weigh   7
weight   7
well-known   (1)
wet   (10)
when   4
whenever   (14)
wherever   (14)
whether   (1)
which   14
while   (3), 4
whisper   (10)
whole   (1)
whole-wheat   (8)
wholesome   (8)
whom   (2)
whose   14
why   1
wild   (1), 5
will   (1), 7
win   1
window   4
wise   (8)
within   (2)
without   (5)
witness   (4)
wives   5
woke up   3
wolf/wolves   5
women   5
won't   3
wonderful   (2), 11
wore   10
worker   4
world   2
world-famous   (11)
worry   (12)
wound   (5)
wrapped   (2)
write   11
write down   (6)
wrong   (1)
wrote   (5), 9, 11

Y

year   1
yell   4
yet   (14)
young   (5)
yourself   4

Z

zebra   (14)
zoo   14

EXPANSION ACTIVITIES

EXPANSION ACTIVITIES

UNIT 1

■ EXPANSION ACTIVITY 1A (page 15)

They take the prize! They're #1!

1. Write the following prepositional phrases on the board: *in the school, in the city, in the class, in the world, in the country, of the summer, on record, in town, on the team.*
2. Read the statements below. Have students write a superlative statement using one of the phrases on the board.

   YOU READ: He never does any classwork or homework.
   THEY WRITE: *He's the laziest student in the class.*

3. Have students share and correct responses with a partner.

Statements:
1. She gives twenty pages of homework every night.
2. There is no crime where I live.
3. He always gets the answer right.
4. Our children know the answer to everything.
5. She's walking on air. She looks like she's in heaven.
6. I have to carry an umbrella all the time here.
7. The weather's always great in July!
8. When is this game going to end?
9. No one will be able to catch us in our sports car.
10. He's always at the doctor's.

(Have students respond using *best* or *worst*.)
11. Lisa wins more races than anyone on her swimming team.
12. Mr. Lincoln always explains things clearly, always corrects homework, and always helps students.
13. Everything Gino makes is delicious.
14. My friend Pedro has never had a car accident.
15. I can't drink this juice. Yechh!
16. Ira takes off, lands, and flies smoothly. Every trip with him is terrific.

17. The picture is clear, the colors are brilliant, and every channel comes in perfectly.
18. Nobody learns anything is this place.

Variation: Form four teams of students. Read the statements below and have teams compete to see which team can say a superlative statement first. If a team makes an incorrect superlative statement, the team that gives a correct response scores a point.

1. The food here is marvelous, but they charge a fortune.
2. She always does what she says she will do.
3. This model has the works, all the equipment you can imagine.
4. This model goes far on a gallon of gas.
5. This child's picture should be on the cover of a magazine.
6. I'll never be able to understand this subject.
7. When you lie down here, you'll fall asleep immediately.
8. There's nothing interesting about this class.

■ EXPANSION ACTIVITY 1B (page 17)

Recommendations and warnings

1. With the class, brainstorm a list of about five things or services that people in your class buy from time to time or are likely to need in the next year or so.
2. Put the following sentence models on the board. Have students complete them before they work in groups.
   a. Where's the best place to ____?
   b. I recommend ____. They have the ____ in town.
   c. Be careful of ____. It's a/an ____ place. They have the ____ in town.
3. Put the students in small groups. Have each group talk about the best and worst places to get the list of things or services in your area. Encourage students to share experiences they have had with the different businesses.
4. Regroup as a class and compare recommendations and warnings. Encourage disagreement and have students give reasons for their opinions.

UNIT 2

■ EXPANSION ACTIVITY 2A (page 33)

He's not tall enough

Read these sentences to students. Have them write a sentence for each numbered item describing the problem and using *enough*.
For example, you say, *I want to send this picture to my sister, but it doesn't fit in the envelope I have.* A student might write, *The envelope isn't big enough.*

Statements:
1. Sammy is four feet tall. The book he wants is on a shelf that is six feet high.
2. The house costs half a million dollars. My salary is $25,000 a year.
3. The car's brakes are bad and the steering wheel isn't working right.
4. I tried to teach my dog to sit, speak and roll over, but he never learned how, even after a year of training.
5. The train takes four hours to get to New York, but I need to be there in two hours.
6. Fatima wants to drive but she is only fifteen.
7. Ralph wants to be on the football team, but he weighs only one hundred twenty-five pounds.
8. The telephone cord won't reach from the living room to the kitchen.

■ EXPANSION ACTIVITY 2B (page 33)

Who gets what?

1. Give students the following information and have them provide a solution for the problem. They can write out the solution or report it orally to the class.
2. Have a class discussion comparing solutions.

Each of the following four families won a new motor vehicle in a contest. Unfortunately, the car dealer forgot to mark the winning tickets with the name of the vehicle. The dealer accepts responsibility for the problem and has agreed to give $20,000 to make the prizes equal. Still the four families cannot agree on who gets which car.

   As a last resort, your group has been called in to resolve the problem. You must assign the vehicles and the cash so that all families will agree to your solution. Your decision is final.

Information on the vehicles: A. pickup truck–25 MPG, $18,600 B. compact car–40 MPG, $11,000 C. station wagon–20 MPG, $23,100 D. van– 25 MPG, $19,700

Information on the families: *Family 1:* couple in their fifties, live far from their plumbing business, three grown children, two grandchildren. *Family 2:* couple in their early forties, both teachers, children 16 and 18, live far from work and schools. *Family 3:* couple in their late twenties, she sells cosmetics door to door, he is a high school baseball coach, three children under 10. *Family 4:* couple in their forties, he's an insurance executive, she's a lawyer, two children, they all like to go camping.

UNIT 3

■ EXPANSION ACTIVITY (page 49)

Going shopping

1. Form groups of three to five students. Tell them they are going to plan and dramatize a situation in a store. (Review the conversations in Listening 17 for ideas, but let students use their imaginations.)
2. Write the following planning questions on the board: *What kind of store is it? Who are the people involved? What's the situation? Are people going to be polite or impolite? What is the result of the conversation?*
3. Have each group role play their situation for the class.

Variation: If the class has sufficient role-play experience, ask students first to discuss and decide on the planning questions they need to answer.

UNIT 4

■ EXPANSION ACTIVITY 4A (page 60)

Drawing floor plans

1. Give students instructions to draw a floor plan. For example:
   A. Draw a rectangle to represent a bedroom.
   Draw a door in the center of the bottom wall.
   Draw two windows in the center of the top wall.
   Draw one window in the middle of the right wall.
   Draw a bed under each window in the top wall.
   Draw a small table between the two beds.
   Draw a closet all along the left wall.
   B. Draw a big rectangle to represent a living room.
   Draw two windows in the center of the top wall.
   Draw one window in the center of the left wall.
   Draw a door in the middle of the bottom wall.
   Put a big couch in front of the two windows.
   Put a coffee table in front of the couch.
   Draw an end table at each end of the couch.
2. After practicing with your example(s), have students their own draw a floor plan and give their classmates instructions to draw it.

■ EXPANSION ACTIVITY 4B (page 60)

Describing actions

1. Have students number their papers from 1–10.
2. Use five interesting objects, for example, a cigar box, a yo-yo, a toy dog, a calculator, and a pair of scissors.
3. Have students watch you manipulate the objects on your desk at the front of the room. After you move an object, give students enough time to write a sentence beginning with "He/She put/took/held…" to describe what you did.
4. Manipulate the objects in the following ways:
   1. Put the cigar box in the middle of the desk.
   2. Put the yo-yo into the box.
   3. Put the toy dog in front of the box.
   4. Take the yo-yo out of the box.
   5. Put the scissors under the box.
   6. Hold the calculator over the toy dog.
   7. Place the dog behind the box.
   8. Take the box off the desk.
   9. Place the dog in the middle of the desk.
   10. Put the dog under the desk.

■ EXPANSION ACTIVITY 4C (page 62)

Checking information in a short talk

1. Have students get pencil and paper ready for note-taking.
2. Tell them you are going to talk about yourself and that they should take notes about what you tell them. Tell them not to worry if they don't understand everything. They will have a chance to check the information.
3. On the board, write questions that students should be able to answer from your talk. For example: *What's my brother's name? Where does he come from? What languages does he speak?*
4. Include information about an individual and a couple you know well. Then have students write answers to the questions on the board. They should check information they are not sure of by asking you a tag question; for example, *Your parents were born in Germany, weren't they?* If there's time, have students write paragraphs about one person or couple you talked about.

■ EXPANSION ACTIVITY 4D (page 62)

You _____, don't you?

1. Form groups of four or six students. Divide each group in half, forming subgroups A and B.
2. Have each subgroup write ten statements they believe are true about the members of the other subgroup.
3. Subgroups take turns checking their statements with the other subgroup, using tag questions.

> Tito comes from Spain. (*written*)
> Tito, you come from Spain, don't you?

UNIT 5

■ EXPANSION ACTIVITY 5A (page 76)

What did they just do?

1. Have students bring in magazine pictures of people doing different things. Select about ten pictures to tape on the wall. Write a number above each picture.
2. Have students look at the pictures and write one or two sentences for each picture about what the people or someone related to the people in the picture *just* did. For example, if the picture is of two people looking at menus in a restaurant, students might write: *They just sat down.* or *The waiter just showed them to their table.*
3. Call on a student to read one sentence. Other students guess which picture the *just*-statement

refers to. The student who guesses the picture correctly reads the next statement. Continue until all students have spoken at least once.

■ EXPANSION ACTIVITY 5B (page 80)

In a youth hostel common room

1. Have students form groups of four to six students. Tell them that they are going to create and dramatize a situation in the common room of a hostel.
2. Have the class brainstorm appropriate planning questions before groups work on the role play. Some might be: Where is the hostel? Who is each traveler? What country does he/she come from? Where has he/she been? Where is he/she going? How is he/she traveling? What topics will the group discuss? Is one person the hostel manager?
3. Set up a living room situation and role play the conversations. In this general situation students should not need to write out their role plays. Encourage them to plan well and improvise during the dramatization.

UNIT 6

■ EXPANSION ACTIVITY (page 93)

How maglev works

If you have students who are interested in science, especially physics, give them the following detailed explanation of how maglev works.

1. Have students discuss the reading with a partner.
2. If they understand it well, have them explain to the class how the magnets work to lift and propel maglev. Students can prepare large copies of the drawings on page 92 and use them in their talk.

How Maglev Works

Both Japanese and German maglev use the forces of magnetic attraction and repulsion to lift the train off the guideway, propel it forward, and stop it. Either attraction or repulsion can be used to lift the train. Both are used to power and stop it. Japanese engineers decided to use repulsion and German engineers decided to use attraction, which makes for important differences in the way the trains look and in the type of guideway they run on.

Japanese maglev runs on a cradle-like track or guideway. (See Fig. 1 on page 92.) The guideway contains a set of coils. The cars contain superconducting magnets. When these magnets pass over the coils, they generate an electrical current in the coils which creates a magnetic field opposite to the magnetic field of the magnets. The repulsive force of the opposite magnetic fields lifts the cars about four inches off the guideway. There are also magnets on the sides of the guideway. They are placed in such a way that when the superconducting magnets on the train pass them, there are always opposite poles in front pulling the train forward (attraction) and identical poles in back pushing it forward (repulsion). In choosing repulsion to lift the train, the Japanese make vehicle and guideway construction simpler and cheaper, but they have to pay the price of a system to freeze the magnets to near-273 degrees Celsius in order to achieve the incredible repulsive force necessary to lift the seven-ton maglev vehicles.

German maglev hooks around a guideway that is a flat rail. (See Fig. 2 on page 92). There are electromagnetic coils in the guideway that receive electric current from a power substation. In the part of the vehicle that curves under the rail, there are battery-powered magnets, 28 per 82 feet of train. Opposite poles are created between the magnets, attracting the hooked part of the train up toward the guideway. At the same time the vehicles are lifted about ½ inch from the guideway. Then, in much the same way as described above for Japanese maglev, attractive and repulsive magnetic forces pull and push the train forward. In choosing attraction to lift the train, the Germans don't have to worry about freezing the magnets, but they have to have sophisticated computers to keep the maglev riding smoothly on its ½ inch cushion of air. If the ½ inch varies even a very little bit, the train will become unbalanced and the ride bumpy.

At present it is not known if these differences will make one type of maglev superior to the other in general or for a specific purpose. Either one or both may be the maglev we know in the next century.

UNIT 7

■ EXPANSION ACTIVITY 7A (page 98)

Learning to drive

1. Have students form groups of three and do a role play in which one student is learning to drive. The other students can be parents, driving instructors, or police officers.
2. Brainstorm planning questions with the whole class.
3. Have groups plan, write, practice, and role play a conversation in which the beginner does something wrong and is confronted by one of the other people.
4. Brainstorm useful language such as:
   Automobile problems/errors: *run a red light, sideswipe a car, make a turn from the wrong lane, have a blowout, drive too fast*
   Warnings/Instructions: *watch out, look out, be careful, Take it easy. Keep your _____ on the _____. Didn't you see that sign? It means you _____.*
   General idioms: *pay attention to, make mistakes, do things right and wrong*

■ EXPANSION ACTIVITY 7B (page 102)

Listing in order of priority

1. In addition to stating and evaluating alternatives, the decision-making process also requires people to know what is important to them, that is to list priorities. Teach students to list what is important to a person in order of priority using Liz's situation.
2. Brainstorm possible considerations for Liz with the class or provide the following: **a.** safety: Liz wants to be safe.   **b.** independence: Liz wants to be independent, to have her own apartment.   **c.** cost: Liz will make a good salary but she won't be able to afford an expensive apartment.   **d.** company: Liz wants friends.   **e.** approval of her family: Liz wants her father and mother to be happy.   **f.** size: Liz needs a studio or a one-bedroom apartment.
3. Have students order these considerations 1–6 on the basis of what is most and least important to Liz.

UNIT 8

■ EXPANSION ACTIVITY 8A (page 112)

Explaining results

1. Have students find pictures in magazines that lend themselves to talking about results. For example:
   a. an accident scene (The small car was going so fast that...)
   b. a child with a prize-winning dog (She took such good care of him that she won the first prize.)
   c. Person learning to skate or ski. (He's such a bad skier, he's going to break his leg.)
   d. A T-shirt with lots of holes. (She's worn it so often that it's falling apart.)
2. Put the pictures on the wall with a number or letter above them.
3. Have students work with a partner and write five sentences using so...that or such a/an...that about different pictures.
4. Have students take turns reading one of their sentences and seeing if classmates can identify the picture they had in mind.

■ EXPANSION ACTIVITY 8B (page 115)

Are you still doing that? (Reentry of gerunds as complements of the verbs: start, begin, stop, and finish)

1. Draw two columns labelled *Activities* and *Projects* on the chalkboard. Brainstorm with students and write in the columns examples of activities and projects they do. For example, *activities*: play the guitar, take music lessons, paint, run a mile a day; *projects*: (re)build something, write a novel, sew/make a dress, clean the house.
2. Above the list of activities write the verbs *start* and *stop/quit*; above the projects write *start* and *finish*.
3. Have students list four activities and projects that they have done or are still doing on a paper and exchange papers with a partner.
4. Students interview their partners and find out whether or not the person is still doing the activities or working on projects. They will use questions such as: *Are you ____ing now? How long have you been ____? On, when did you finish/stop ____ing?*

5. Have students write a paragraph using the information their partners gave them.

UNIT 9

■ EXPANSION ACTIVITY 9A (page 128)

Library project on American holidays

If your students have access to English encyclopedias or other sources of information on American holidays, have individuals or groups read about different holidays and share important details with the class.

■ EXPANSION ACTIVITY 9B (page 131)

Reading about Thanksgiving

If your students lack background knowledge about the American holiday, Thanksgiving, reproduce this reading and go over it in class before doing *Reading 17*.

Pre-reading questions

1. What is the purpose of Thanksgiving?
2. Why did the pilgrims celebrate the first Thanksgiving in Massachusetts Colony?
3. What kind of celebration did they have?
4. What similarities are there between the way the pilgrims celebrated their thanksgiving day and the way it is celebrated today?

Thanksgiving: the Oldest American Holiday

Thanksgiving, the day that Americans have set aside to give thanks as a nation for their national and personal blessings, is celebrated on the fourth Thursday of November each year. It has not always been officially celebrated by the entire nation, but we can consider it the oldest U.S. holiday because its roots go back to the arrival of the first European settlers in Massachusetts.

In the fall of 1620, about 100 pilgrims arrived safely at Plymouth, Massachusetts, after a three-month voyage from England in a small ship named the *Mayflower*.

Life on land was more difficult than during the ocean trip. Of the 102 pilgrims who landed safely, almost half died during the first winter. In the spring the survivors worked hard and planted crops that gave them a good harvest. In the fall of 1621, they

had plenty of food to eat, they had made friends with the Indians in the area, and they were ready for the coming winter. So in October of 1621, William Bradford, the governor of the colony, proclaimed the first Thanksgiving in Massachusetts to thank God for their success in their first year. About 90 Indians joined the pilgrims for three days of celebration. There were games, Indian dances, and all kinds of good food including wild turkey, duck and geese, and Indian corn bread.

There have been many Thanksgiving days since that famous one in 1621, and Thanksgiving has been celebrated on many different days. President George Washington made November 26 a national day of Thanksgiving in 1789, but not all states celebrated it, and some people didn't celebrate it on that day. In 1863, President Abraham Lincoln proclaimed Thanksgiving the last Thursday in November. In 1939, President Franklin D. Roosevelt moved it to the third Thursday and finally in 1941 to the fourth Thursday in November, where it is today.

Even though Thanksgiving has been celebrated on different days in November, Americans continue to celebrate it in a way similar to the first Thanksgiving in Massachusetts. People give thanks for their blessings, each in his or her own way. Families and friends still gather and eat together. They usually have turkey and other foods that the pilgrims ate. And many still enjoy games, but they don't usually participate. Most people prefer to go to a local high school football game or to watch college or professional football games on television.

UNIT 10

■ EXPANSION ACTIVITY (page 134)

Texas montage

1. Begin work on a mural or bulletin board about Texas. You or students can write to the Office of Tourism, State Capital, Austin, Texas, for a map and travel brochures. You can also write to companies with offices in Houston, Dallas, and other cities. Universities will send recruitment brochures with lots of pictures. Have students watch for pictures of life in Texas in magazines and newspapers.

2. When the material is assembled, have students decide what they want to put in the mural or on the bulletin board. Small groups can be in charge of different parts of the project. You will have several opportunities to refer to the mural or bulletin board as you talk about the Logans' new life in Texas in Units 10-12.

UNIT 11

■ EXPANSION ACTIVITY 11A: (page 149)

What did you use to think?

Have a class discussion about misconceptions students had or things they used to believe when they were children. For example, *I used to think that I could fly.* Keep a record of the misconceptions on the board and find out by a show of hands which are the most common in your class.

■ EXPANSION ACTIVITY 11B: (page 149)

Changes

1. Have students talk about changes in their lives in a small group. They should talk about how things used to be, how they are now, and what caused the change.
2. Write some of the following incomplete sentences on the board to guide the small group conversation.
   • Before I got married, I used to _____.
   • Before I came to the United States, I used to _____.
   • When I was in elementary/high school, I used to _____.
   • Before I started working at ____, I used to _____.

■ EXPANSION ACTIVITY 11C (page 151)

A terrible interview

1. Have students review Units 10 and 11 and list areas in which a person will be judged for a job. They should come up with a list similar to this: *education, work experience, goals, personality, interests, behavior during the interview, clothing worn to the interview, communication skills, specific things he/she said during the interview.*

2. Have students use their list to write a paragraph about John J. Joke who was the worst applicant for the programmer's job at the Dallas Electric Company. Have students describe John's background and behavior in order to show that he was definitely the worst candidate for the job.
3. Have students read their compositions aloud in small groups and chose the best in their group for reading to the whole class.
4. End with a discussion of sure ways to lose a job or a role play of John J. Joke's interview.

UNIT 12

■ EXPANSION ACTIVITY (page 164)

What to look for in a college, or a vocational or technical school

1. Have students form small groups. Give them this list of things to consider when picking a college, or a vocational or technical school.

What to look for in a college
   a. good courses
   b. interesting neighborhood/city
   c. good teachers/faculty
   d. good library
   e. good laboratories
   f. low tuition
   g. many extracurricular activities
   h. prestigious name
   i. safe surrounding area
   j. good sports facilities
   k. long vacations
   l. good social life

2. Tell students to talk about the considerations and list them in order of importance from most important to least important.
3. Have secretaries write the lists on the board. Compare the lists. Were they nearly the same? Were there surprises? Have group members defend their choices.

LISTENING SCRIPTS

Listening Scripts

UNIT 1

17 Listening (page 17)

First Listening

Listen to the example:

If you love Carmen's Boutique in town, you can now enjoy shopping at Carmen's new location at the Winfield Mall. At the mall, you can continue to count on the best quality for the price and the same personal service. To celebrate the opening of her new store and the new mall, Carmen is offering up to 15% discount on the latest spring fashions. That's right—15% on all the new lines. So stop in soon at Carmen's new location next to the Winfield National Bank.

Answer: The answer is #27— Carmen's Boutique.

Now listen to the other ads and identify the stores.

• Opening this weekend in the new Winfield Mall is Winfield's newest fast food restaurant— Chicken Delight. Maybe you ate yesterday at the other chicken place in town, but you didn't eat chicken as delicious as Chicken Delight. Our chicken is just as good as the chicken you make at home. So next time you're in a hurry or just want to take it easy, stop at Chicken Delight, next to the new Warner's Department Store. Enjoy your meal in our comfortable family surroundings or pick it up to take home. Either way, you will be eating the best chicken in the world.

• Next time you need furniture, think of Ray's Unfinished Furniture— across from Nelson's Pharmacy in the new Winfield Mall. At Ray's you'll find the largest selection of unfinished furniture in the Winfield area, and of course without the high prices of other furniture stores. We'll teach you what you need to know about paints and varnishes so you can have beautiful furniture at half the price. For a limited time only, everything in the store at 25% off to celebrate the Grand Opening. Remember, the only reason we don't finish it—is that *you* can.

• Opening this week at the new Winfield Mall, a new kind of men's clothing store. Nothing in the store over $21.95. That's right, folks, the best buys on all

casual men's clothing— shirts, pants, swim suits— everything! And no price higher than $21.95! Who are we? We're called "$21.95," and we're located right next to the exit to Bell's Supermarket. So stop in to see us when you come to see the new Winfield Mall.

• Is there a wedding, a birthday, or an anniversary coming up in your family? Look no further than The Gift Box, where you'll find the largest selection of imported gifts in the area. Over 50% of our stock is imported so you're sure to find something new and different for the people on your list. And to celebrate the Grand Opening, if you are one of the the first 100 customers who come in and tell us that they heard this ad on the radio, there's a very special surprise gift for you. Just give the cashier the winning words "no two of a kind" and you'll get your gift. Don't delay. Only 100 free gifts at The Gift Box.

Answers: First and Second Listening:

Store #1, Ray's Unfinished Furniture 1. Superlative claim: the largest selection of unfinished furniture in the Winfield area 2. Obvious exaggeration: no 3. Special offer: 25% off everything in the store **Store #18,** Chicken Delight 1. Superlative claim: the newest fast food restaurant, the best chicken in the world 2. Obvious exaggeration: the best chicken in the world 3. Special offer: no **Store #23,** The Gift Box 1. Superlative claim: the largest selection of imported gifts in the area 2. Obvious exaggeration: no 3. Special offer: 100 gifts for customers who say "no two of a kind" **Store #29,** "$21.95" 1. Superlative claim: the best buys on casual men's clothes 2. Obvious exaggeration: no 3. Special offer: no

UNIT 3

17 Listening (page 49)

Conversation 1

SALESPERSON: May I help you?

CUSTOMER: Yes. I'm looking for a pattern and some fabric to make a party dress for my daughter. I'd like it to be pretty, but a strong, washable fabric.

SALESPERSON: You can't beat cotton. We have some beautiful 100% cotton fabrics right over

here. ... How do you like this white one? Aren't the little flowers pretty?

CUSTOMER: It *is* beautiful, but my daughter's favorite color is yellow. Do you have something similar in yellow?

SALESPERSON: What about this one? It's light weight, but it's strong too.

CUSTOMER: That's perfect. I can just see her in it.

SALESPERSON: Good. Let's go over and have a look at the pattern books.

Conversation 2

SALESPERSON: Good afternoon. Can I help you?

CUSTOMER: I'd like to return these slacks for a credit on my charge account.

SALESPERSON: What seems to be the problem?

CUSTOMER: I just don't like them. It's the style, I guess. But it really doesn't matter, does it? Just give me credit on my account.

SALESPERSON: No problem, ma'am. Glad to help. Just a minute. I'll be right back.

Conversation 3

CUSTOMER: There's never anyone to help you in this department.

SALESPERSON: I'd be glad to help if I can, sir.

CUSTOMER: Oh, there you are. Yes. I want to exchange this suit. It doesn't fit right.

SALESPERSON: No problem. Do you have the sales slip?

CUSTOMER: No, I don't. I threw it away.

SALESPERSON: Did you buy the suit recently, sir?

CUSTOMER: About a month ago, but I haven't worn it. I tried it on once, but I didn't like it.

SALESPERSON: I'm very sorry, sir, but we can't accept any merchandise that isn't accompanied by the sales slip.

Conversation 4

CUSTOMER: Excuse me. Where are the polo shirts that were advertised on sale?

SALESPERSON: We don't have any polos on sale.

CUSTOMER: Today's paper advertises 100% cotton polos for $15.

SALESPERSON: Look I know this department. There are no polos on sale. I think that was last week.

CUSTOMER: I have a copy of the paper right here.

Would you please find the manager for me?

SALESPERSON: He's not here today. You'll have to come back tomorrow.

Conversation 5

CUSTOMER: Excuse me, ma'am. (pause) Excuse me, ma'am. (louder)

SALESPERSON: Oh, I'm sorry. Daydreaming, I guess. What can I do for you?

CUSTOMER: I'd like to exchange this sweater. It's too small for my wife, and she doesn't like red.

SALESPERSON: Do you have the sales slip?

CUSTOMER: Yes, right here.

SALESPERSON: Very good. Now what size and color would you like?

Answers: First and Second Listening: **Conversation 1:** *Salesperson:* polite *Customer:* polite *Problem:* to select fabric for daughter's dress **Conversation 2:** *Salesperson:* polite *Customer:* impolite *Problem:* to return slacks with credit on a charge account **Conversation 3:** *Salesperson:* polite *Customer:* impolite *Problem:* to exchange a suit without a sales slip **Conversation 4:** *Salesperson:* impolite *Customer:* polite *Problem:* to find the shirts that are on sale **Conversation 5:** *Salesperson:* polite *Customer:* polite *Problem:* to exchange a sweater with sales slip

UNIT 7

13 Listening (page 102)

Use this example twice, once before the First Listening and once before the Second Listening.

A: So are you coming with me Saturday?

B: I'd like to go to the beach, but I really should clean the house. I haven't cleaned it in a month.

A: C'mon. Don't be silly. The house can wait.

B: True, but if I don't do it this weekend, I'll have to do it during the week. And I'm tired after work.

A: So stay home and clean the house if you want, but if I were you I would go to the beach. You shouldn't pass up an opportunity like this.

B: Well... Mmm... I guess you're right. I'll be ready in a minute.

Answer: First Listening: Decision/problem: what to do on Saturday

Answer: Second Listening: Alternatives: clean the house OR go to the beach; The person decides to go to the beach.

Conversation 1

A: What movie should we go to this weekend?

B: We could go to "Return of the Sea Monster." They say it's pretty good.

A: I heard it wasn't that hot. I'd rather go to "Lost Love." My sister says it's beautiful. It's at the Washington.

C: We could also stay home and watch something on TV. It's cheaper, and I'm almost broke.

B: That's not a bad idea. I don't think "Return of the Sea Monster" or "Lost Love" sound like they're worth the money.

A: OK with me. Let's send out for a pizza.

Conversation 2

DICK: Wow! Do I have a problem! I really put my foot in my mouth this time.

STAN: What's the matter, Dick?

DICK: I can't go to the basketball game with you Saturday. I told my mother I would take her to the symphony. Now what should I do?

STAN: That's easy. Just tell her you can't go. You have to work.

DICK: She knows I never work on Saturday night. I'll hurt her feelings. Maybe I could get my sister to take her.

STAN: Yeah, or maybe you could get tickets for Thursday night instead. The orchestra plays Thursdays and Saturdays, doesn't it?

DICK: Yes, but I think I'll call my sister first.

Conversation 3

BILL: So what are we going to get Mom for her birthday?

SUE: I have only about five dollars. How about you?

BILL: That's two more than I have. What can we possibly get for only $8.00? All I can think of is flowers.

SUE: I'm sure she would like flowers, but what about a book? She loves to read.

BILL: Yeah, or maybe we could get two or three of her favorite magazines.

SUE: She buys the magazines herself. What kind of books does she like to read?

BILL: You should know that better than I.

SUE: OK. Let's see if we can find a good biography in paperback. I know she'll like that.

Conversation 4

HAL: Frank, I don't know what to do. I'm spending too much money on my car. It costs me $20 just to change the oil.

FRANK: Well, one thing you could do is learn how to change the oil yourself. I'd be glad to teach you if you want.

HAL: Yeah, but that's so messy. Your hands get all dirty. You never really get them clean.

FRANK: That's not true, but anyway if you don't like that idea, you could try to find a cheaper garage. Maybe someone who is just starting a business.

HAL: That takes a lot of time. As usual, I probably won't do anything. I just like to complain.

Conversation 5

MARY: Oh, Dan. I'm having such a problem with the kids. Now they won't clean their rooms or do anything.

DAN: You're too nice. You're not tough enough on them. Tell them they can't go out until they clean their rooms and you'll see what happens.

MARY: I've tried that. It doesn't do any good. Any other ideas?

DAN: Clean their rooms for them.

MARY: Are you kidding? Be serious.

DAN: I told you. Stand at the door. Tell them they can go out when their rooms are clean. It's very simple. You have to be strong and patient.

Answers: First and Second Listening:

Conversation 1: *Decision:* what to do this weekend *Alternatives:* go to a movie OR stay home and watch TV; They decide to stay home and watch TV.

Conversation 2: *Problem:* Dick wants to go to a basketball game, but he told his mother he would take her to the symphony. *Alternatives:* get his sister to take her OR get tickets for Thursday; He decides to get his sister to take her.

Conversation 3: *Decision:* what to get mother for her birthday *Alternatives:* flowers OR book OR magazine; The people decide to look for a book.

Conversation 4: *Problem:* spending too much on the car *Alternatives:* learn how to change the oil OR find a cheaper garage; Hal probably won't so anything.
Conversation 5: *Problem:* Kids won't clean their rooms. *Alternatives:* tell the kids they can't go out until they clean their rooms OR clean the rooms for the kids; There is no information about which alternative Mary will choose.

UNIT 8

16 Listening (page 116)

LIZ: Hello.

LENORE: Hi, Liz. This is Lenore.

LIZ: Lenore! What a surprise! It's been ages.

LENORE: Yes. Too long. How's everything?

LIZ: Just fine. Are you calling from school?

LENORE: Yeah. I'm taking a break from studying. I thought I would catch up on the news, so I called you in Winfield and your mother gave me this new number. She says you've got a new job, but she didn't give me any of the details.

LIZ: Yeah, I started at Worldwide Airlines a month ago. I'm a ticket agent. I just had to do something more interesting than find phone numbers in a data base.

LENORE: And how are folks taking your move to New York?

LIZ: They've been great! Oh, they were a little worried when I was thinking of living by myself, but now that I have a roommate, no problem. Dave is the one who's giving me problems.

LENORE: Dave? Somebody new?

LIZ: Didn't I tell you about Dave? I've been going out with him for a couple of months now. He's a student at Winfield Community College — studying communications.

LENORE: So what's his problem?

LIZ: Oh, he didn't have any objections to my changing jobs, but when I told him I wasn't going to live in Winfield anymore, you should have seen his reaction. Can you believe it? He wanted me to commute from Winfield every day. Gosh, if I did that, I wouldn't have time to enjoy New York.

LENORE: Well, give him time to get used to the idea. So how do you like New York? Have you done anything interesting?

LIZ: Yeah, thanks to my friend Sue. When I was living with her I went to a couple of free concerts and we saw a fantastic dance group called The Dance Theater of Harlem. They're a group of dancers who do both modern dance and ballet.

LENORE: Sounds great! How would you like a visitor?

LIZ: Terrific. When can you come? How about next weekend?

LENORE: How about the weekend after that? I've got three exams and a couple of projects before the end of the month.

LIZ: OK. I'll expect you the first weekend in April. I'll call you again before then. Bye bye.

Answers to the First and Second Listening: 1. F 2. NG 3. T 4. F 5. T 6. From Elinor, Liz's mother. 7. Dave wants Liz to live in Winfield and commute to New York City 8. She has gone to a couple of free concerts. She has seen the Dance Theater of Harlem. 9. She has three exams and a couple of projects. 10. March

UNIT 9

16 Listening (page 130)

Conversation A

A: Sure we should invite the men. I don't care if people don't usually invite men to this kind of party. Fathers are just as important as mothers.

B: OK, we'll invite the men. When should we have the party?

A: How about next Sunday afternoon? I think almost everybody can make it then.

B: Good idea. Does Maribelle know we're planning this?

A: No, but I'll talk to Tom. He can take her out somewhere for lunch. After lunch he can say he wants to stop by to see me for a minute.

A: That's a good idea. She'll never suspect anything since Tom visits you at least once a week.

Conversation B

A: What are you planning for Betsy's birthday, Luellen?

B: I haven't really thought about it, and it's next weekend. Billy's birthday is soon, too, isn't it?

A: Yeah, next Friday, the 28th.

B: Really? Betsy's is Sunday. Let's have one party for the two of them on Saturday. That way we can share the work.

A: That's a great idea. I never look forward to trying to keep a group of small children busy and happy at a birthday party. Where shall we have it?

B: We can have it at my place, no problem. We've got a park right across the street, so all the games can be over there. Then we can come back to the apartment for the cake and ice cream. The only problem will be if it rains.

A: I'll think of something to do in the apartment if it rains, but let's not worry about that. It doesn't rain much at this time of year.

Conversation C

A: Hi, Bill. It's Mom. How's everything?

B: Fine. How's everything with you?

A: Just great, especially after that fantastic party you had for Dad and me. I know we said thank you that night, but I still can't believe it. We hadn't seen some of those friends in a long time. And the food and the music were terrific, too. You really went out of your way.

B: It was a lot of work, Mom, but you know Ann and I would do anything for you and Dad. And it isn't every day that people celebrate forty years together. We really wanted to say thanks for everything you've done for us.

A: Well, son someday you'll know how good it is to hear that. Dad and I thank you again.

Conversation D

A: Ladies and gentlemen, at this time I'd like to ask our guest of honor, Sara Randall, to come to the microphone. Sara...
Sara, you've heard the thoughts of some of your colleagues and former students. They have said it all. I really cannot add anything more. So let me just present this small token of our love and respect for you, a thank you for all you have done for our school. Let me read the inscription on this beautiful silver plate.
To Sara Randall, colleague, teacher, and friend upon her retirement after thirty successful years at Winfield High School. In

gratitude for everything you have taught us about how the lessons of history must be applied to the future.

The Faculty and Students
Winfield High School
June 12, 1991

SARA: Thank you all so very much. This has been a wonderful evening, and this beautiful plate will keep the memory of it clear in my mind for years to come. As you know, I'm not one for speeches, so let me just say that I have enjoyed my thirty years here at Winfield very much, and I see no reason why my next thirty years in retirement won't be just as good. Thank you everyone.

Answers: First and Second Listening:
Conversation A: baby shower 1. F 2. T 3. T 4. NG **Conversation B:** birthday party 1. F 2. NG 3. F 4. F **Conversation C:** wedding anniversary 1. F 2. NG 3. NG 4. F **Conversation D:** retirement party 1. F 2. T 3. F 4. NG

UNIT 12

14 Listening (page 164)

SAM: Hello. #

SAM: Well, what do you know. What a surprise! How's Texas? Still hot? #

SAM: No kidding! Over 100 degrees. Wow! I bet you spend a lot of time at the pool. # You've got a new best friend, too. That's great. # OK. Put her on. #

SAM: Of course, I'm OK, Mom. # No, I don't. # Yes, I eat well. # No, I decided not to go to summer school. # Yeah # Uh huh. # What about you? How's the job going? #

SAM: Yeah. # I'm sure. # Uh huh # Take it easy. You'll get used to it. Have you found a house yet? #

SAM: You'll find one. Don't worry. # Yeah, it's never easy. And Dad? Everything going well with him? # Oh, hi, Dad. # Yeah, I'm fine. # No, no problems. What's new? #

SAM: That's too bad. Well, at least it got you to Texas. Now maybe you'll have to buy a new one # Yeah, I know you never buy new ones. # You'll find a good used one I'm sure. # Uh huh # Is Bob there? #

SAM: Good. # And don't worry about me, Dad. I'll be fine. #

SAM: Hi, Bob. How's everything? #

SAM: I just wanted to tell you to save some money. Don't spend it all on the girls down there. #

SAM: I mean I've got two weeks in December. # I thought I might come for Christmas. I could help you find the right car if you want. #

SAM: I hope so. Have you decided what to do about college yet? #

Sam: Yeah, you might be better in a smaller place. # Uh huh # Listen, Bob, I have to get to work. Put Mom on again, OK? #

SAM: Bob will give you the news, Mom. I just wanted to say good-bye. I've got to get to work. Say good-bye to Dad and Lisa for me. #

SAM: I miss you all, too. I'll call in a couple of weeks. Bye now.

Answers: First Listening: Order: Lisa 1, Adela 2, Tom 3, Bob 4. *Topics:* Lisa: a, c, g; Adela: h, f, b; Tom: e; Bob: d, e, g. *Answers: Second Listening:* 1. T 2. T 3. F 4. NG 5. F 6. T 7. T 8. T

WORKBOOK ANSWER KEY

Workbook Answer Key

UNIT 1

A. 1. improvements 2. safe 3. luxury 4. sponsored 5. economical 6. latest 7. creative 8. convenient 9. jointly 10. exaggerate

B. 1. auto show 2. furniture show 3. pharmacy 4. sporting goods store 5. home improvement exhibit 6. amusement rides 7. fashion show 8. bank

C. (Answers will vary.)

D. (In some cases, more than one answer is correct.) 1. won't 2. may not / might not 3. will / might / may 4. may not / might not / won't 5. won't / may not / might not 6. will 7. won't 8. may / might; will

E. 1. Would you rather go to a movie or to a large party? 2. Would you rather read a book or watch TV? 3. Would you rather play a sport or watch a sport? 4. Would you rather go to a small quiet restaurant or to a comedy show? 5. Would you rather go to a park or to a shopping mall? 6. Would you rather go to the ocean or the mountains? 7. (Questions will vary.)

F. (Answers will vary.)

G. (Possible answers. Answers will vary.) 1. A: Would you like to go with me to a late movie? B: Thanks, but I'd rather not. I have to get up early tomorrow. A: Come on. It's a great new comedy. I think you'd like it. B: I'd really like to go, but I'm tired and I'd rather go another time. How about tomorrow night? 2. A: Why don't we go play tennis this afternoon? B: No, thanks. It's too hot. A: Let's play a night game, then. How about 8:00? B: Sure. That sounds better. I'll see you then. 3. A: Do you want to go to an antique car show with me? B: Well, it sounds like fun, but I have some chores to do. A: But today is the last day of the show. I'd rather not go by myself. Come on. It's supposed to be great. B: Well, OK. I'm sure it'll be fun. Let's meet at noon. 4. A: Would you like to go to lunch? We could go to a pizza shop. B: Well, I guess so, but I'd rather not eat pizza. How about ...? A: Sure, that sounds fine.

H. (Answers to the questions will vary.) 1. closest

2. most luxurious 3. newest 4. most reliable 5. most crowded 6. most reasonable 7. most convenient 8. most helpful 9. best 10. most uncomfortable

I. (Answers will vary.)

J. (Answers will vary.)

UNIT 2

A. 1. c 2. b 3. a 4. a 5. c 6. a 7. a 8. b

B. (Answers will vary.)

C. (Answers will vary.)

D. (Answers will vary.)

E. 1. B: She was in Breakfast Club, wasn't she? A: She's a good actress, isn't she? B: She's always better than you expect, isn't she? 2. A: You weren't in class yesterday, were you? B: It was hard, wasn't it? 3. A: Your older brother is a teacher at the high school, isn't he? A: But your brother's name is Jose Blanco, isn't it? B: It's confusing, isn't it? 4. A: You aren't going away this weekend, are you? B: It's her birthday, isn't it?

F. 1. T 2. T 3. T 4. F If you run out of gas the engine won't work. 5. T 6. F If you have a flat tire, you'll probably find a spare tire in the trunk. 7. T 8. F If you want to check the car behind you, look in your mirror. 9. F When you come to a stop sign, you will use your brake to slow down. 10. T

G. (Note: Usually more than one answer is possible.) 1. The School Street apartment is more expensive than the Willow Street apartment. The River Road Apartment is the most expensive apartment. 2. The School Street apartment is more convenient to the bus stop than the Willow Street Apartment. The River Street apartment is the most convenient to the bus stop. 3. The School Street apartment is the closest to the school. 4. The School Street apartment is in the best condition. 5. The River Road apartment is cleaner than the School Street apartment. The Willow Street apartment is the cleanest one. 6. The River Road apartment is the most modern one. 7. The School Street apartment is cheaper than the River Road one. The Willow Street apartment is the cheapest. 8. The School Street apartment is the brightest.

H. (Answers will vary.)

I. 1. sadly 2. beautifully 3. well 4. creatively

5. considerate 6. quickly 7. nervously 8. angrily 9. good 10. busy

J. (Answers will vary.)

UNIT 3

A. 1. sat down 2. come back 3. fill out 4. take off 5. pick out / look for 6. put out 7. filled up 8. came in 9. try on 10. looked at 11. blow out 12. put back

B. (Answers include five of these sentences.) Tomorrow Joseph is going to fill a job application out at the radio station. "It's so hot in here. Why don't you take your coat off?" Sachiko went to the store to pick some new curtains out, but she didn't find what she wanted. It took the firefighters about three hours to put the fire out downtown. The gas station attendant filled the car up with gas and then asked for $17. The customer asked if she could try some black shoes on in a size seven. The little girl was laughing so hard that she couldn't blow her birthday candles out. Cristina decided to put the green suit back because it was the wrong style for her.

C. 1. afford 2. sew 3. make ends meet 4. pattern 5. style 6. fabric 7. fit

D. 1. A: New York City is the capital of New York State, isn't it? B: No, it isn't. Albany is the capital. 2. A: Margaret Thatcher was the Prime Minister of England, wasn't she? B: Yes, she was. OR A: Margaret Thatcher is the Prime Minister of England, isn't she? B: No, she isn't. She was the Prime Minister until 1990. 3. Mount Everest is in Nepal, isn't it? B: Yes, it is. 4. John Kennedy was President of the United States in 1970, wasn't he? B: No, he wasn't. He was President from 1960-1963. 5. A: Zimbabwe is north of South Africa, isn't it? B: Yes, it is. 6. A: Hong Kong is an island, isn't it? B: No, it isn't. 7. A: Leonard Bernstein was a famous actor, wasn't he? B: No, he wasn't. He was a famous composer/conductor. 8. The Amazon jungle is in Chile, isn't it? A: No, it isn't. It's in Brazil.

E. (Answers will vary.)

F. 1. himself 2. she; it; herself 3. me; I 4. They 5. herself; her 6. We 7. himself; him 8. themselves 9. themselves 10. herself; she

G. 1. You should take it off. 2. You should call him/her back. 3. You should throw it out. 4. You

should pick it up. 5. You should turn it up. 6. You should take it back. 7. You should turn it off. 8. You should put them back. 9. You should sit down. 10. You should stand up.
H. (Answers will vary.)
I. (Answers will vary.)

UNIT 4

A. *Across.* 2. neighbor 4. yard 6. bedroom 7. apartment 11. deposit 12. window 14. lease 15. utilities 17. dining 18. tenants 19. studio 20. refrigerator 21. owner *Down.* 1. landlord 3. rent 5. vacant 8. expensive 9. modern 10. unfurnished 13. convenient 16. sign
B. 1. visited 2. was staying; saw 3. was; was 4. saw; needed 5. spoke 6. said 7. went 8. was looking at; ran into; gave 9. were; had 10. was painting; dropped; was 11. was working; came 12. was; felt
C. (Answers will vary.)
D. (Answers will vary.)
E. (Drawings should match the written description given in workbook.)
F. (Answers will vary.)
G. 1. doesn't it; 2. isn't it; 3. doesn't it; 4. isn't there; 5. does it; 6. do you; 7. wasn't she; 8. do you; 9. isn't it
H. Mr. White speaks lines a, b, d, i, j, k, l. Tran speaks lines c, e, f, g, h, m. The completed dialogue is as follows. Tran: Yes, it is. Nice big windows. Could you show me around, please? Mr. White: Certainly. The kitchen's in there, with a door to the back stairs. Tran: And are the appliances included? Mr. White: Yes. The stove and refrigerator stay here. That table belongs to the tenant, though. In fact, except for the kitchen appliances, the apartment is unfurnished. But you have your own furniture, don't you? Tran: Yes, I do. And the bedrooms are down this hall, aren't they? Mr. White: Yes, two bedrooms and a bath. Tran: The bathroom ceiling looks cracked. Has there been a problem with leaks? Mr. White: Yes, the pipe upstairs broke, but that has all been fixed. Someone's coming tomorrow to repair the ceiling. Tran: That's good. And so the rent is $300 a month, right? Mr. White: Yes, plus a security deposit of $300. You're looking for something for next

month, aren't you? Tran: Yes, I am. I'm very interested in this apartment. Can I call you this afternoon? Mr. White: Yes, I'll be home all afternoon.

UNIT 5

A. (Answers will vary.)
B. arrived, was, have been, have been, have gained, have... gained, have met, have done, took, rented, were taking, saw, had been, rained, stayed, studied, have ... spoken, was
C. 1. left 2. hasn't spent 3. has been, hasn't been 4. bought, has broken 5. spoke, told 6. drove, didn't have, were/felt 7. hasn't seen 8. lost, found 9. has written, hasn't gotten 10. didn't feel, went
D. 1. Have you lost weight? 2. Answer will vary. 3. Have ... visited you recently? 4. Yes, they have. 5. Has it rained much this month? 6. Answer will vary. 7. Have you gotten a letter from ... lately? 8. Answer will vary.
E. (Answers will vary.)
F. (Answers will vary.)
G. (Answers will vary.)

UNIT 6

A. (Answers will vary.)
B. Possible questions. 1. Where has your mother traveled to? What cities did she go to in Japan? 2. Have you written many letters to your parents? 3. Where have you been on vacation? What did you do there? / What did you enjoy doing there? 4. Where have you been? 5. What has ... written lately? When did he write his last book.
C. (Answers using *since* will vary, according to the current year. They follow the example.) 1. B: Greg Brown has worked there for five years. 2. A: How long has Maria Rodriguez worked in Customer Service? B: She has worked there for 5 years. 3. A: How long has Vinh Nguyen worked in Sales? B: He has worked there for 10 years. 4. A: How long has Kim Son worked in Accounting? B: She has worked there for 10 years. 5. A: How long has Al Sheppard worked in Design? B: He has worked there for 20 years.
D. 1. Swimming 2. Driving 3. Eating 4. running 5. listening 6. meeting 7. Speaking

8. cooking 9. Studying 10. Opening 11. washing 12. Watching 13. Typing 14. fixing 15. Finding
E. (Answers will vary.)
F. (Answers will vary.)
G. (Answers will vary.)

UNIT 7

A. 1. Sounds good to me 2. has gone up 3. sorry 4. get to the point 5. none of my business 6. looking forward 7. let me know 8. making ends meet 9. I can't believe it! 10. going on 11. can't help 12. in some ways 13. What ... for 14. Forget it!
B. Possible answers. Picture A has a square around the circle in the center. Picture B has a rectangle around a square in the center.; Picture A has a rectangle above the triangle on the right. Picture B doesn't.; Picture A has a diamond in the center bottom. Picture B has a circle.; Picture A has a circle on the left. Picture B has a diamond.; Picture A has an octagon in the top center. Picture B has a pentagon.; Picture A has seven shapes in it. Picture B has six.
C. Possible questions. 1. Have you eaten ... yet? 2. Have you painted ... yet? 3. Has ... graduated from ... yet? 4. Has she bought a/an ... yet? 5. Have they gotten married yet?
D. 1. A: Has she picked up her tickets yet? B: No, she hasn't. 2. A: Has she reserved a hotel room yet? B: Yes, she has already reserved one. 3. A: Has she bought a bathing suit yet? B: Yes, she has already bought one. 4. A: Has she finished the sales report for Mr. Holt yet? B: No, she hasn't finished it yet. 5. Has she gone to the bank yet? B: Yes, she has already gone to the bank. 6. A: Has she packed her suitcases yet? B: No, she hasn't packed them yet. 7. A: Has she stopped the mail yet? B: No, she hasn't stopped the mail yet. 8. A: Has she renewed her passport yet? B: Yes, she has already renewed her passport.
E. (Answers will vary.)
F. 1. d 2. g 3. e 4. a 5. b 6. c 7. f 8. h
G. Possible answers. Alonso could look for another job that offers training on the job. He could take the two-year program at night. He could work his night job on the weekends so he could take the

night classes during the week. He could quit his night job. He could try to get a loan to pay for the course. He could borrow some money from his family. He could live with his parents or relatives to save money.

H. Possible answers. If he quits his night job, he won't have enough money. If he doesn't change jobs or get training, he will be bored. If he goes to night school, he may have to quit his night job. If he goes to night school and keeps his night job, he will be very busy. If he gets a loan for school, he will have to pay it back with interest.

I. (Answers will vary.)
J. (Answers will vary.)
K. (Answers will vary.)
L. (Answers will vary.)
M. (Answers will vary.)

UNIT 8

A. 1. The people have been waiting for the bus for 30 minutes. 2. Nancy has not been feeling well lately. 3. The Thomases have been thinking about moving to St. Louis. 4. Leo has been looking for a job for two months. 5. The basketball team has not been playing well this season. 6. Maria has been working on a math problem for a long time. 7. Andre has been cooking all day. 8. The Richards family has been vacationing in Vermont every summer since l985. 9. Mach Lin has been reading an excellent book all weekend. 10. Paulo has lived in the United States for 3 years.

B. (Answers will vary.)
C. 1. hasn't made 2. has been studying 3. has known 4. haven't told 5. has been driving 6. has been waiting; hasn't arrived 7. has written 8. has been playing 9. have lived/have been living 10. has visited
D. 1. haven't written 2. have lived; have been living 3. have been 4. haven't seen 5. went 6. bought 7. haven't gone 8. haven't had 9. arrived 10. has stolen 11. haven't seen 12. took 13. cost 14. was 15. drove; was driving 16. have changed 17. got 18. have learned/have been learning 19. have talked/have been talking 20. have ... been 21. Have ... seen 22. wrote 23. told 24. were/have been 25. had met

E. 1. TOM: Not so good. I haven't been feeling well lately. MARIE: Why not? Have you been sick? TOM: No, I've just been tired. I have been working too hard. MARIE: What have you been working on at the office? TOM: I have been working on a big report. I have to finish it next week. MARIE: You'll probably feel better next week. 2. MARK: Hi. I haven't seen you since graduation. How have you been doing? JOAN: Fine. I have been working as a salesperson recently. MARK: Where do you work? JOAN: Downtown, at Robertson's Computers. MARK: That's great. How long have you been working there? JOAN: I have been working there for three months. I really enjoy it./ I have really been enjoying it.

F. (Student answers with *that...* will vary.) 1. so 2. so 3. such a 4. such 5. so 6. such a 7. so 8. such an 9. so 10. so
G. Possible answers. 1. I don't/can't believe it! What a surprise! That's terrific! 2. You're kidding! Where did you hear that? That's terrible. 3. I can't believe it. I'm so sorry to hear that. 4. That's wonderful! I can't believe it! Are you sure? I thought he has been going to Columbia University. 5. That's terrific! You're kidding! 6. Are you sure? 7. What a... 8. Really? I didn't know that. 9. That's too bad. Where did you hear that? 10. That's too bad.
H. 1. f 2. j 3. g 4. e 5. a 6. i 7. h 8. d 9. c 10. b
I. (Answers will vary.)
J. 1. have been looking 2. have heard 3. have received/have been receiving 4. have received/have been receiving 5. was 6. called 7. was 8. read 9. have taught/have been teaching 10. taught 11. has happened 12. came 13. made 14. did ... make 15. has made 16. have been doing 17. have been

UNIT 9

A. (Answers will vary.)
B. 1. neat 2. not a bad idea 3. suppose 4. wild 5. What's up? 6. senior prom 7. lend
C. 1. A: Is this shirt Pierre's? B: Yes, it's his. 2. A: Is this cassette tape yours? B: No, it isn't mine. It's Juan's. 3. A: Are these tickets the Logans'? B: Yes, they are theirs. 4. A: Is this cup of tea Andy's? B: No, it isn't his. It's Sue's.

5. A: Is this money Carol's? B: Yes, it's hers. 6. A: Are these sandwiches the children's? B: Yes, they are theirs. 7. A: Is this magazine ours? B: No, it's not ours. It's Tim's. 8. A: Is this luggage Becky's? B: Yes, it's hers.
D. 1. his 2. mine 3. hers 4. ours 5. theirs
E. (Answers will vary.)
F. 1. Susan saw her dog chasing a car down the street. 2. We listened to the two politicians talking about crime. 3. He saw the children swimming in the pool. 4. The coach watched the players practicing their kicks. 5. The teacher heard the students discussing plans for a party./ The students heard the teacher discussing plans for a party. 6. Dave watched the mechanic fixing the brakes on his car. 7. Ana saw a thief stealing a car. 8. The crowd watched the firefighters putting out the fire./The crowd watched the firefighters putting the fire out.
G. (Answers will vary.)
H. (Answers will vary.)
I. 1. One; another 2. One; The others 3. One; The other 4. One; The other 5. One; The others 6. One; The other 7. Others 8. One; The other
J. (Answers will vary.)
K. Answers will vary. Possible answers. 1. KIM: May, I need an evening gown for the prom. Could I borrow yours? MAY: Sure, you can borrow it. But you should try it on first. It may be too big. KIM: Thanks. I'll try it on. 2. TRAN: I really need a car for the prom. Could I borrow yours? VINH: I'm sorry but I'd rather not lend it to you. You're a bad driver. And besides, my car isn't working well right now. Why don't you borrow Dad's? TRAN: I guess I could ask him. 3. MRS. WILSON: My daughter is going to the prom and I really want to take pictures. Could you lend me your video camera? MR. ANTONIO: Sure. I would be happy to let you use it. When you come by to pick it up, I'll show you how to use it.

UNIT 10

A. 1. opening 2. job/position 3. job/position/opening 4. experience 5. application 6. application 7. interview 8. applicants 9. apply 10. position/job/opening 11. interview 12. references 13. transcript

14. interview
B. (Answers will vary.)
C. 1. c 2. d 3. e 4. b 5. f 6. a
D. 1. fill out; fill in 2. turn...down 3. tried...on; send...back 4. look over 5. give...back 6. leave out 7. turn in 8. put...out 9. picks up 10. turn off 11. take...back 12. pick...out 13. put away 14. took...off 15. blew out
E. 1. A: Has he sent the application back to Warner's yet? B: Yes, he has. 2. A: Has he had a second interview at Warner's yet? B: No, he still hasn't had a second interview there. 3. A: Has he had a second interview at Electric Supply Company yet? B: Yes, he has. 4. A: Has he sent the application back to Greene's yet? B: No, he still hasn't sent it back. 5. A: Has he received a call for an interview at Builders Supply Company yet? B: Yes, he has. 6. A: Has he gone to his first interview at Builders Supply Company yet? B: No, he still hasn't gone there.
F. 1. didn't he? Yes, he did. 2. didn't he? No, he didn't. 3. didn't he? Yes, he did. 4. did he? No, he didn't. 5. didn't they? No, they didn't. 6. didn't he? Yes, he did. 7. did he? No, he didn't. 8. didn't he? Yes, he did.
G. 1. didn't you 2. didn't you 3. do you 4. aren't you 5. don't you 6. didn't you 7. weren't you 8. did you 9. weren't you 10. don't you
H. Possible answers. 1. I think so./I hope so. 2. I don't think so./I hope not. I don't think so. 3. I guess not./I don't think so. 4. I guess so. 5. I don't think so./I hope not. 6. I don't think so./I guess not. 7. I think so. 8. I don't think so.
I. 1. disorganized 2. persevere/keep going 3. hardworking/industrious 4. dishonest 5. imaginative/creative 6. uncooperative 7. enthusiastic 8. dependable/responsible 9. take the initiative 10. keep going 11. creative/imaginative 12. irresponsible
J. (Answers will vary.)
K. (Answers will vary.)

UNIT 11

A. 1. keep records 2. encouraged 3. put...talent to work 4. find out 5. supervises 6. customized

7. greeted 8. gets...excited
B. (Answers will vary.)
C. (Answers will vary.)
D. (Answers will vary.)
E. (Answers will vary.)
F. 1. Have you ever used a calculator? 2. Have you ever explained delays to customers? 3. Have you ever worked with difficult customers? 4. Have you ever used a computer? 5. Have you ever sold airplane tickets? 6. Have you ever worked in a stressful job? 7. Have you ever trained new employees?
G. (Answers will vary.)
H. (Answers will vary.)
I. for giving; in learning; about selling; at finding; by saying; to talking
J. (Answers will vary.)
K. (Answers to questions will vary.) 1. When are you happiest? 2. When are you saddest? 3. When are you most energetic? 4. What are you proudest of? 5. What are you most enthusiastic about?
L. (Answers will vary.)
M. (Answers will vary.)

UNIT 12

A. 1. sick and tired 2. pretty big step; make a go of it 3. take a break 4. risky 5. heard from your folks 6. check it out 7. look up 8. values
B. (Answers will vary.)
C. 1. He has been very busy at his job recently, hasn't he? 2. He hasn't had much time to study, has he? 3. He should study more, shouldn't he? 4. He won't pass his final English test, will he? 5. He will have to repeat the course, won't he? 6. He can still change the situation, can't he? 7. He shouldn't give up, should he?
D. 1. it's a seven-passenger car 2. she's a four-year-old girl 3. it's a two-car garage 4. it's a fifteen-pound turkey 5. it's a nine-woman team 6. it's a twenty-dollar radio 7. it's a five-day vacation 8. it's a 10-kilometer race 9. it's a one-year course 10. it's a two-hour class
E. 1. right here/right with you 2. right away/right now; right away/right now 3. right there/right here 4. right after 5. right across 6. right now/right away

F. (Answers will vary.)
G. 1. A: Did Tran have a house in Dallas? B: No, he didn't. He had an apartment. 2. A: How long has Tran lived in Chicago? B: He has lived there since 1991/for ... years. 3. A: When did he move to Chicago? B: He moved there in 1991. 4. A: How long will he live in an apartment? B: (Answers will vary.) 5. How long has he worked as an engineer? B: He has worked as an engineer since 1985/for ... years. 6-10: (Questions and answers will vary.)
H. Answers will vary. Possible answers. 1. He will have to save a lot of money/get a loan. 2. He might not have as much free time because he will have to take care of his house. He might be more worried about money because he will have a big responsibility. He might have more room in a house. 3. She should talk with other people who have import businesses. She should find out if there are any organizations for import businesses. She should look up information in the library. 4. She could import clothing, art work, rugs, furniture, jewelry. 5. She may not have enough money. She might not know who to buy from. She might not understand the laws. She might have trouble finding a good store to rent.
I. (Answers will vary.)
J. 1. c Cristina got married, didn't she? Cristina has lived in the U.S. for three years, hasn't she?
2. d Gino is thinking about opening his own restaurant, isn't he?
3. e Liz got a job as a ticket agent, didn't she?
4. h The Logan family moved to Dallas, didn't they?
5. g Adela got a job at Dallas Electric Company, didn't she?
6. b Tom became a partner in a travel agency in Dallas, didn't he?
7. f Mike graduated from high school, didn't he?
8. a Bob got a part-time job in Dallas, didn't he?
K. (Answers will vary.)